AF574234

POOLS FROM ABOVE

BRAD WALLS

POOLS

FROM ABOVE

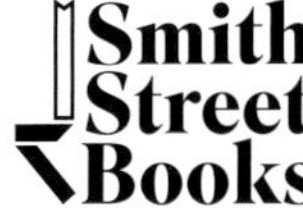

INTRODUCTION

Produced over a span of three years in four countries, *Pools From Above* is the culmination of my long journey to discover the beauty in commonplace landscapes seen from unexpected vantages.

Initially inspired by my travels throughout Southeast Asia and Australia, I began capturing bodies of water to document holiday memories. It wasn't until picking up *Splash: The Art of the Swimming Pool* by Annie Kelly that I invested time into curating my own series. As I turned each page of Kelly's book, a wave of nostalgia washed over me, taking me back to summer days swimming in my childhood pool. Paying homage to Kelly, I chose to explicitly experiment with negative space, compositional balance, leading lines and symmetry. As such, the series emphasises the pools' less appreciated elements that I fell in love with – their curves, sharp edges, diverse blue hues and the way elongated shadows play against their surfaces. This is all lost without an alternate viewpoint.

As much as I'm drawn to their visual features, I've come to learn that pools have distinct personalities – some evoking a sense of tranquillity, others a more solemn feeling. Pools, often appreciated merely as architectural objects, retain an innate ability to trigger involuntary memories. For me, they can evoke the smell of my favourite food, or resurrect memories of my holidays.

As I look back at the 89 images, I'm reminded that the most harmonious visual elements of our world remain hidden to us – until we view them from a new perspective.

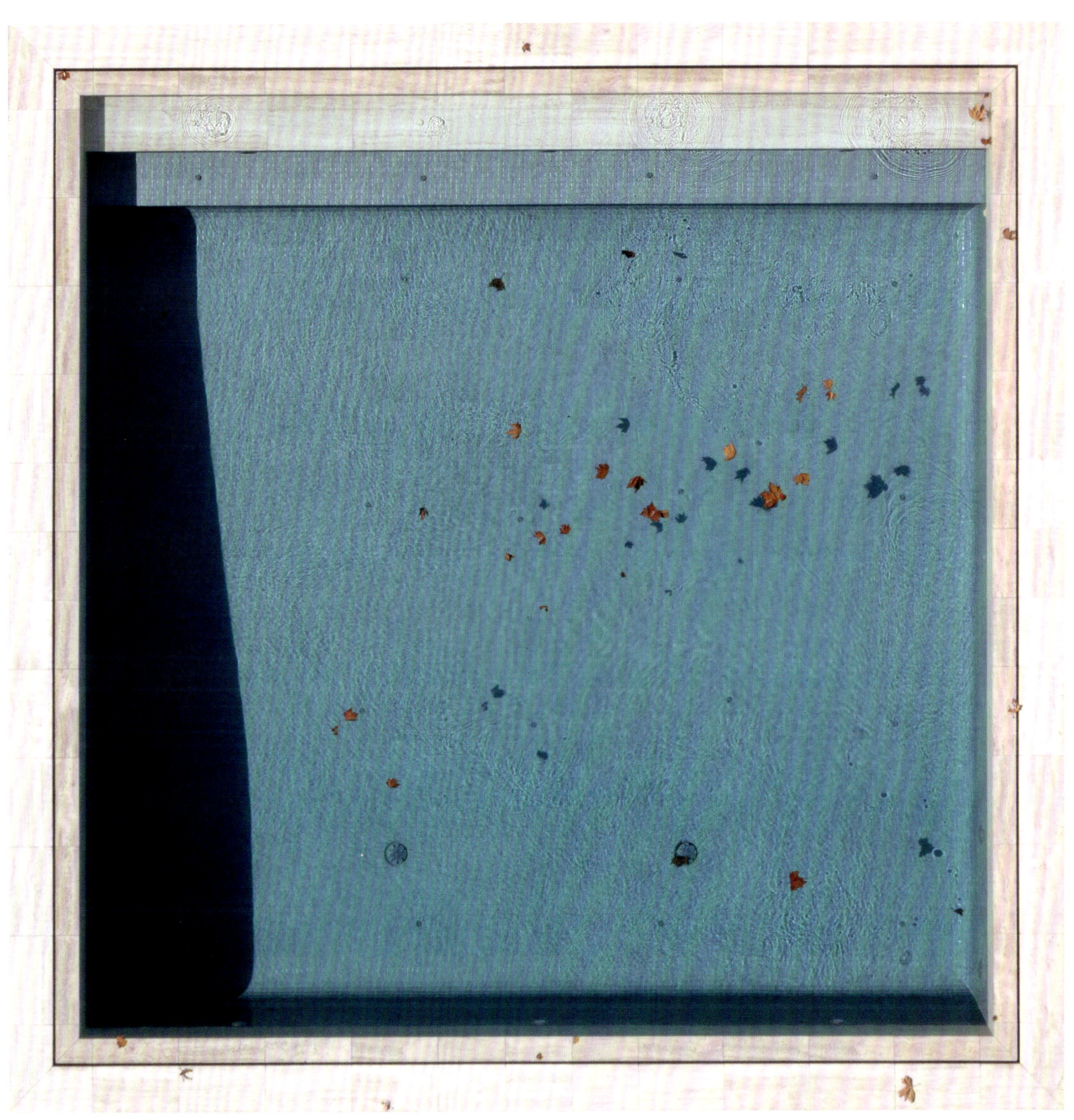

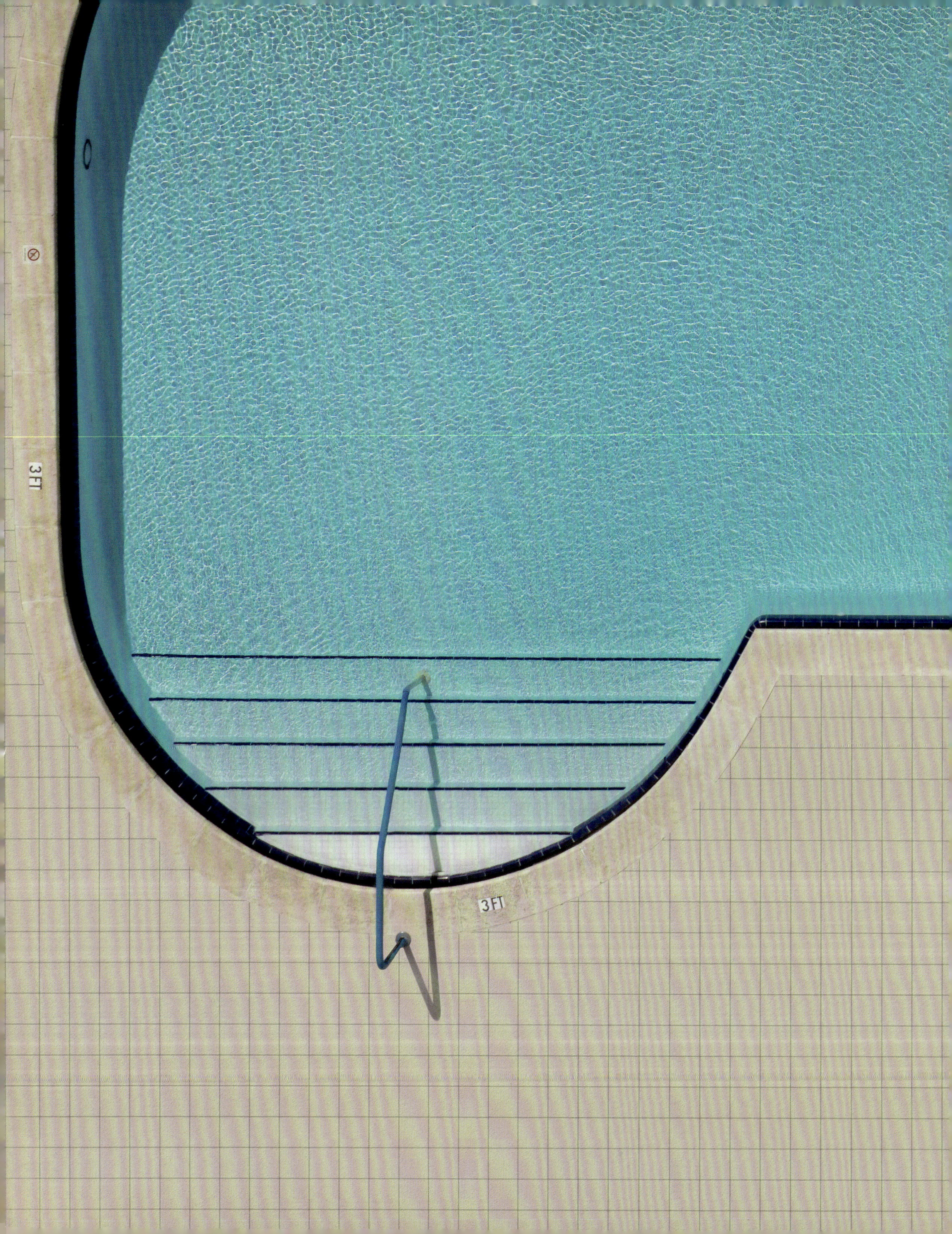
3FT
3FT

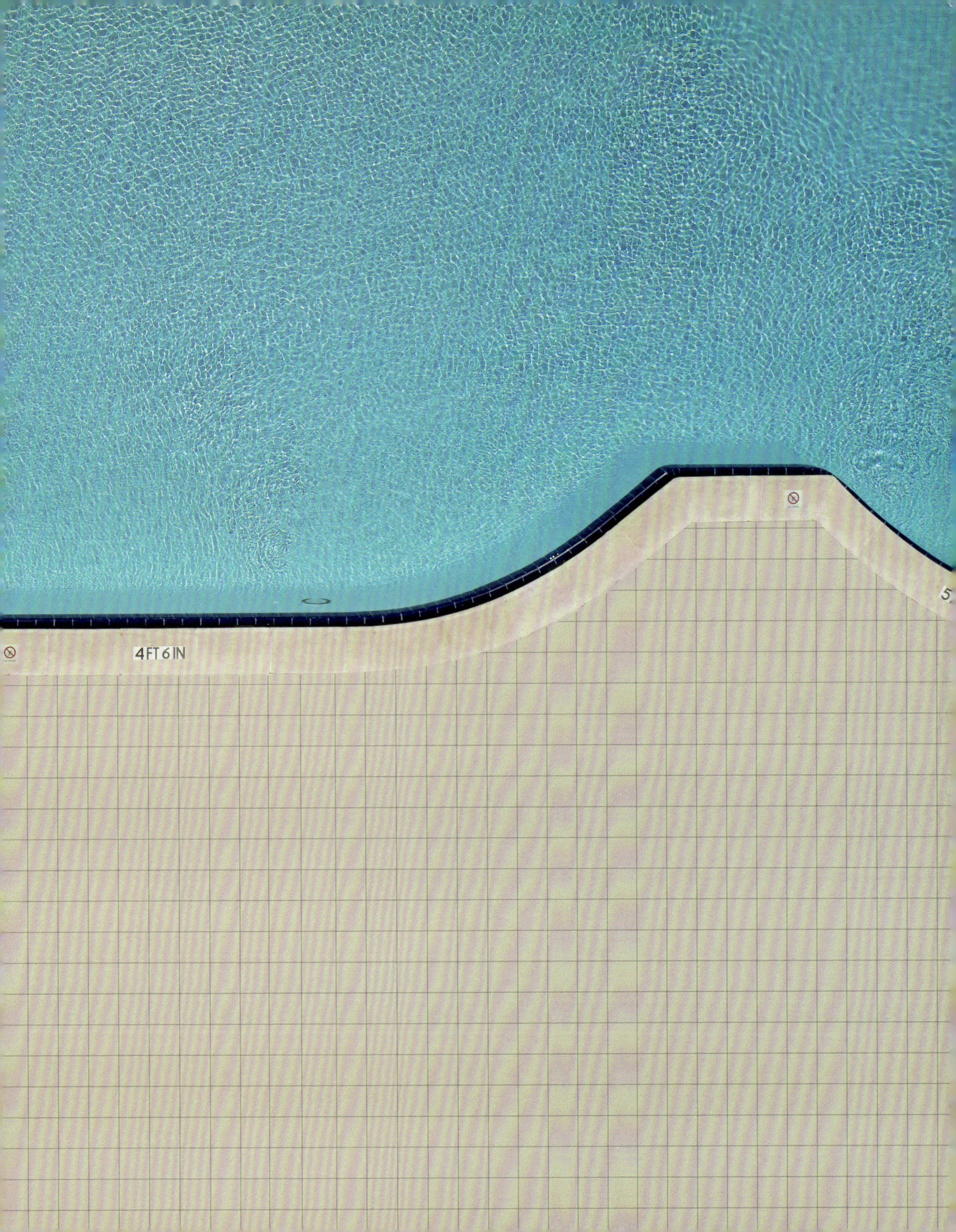
4FT 6IN

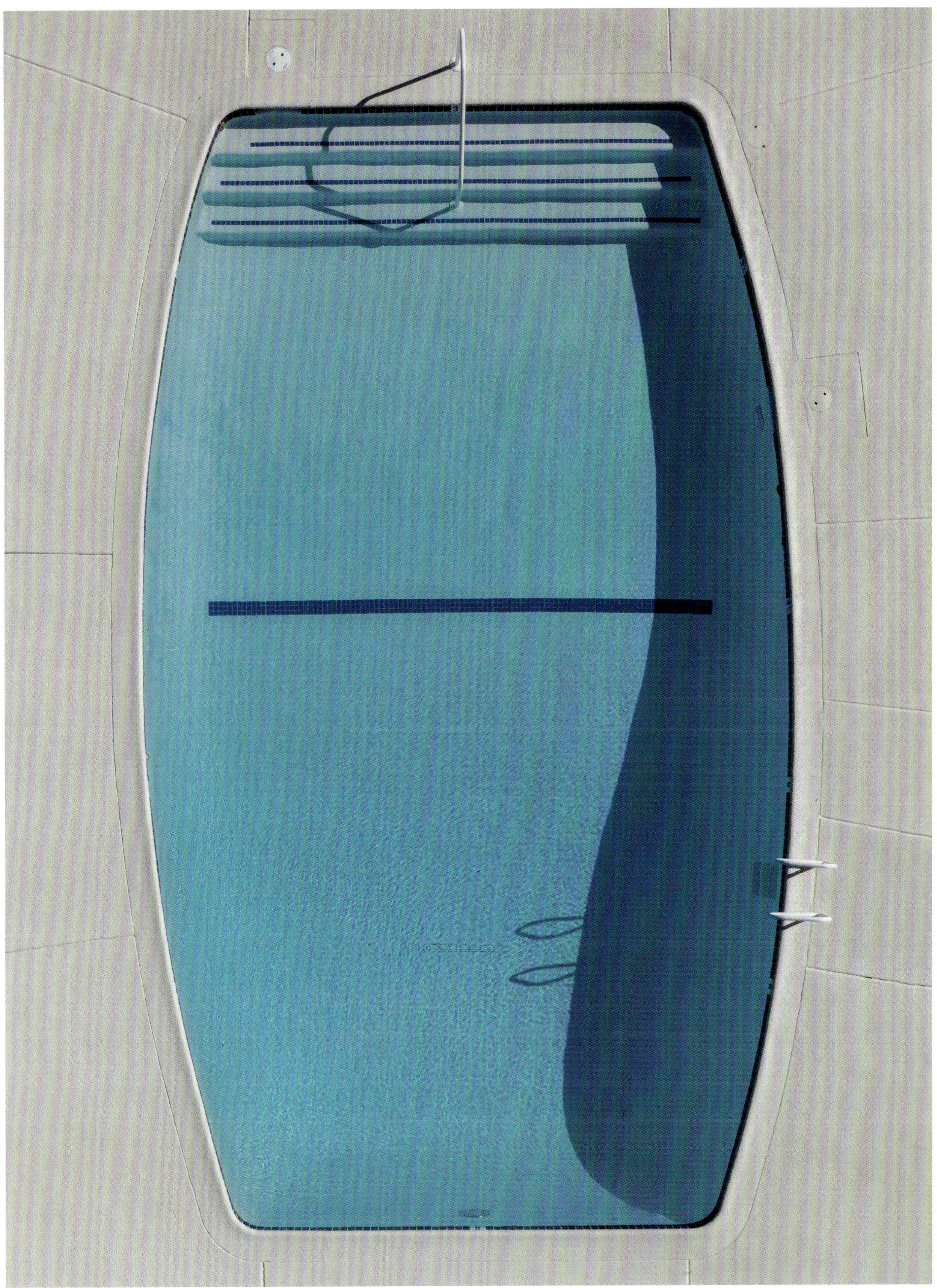

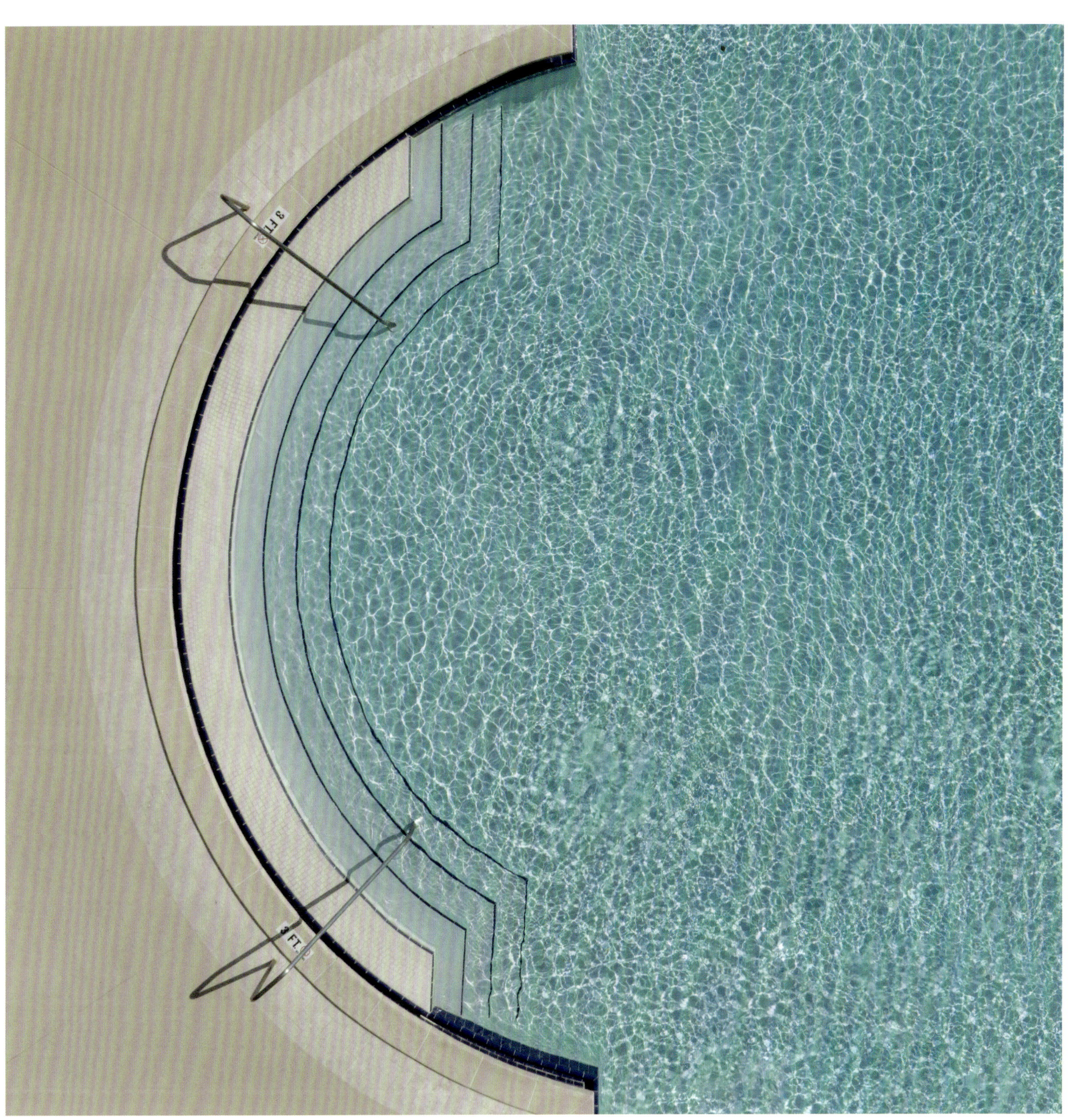
3 FT
3 FT

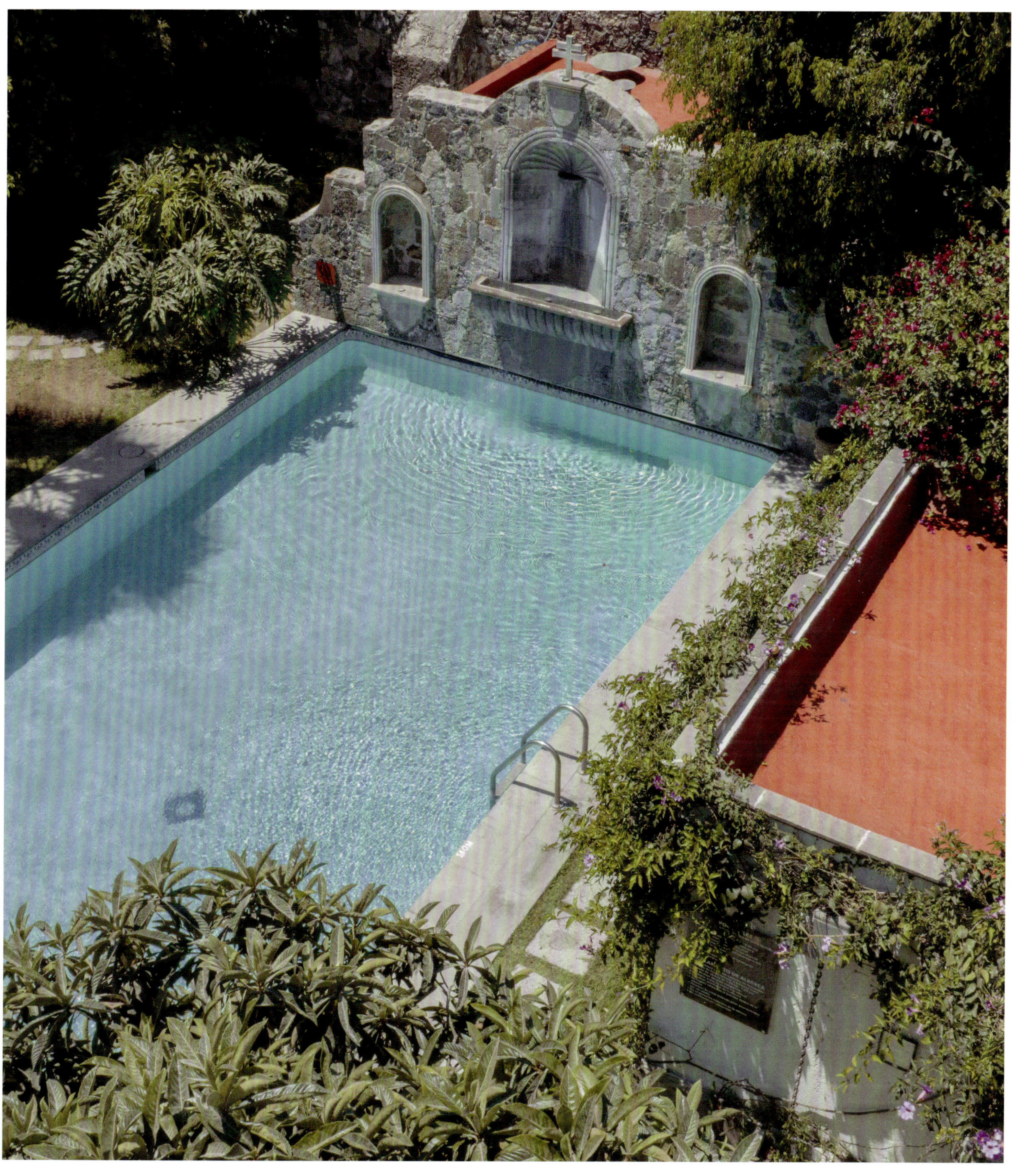

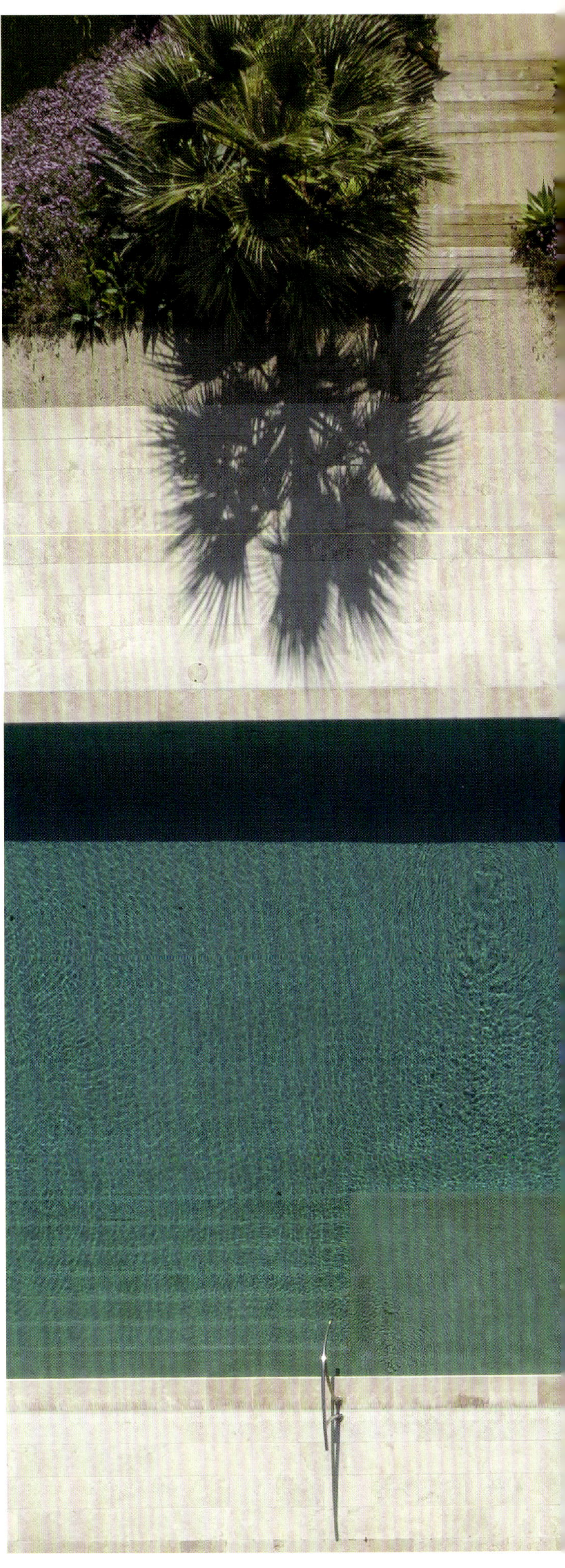

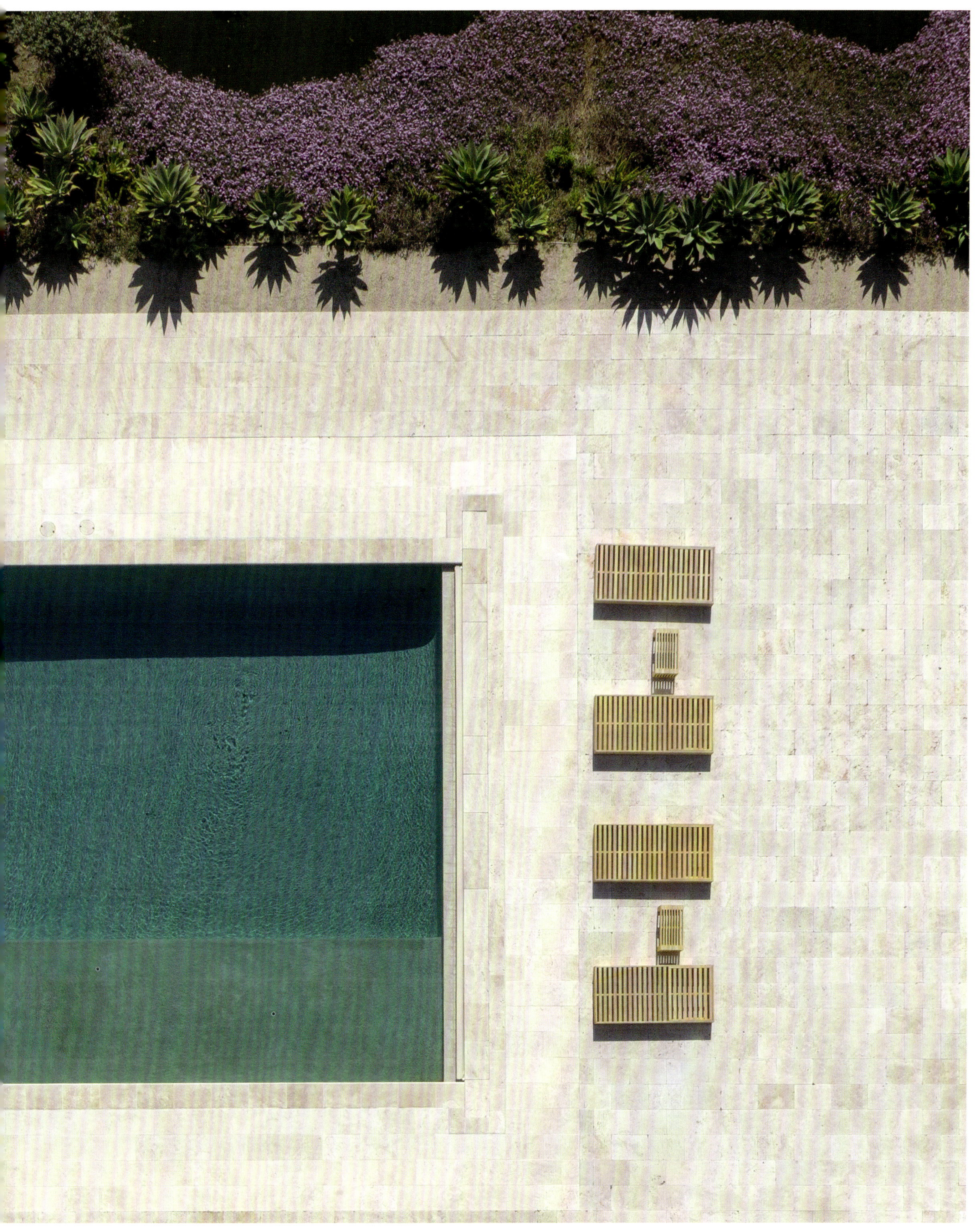

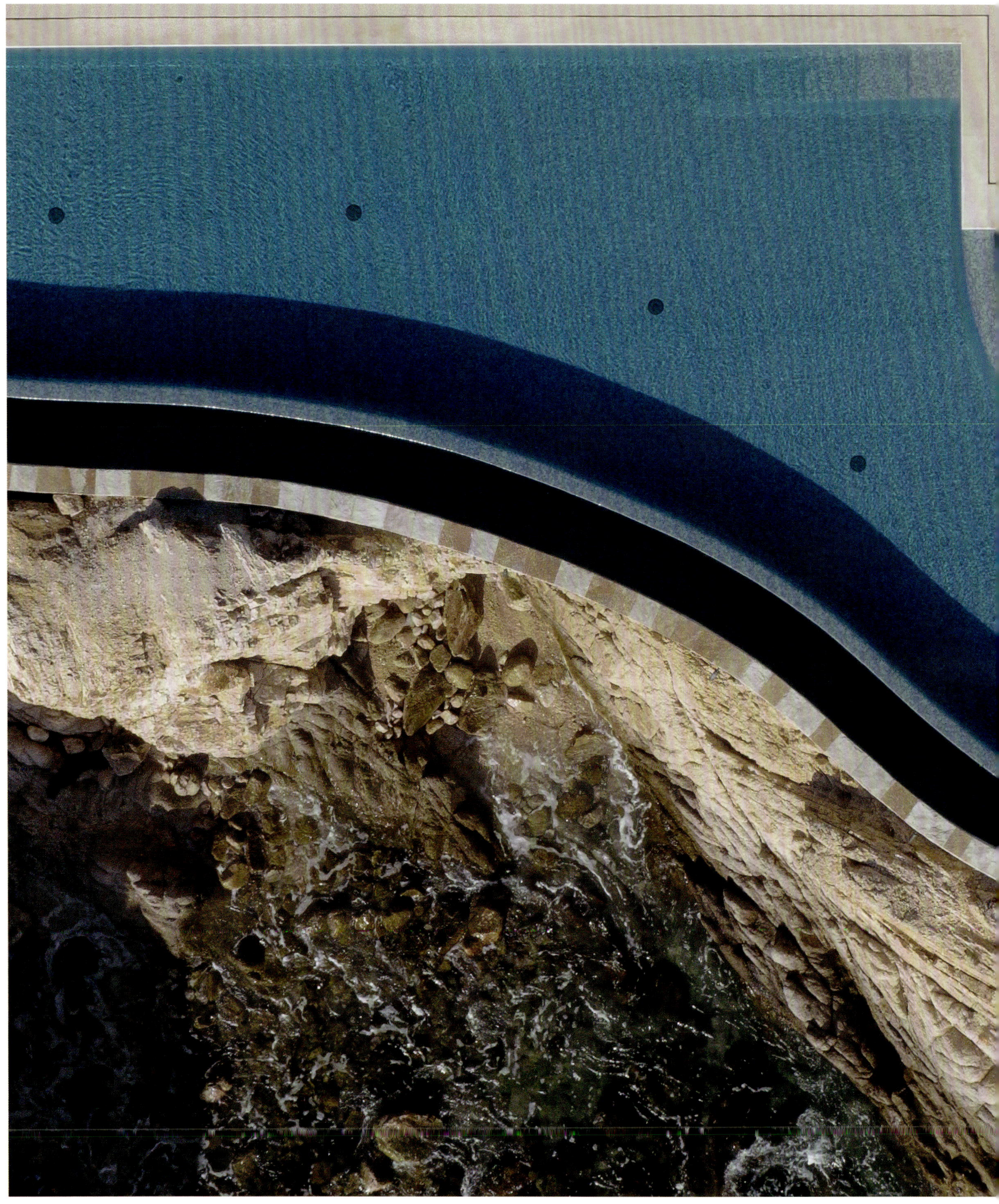

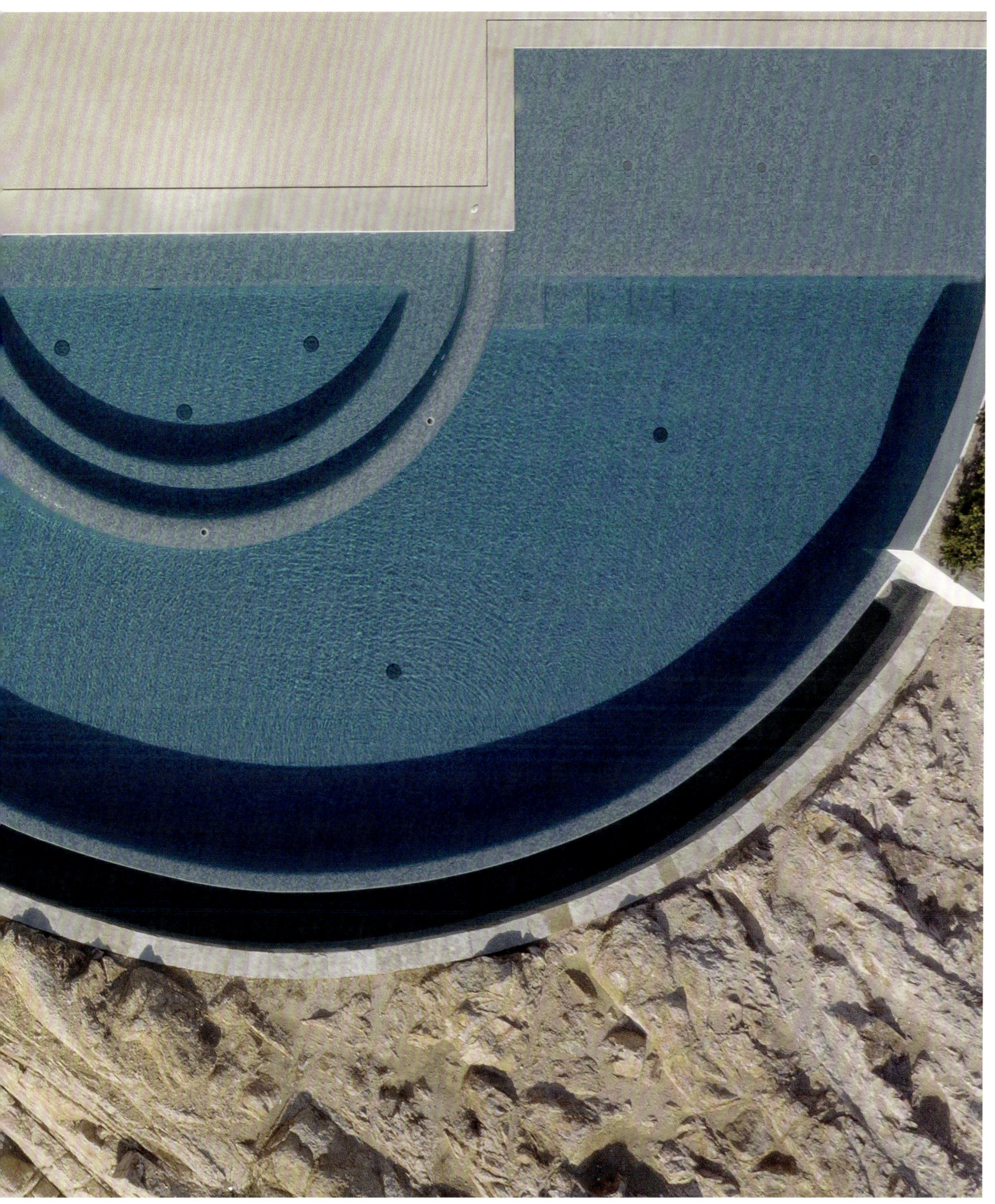

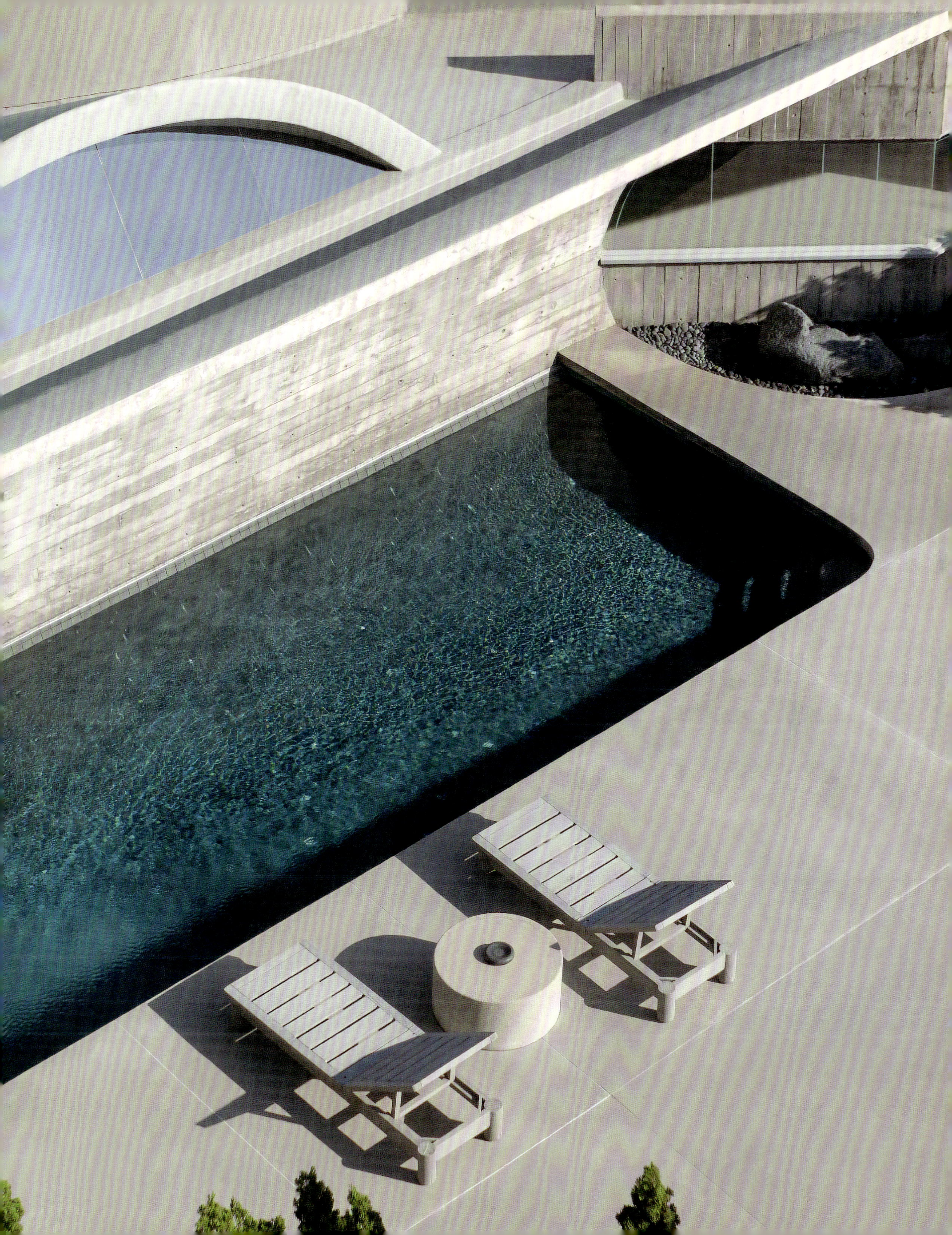

MALIBU, CALIFORNIA
USA

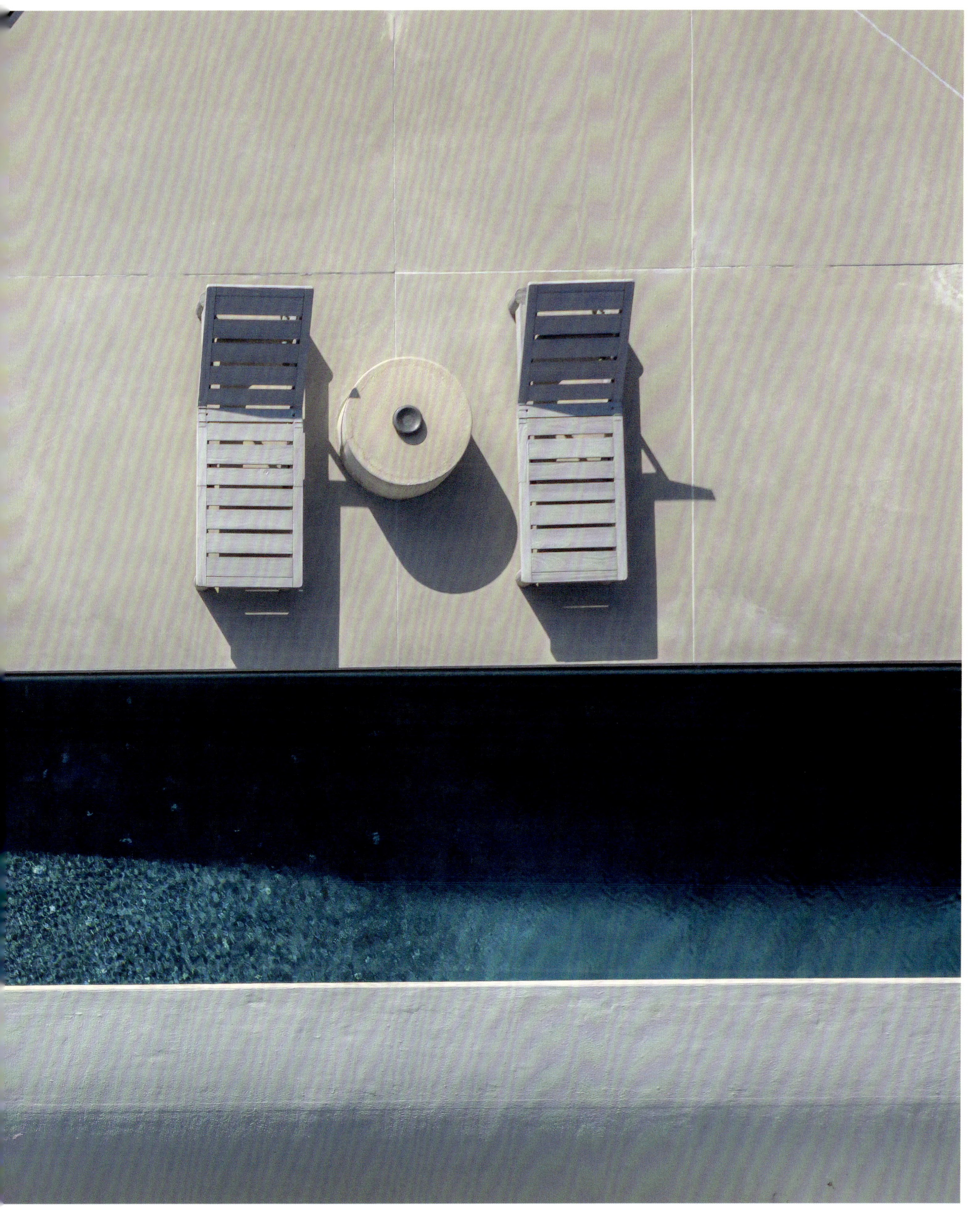

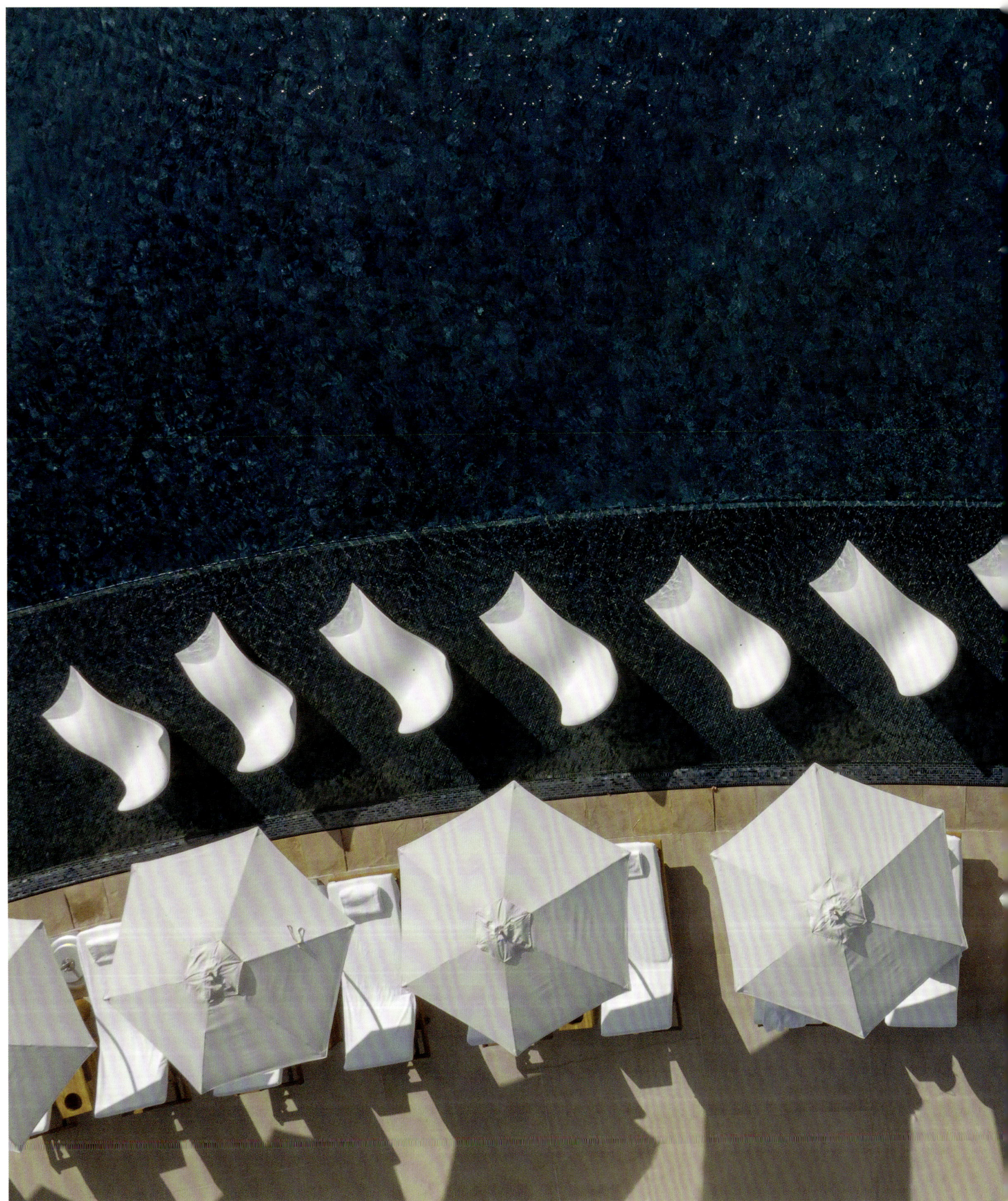

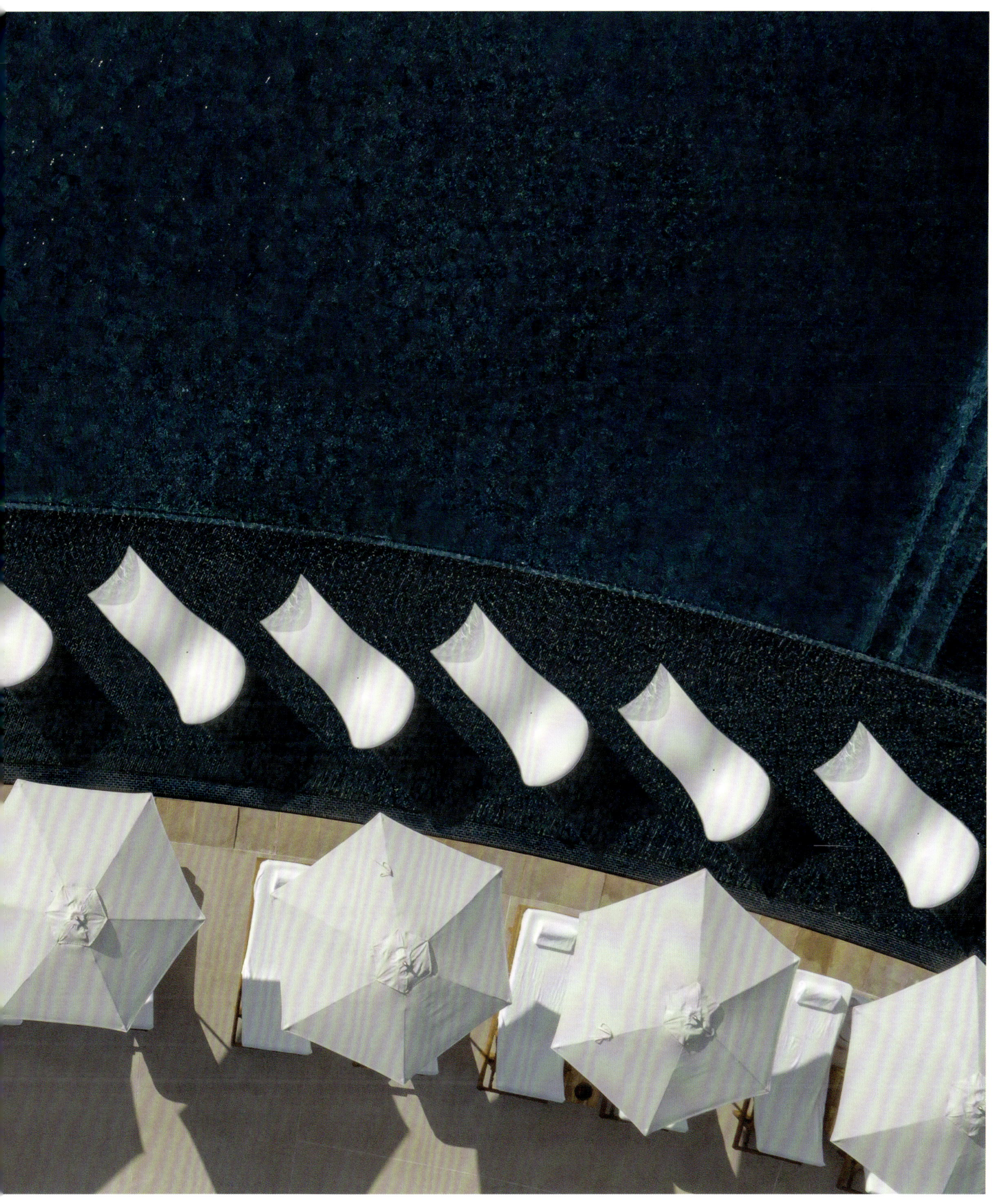

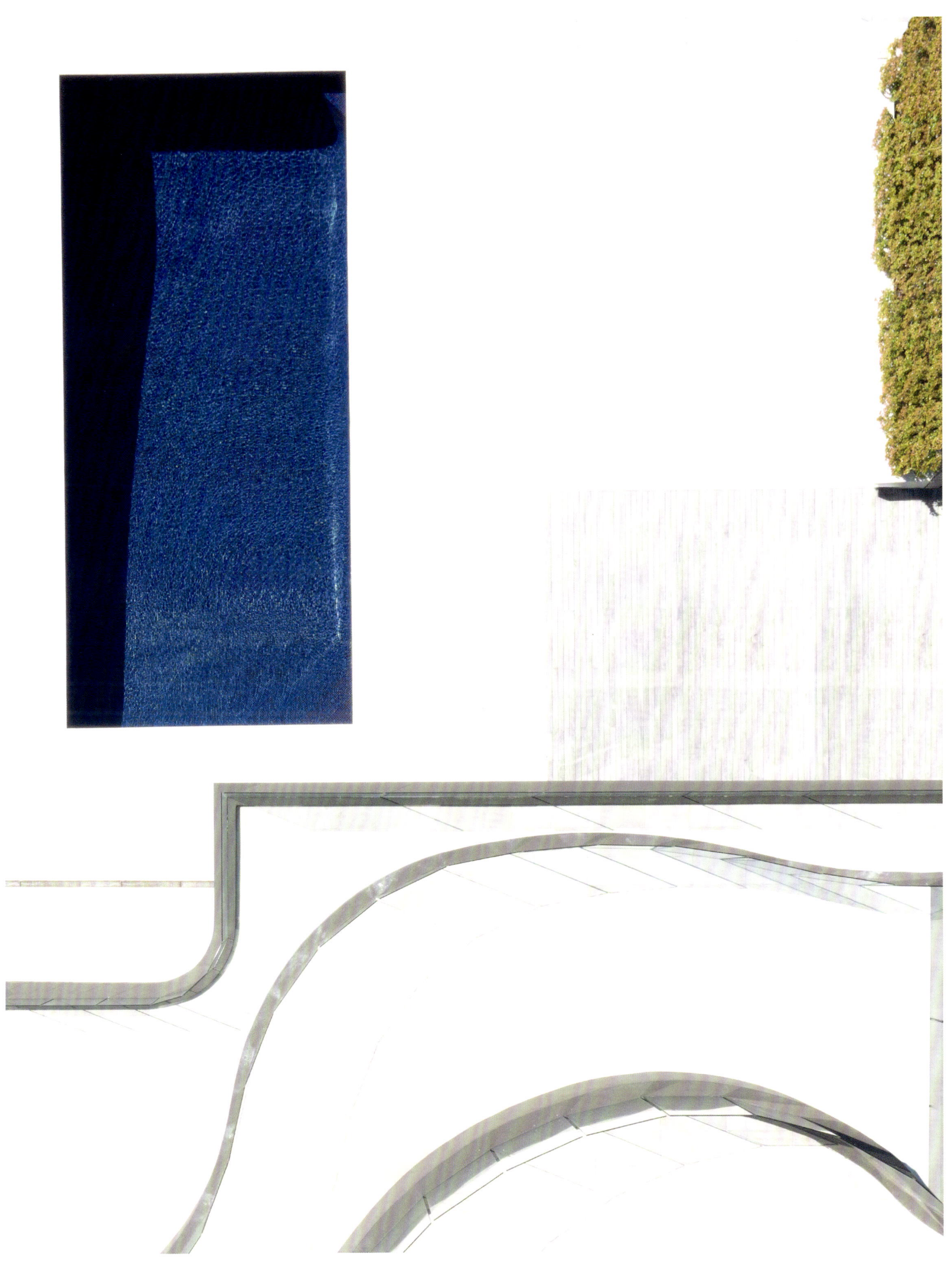

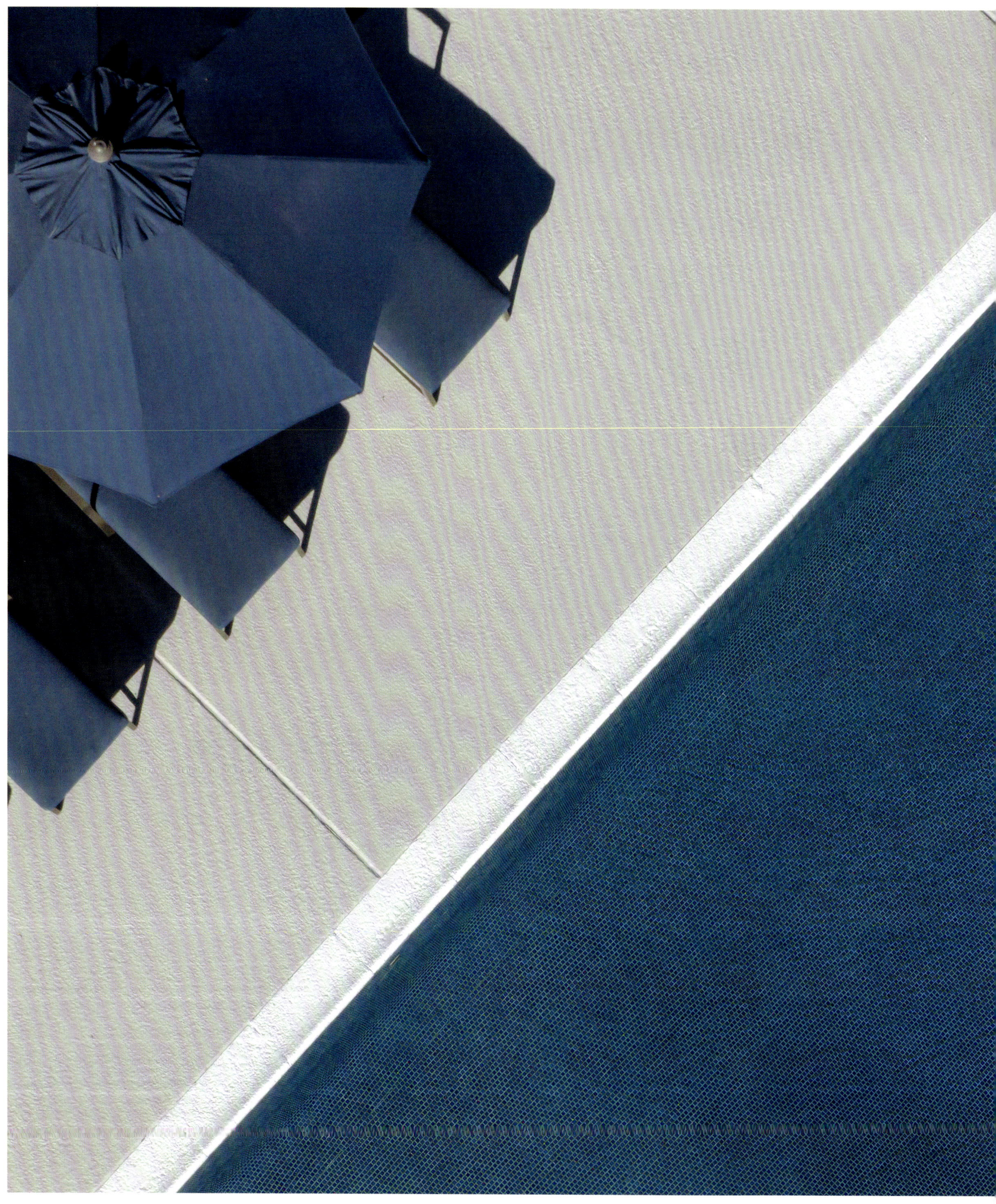

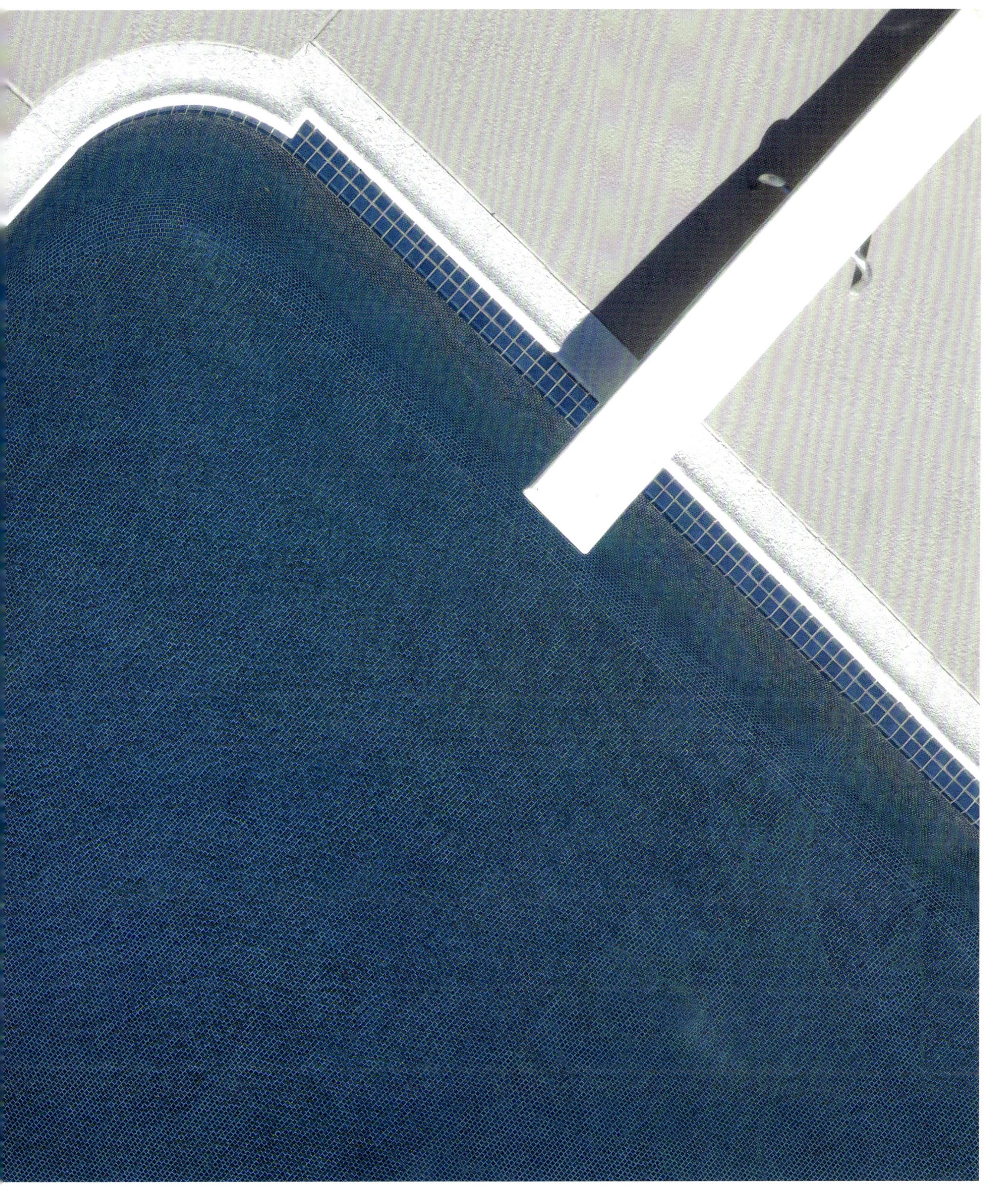

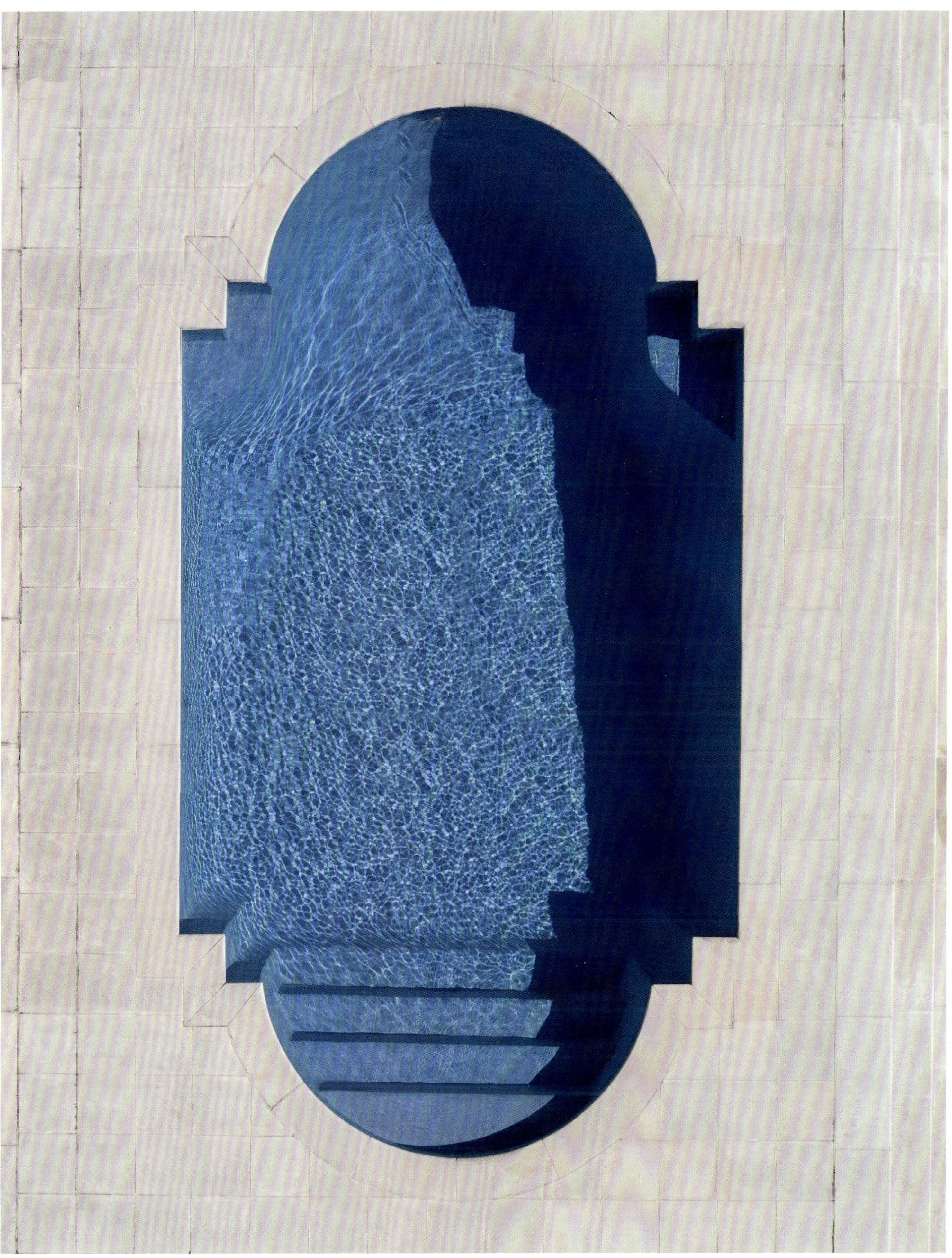

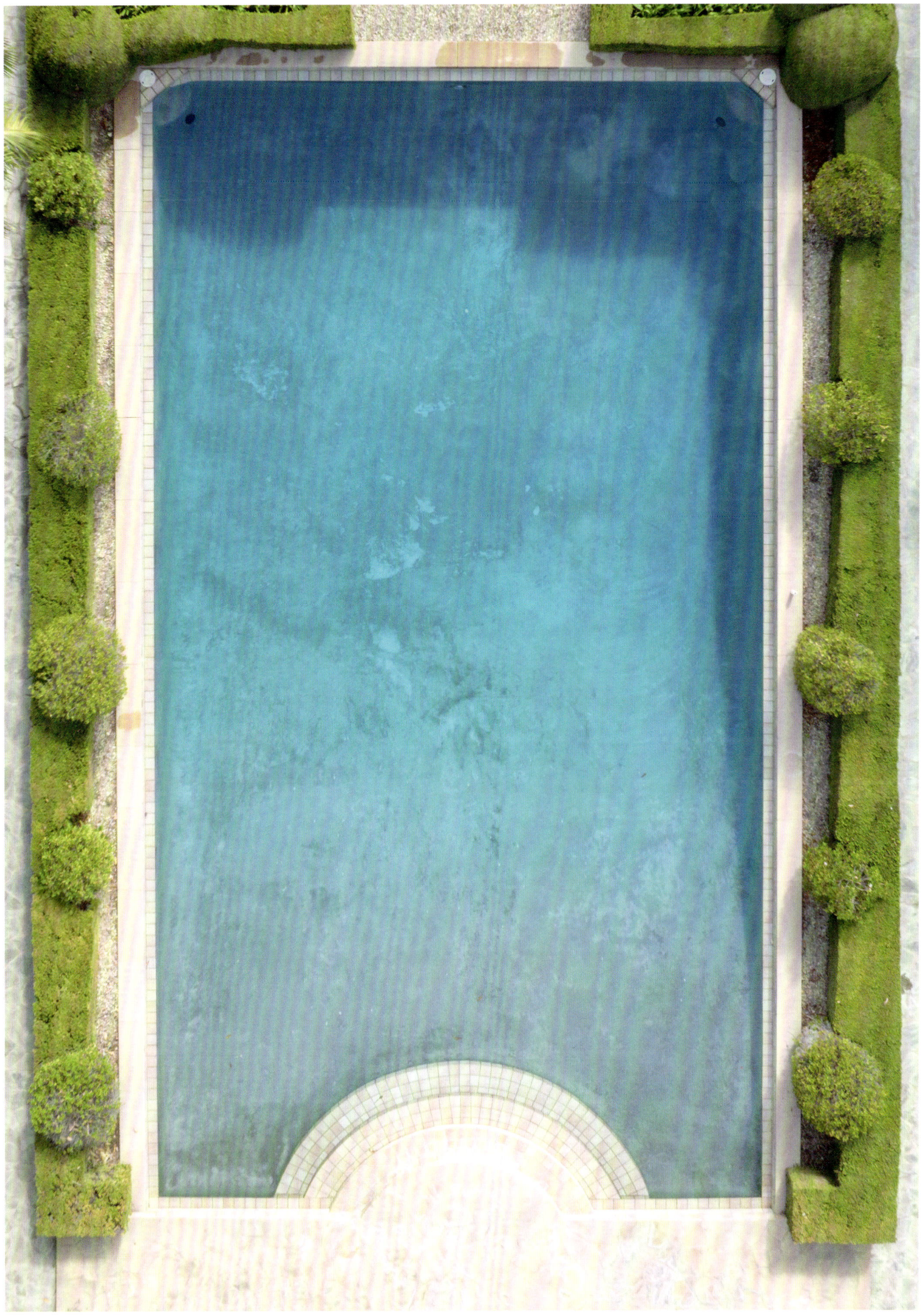

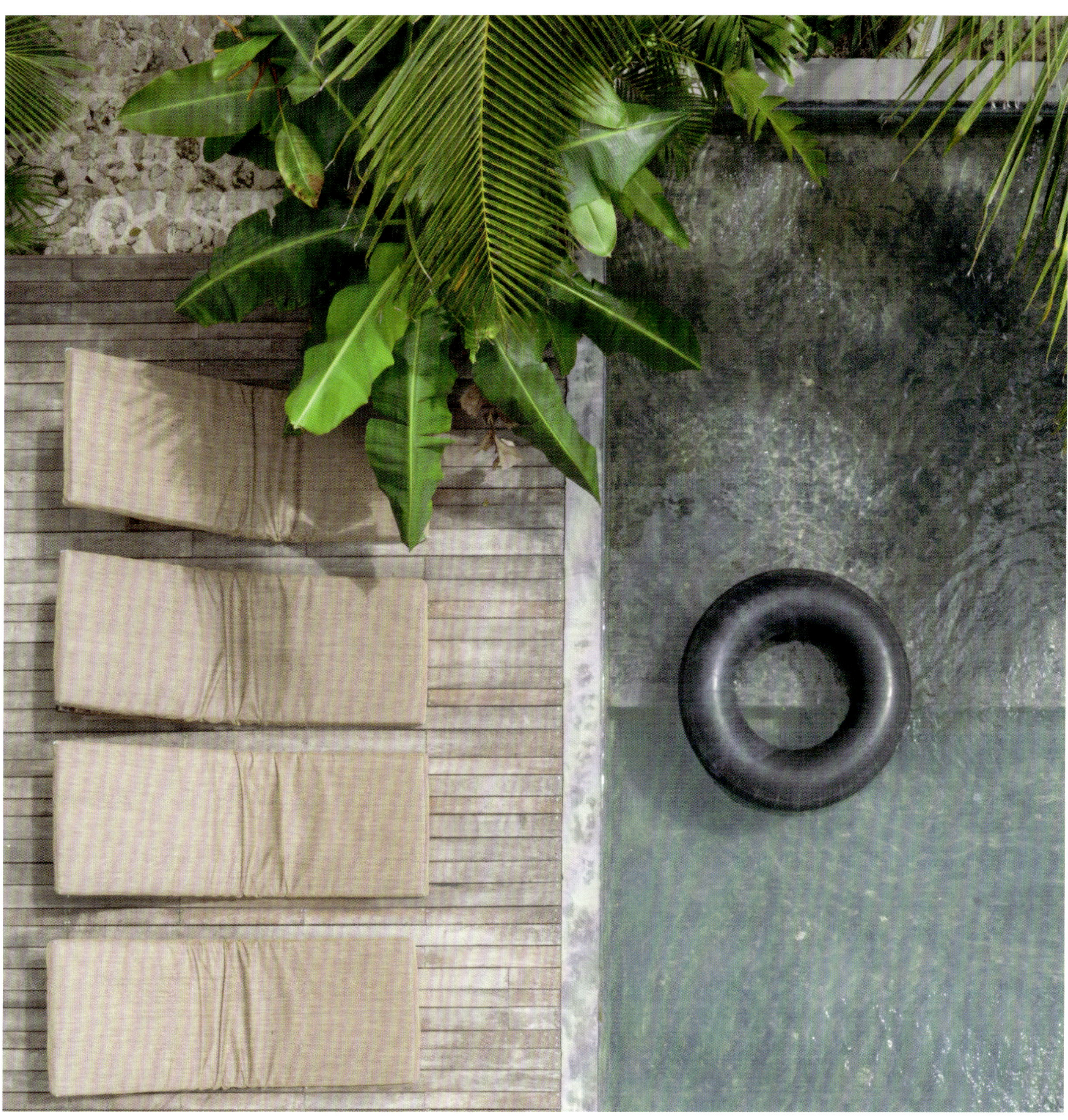

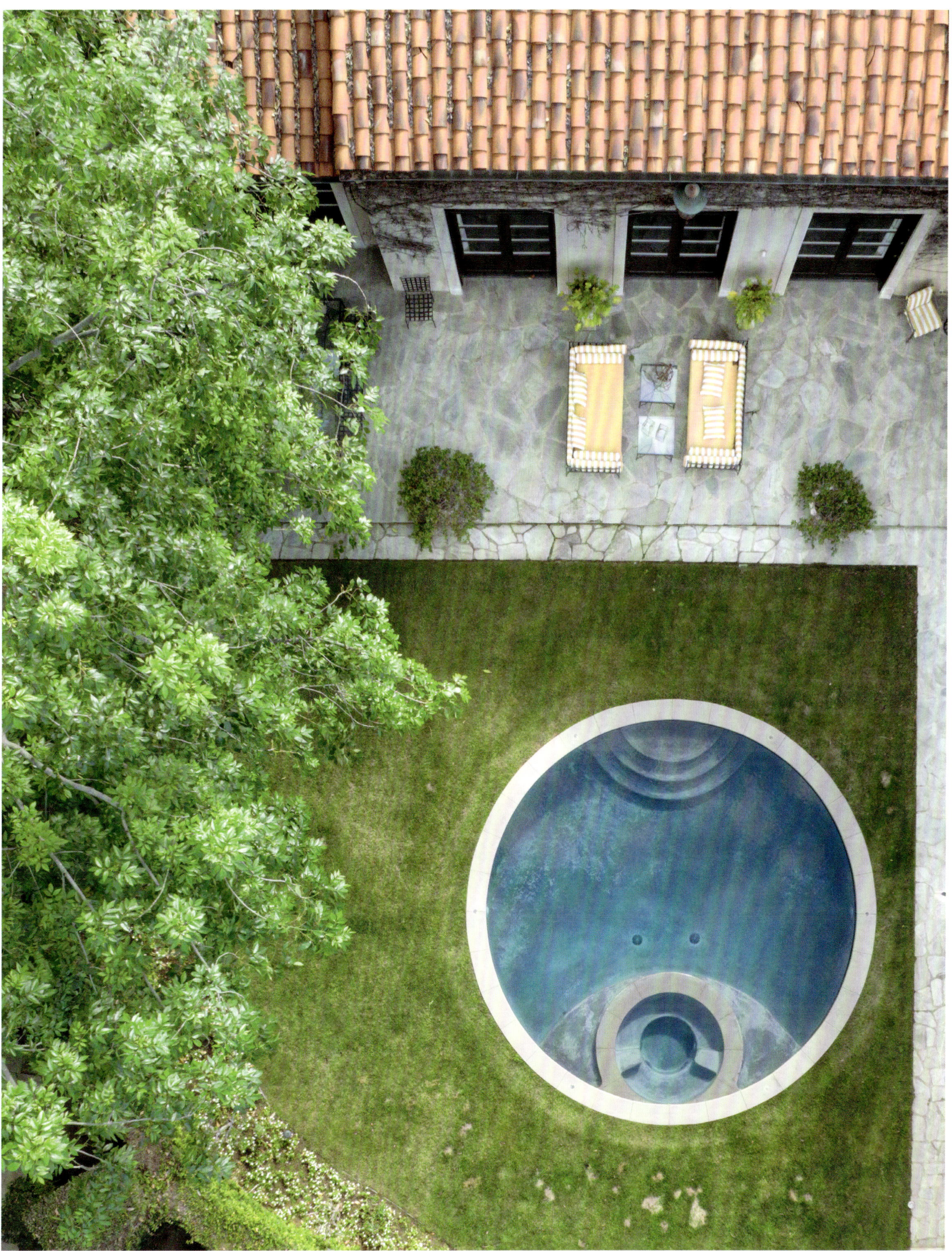

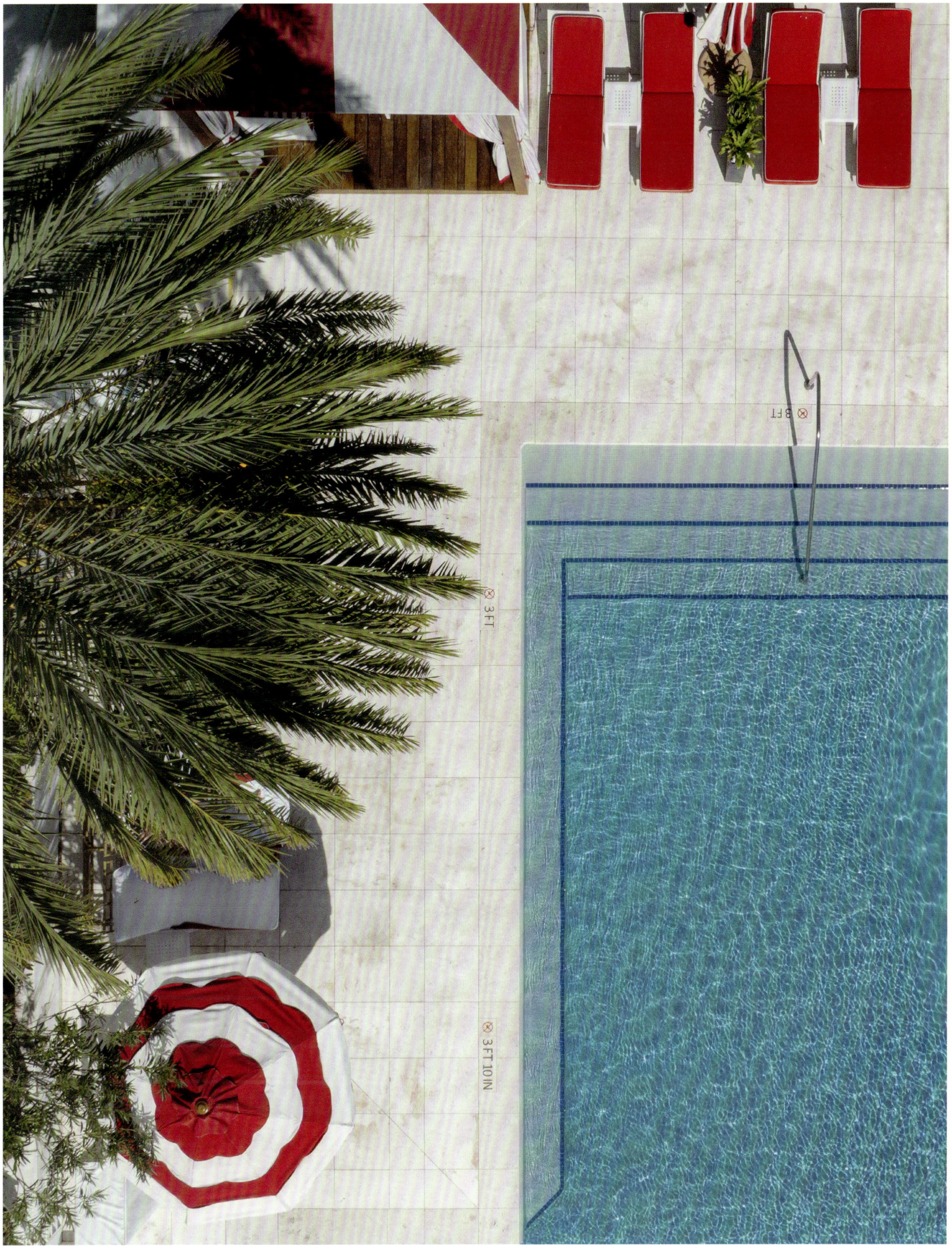
3FT
3FT
3FT 10IN

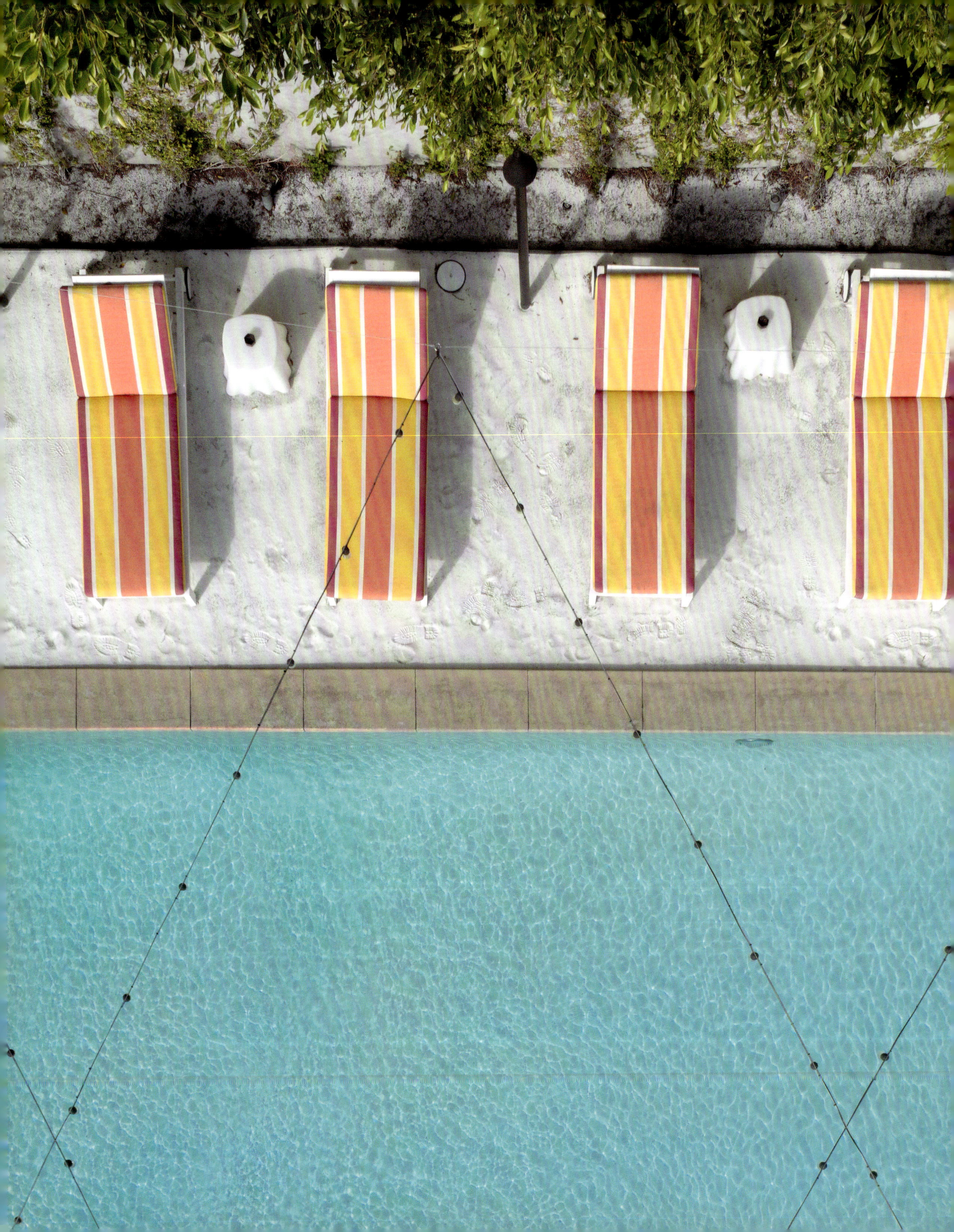

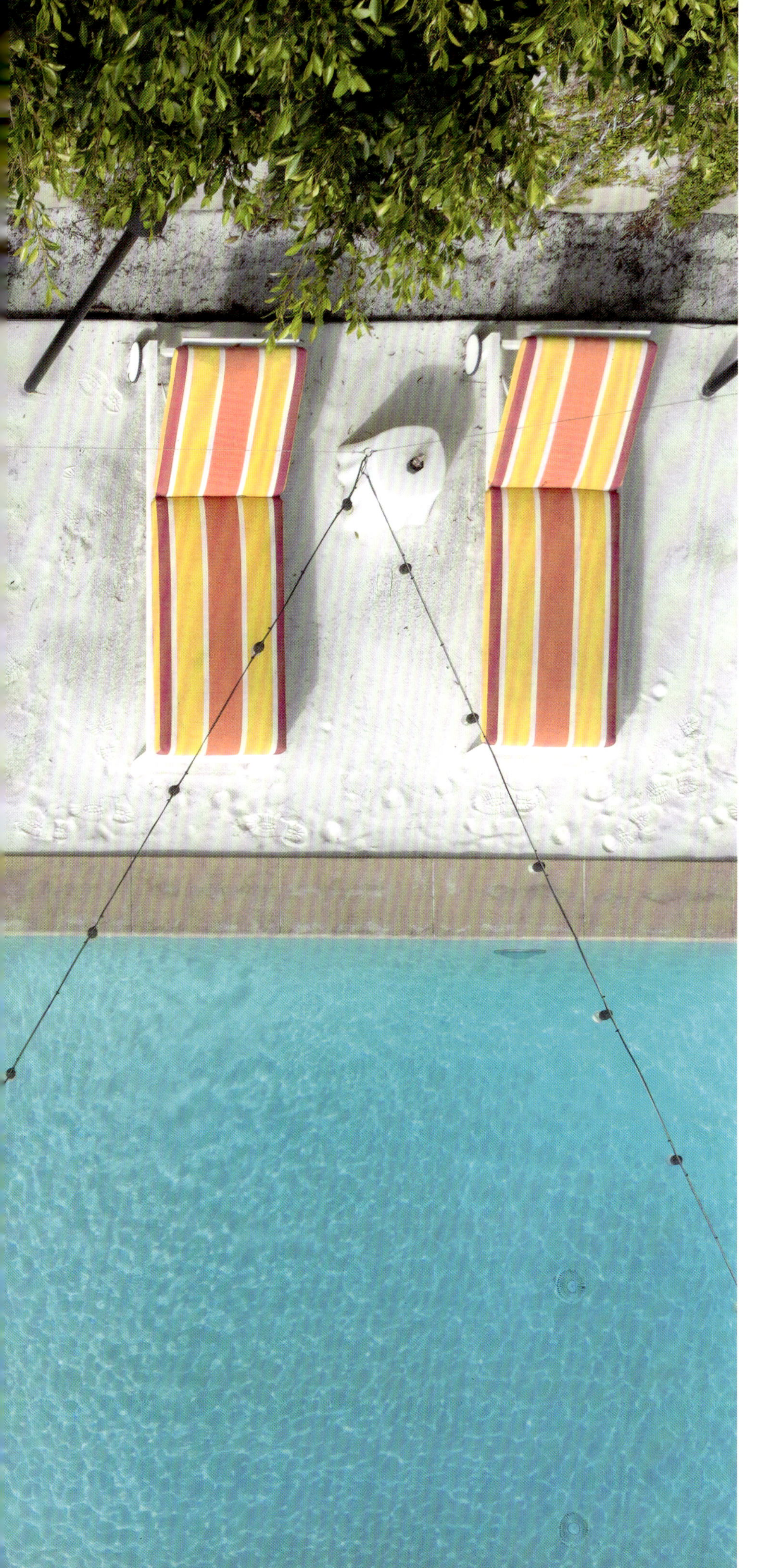

PALM SPRINGS, CALIFORNIA – USA

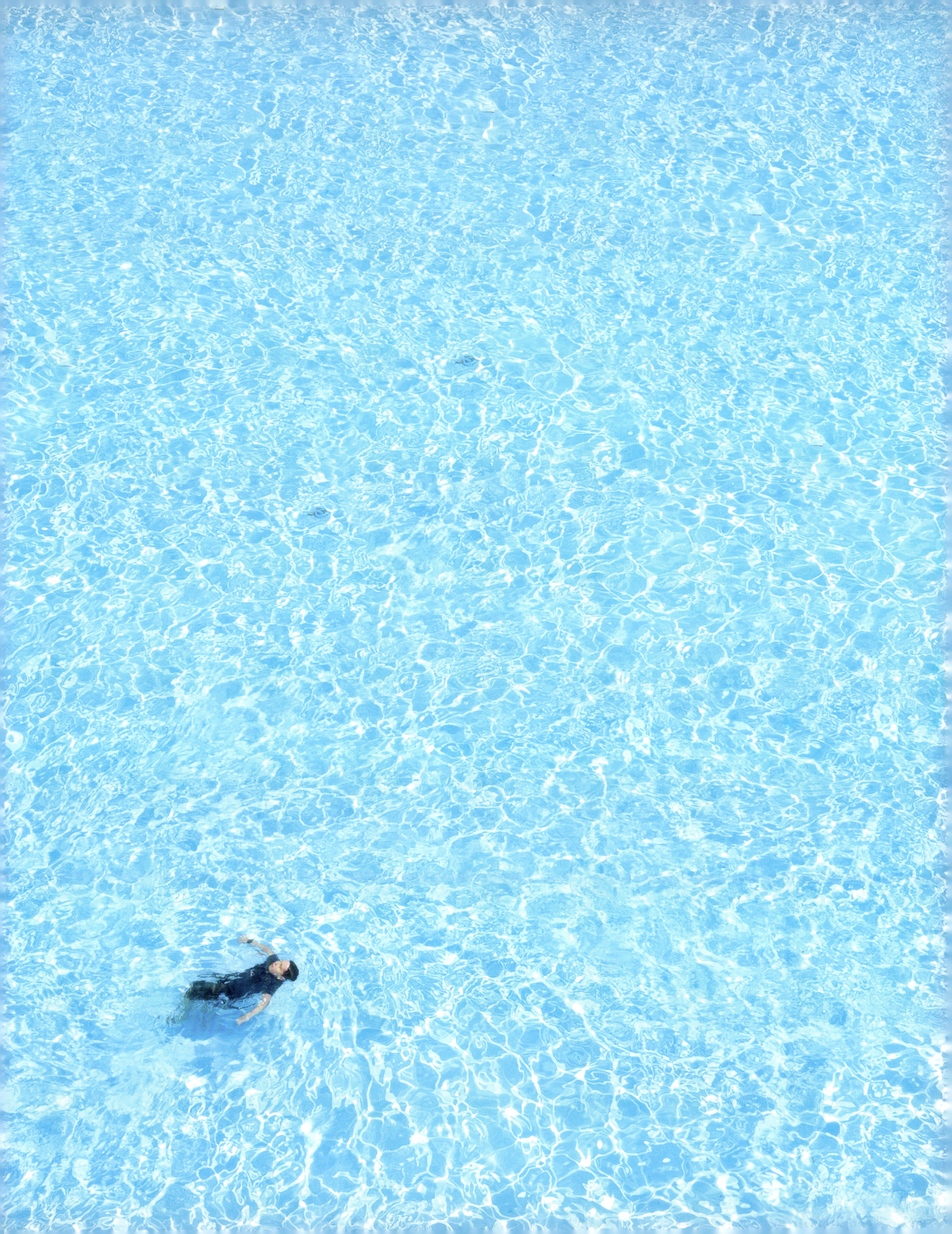

VAUCLUSE, NSW
AUSTRALIA

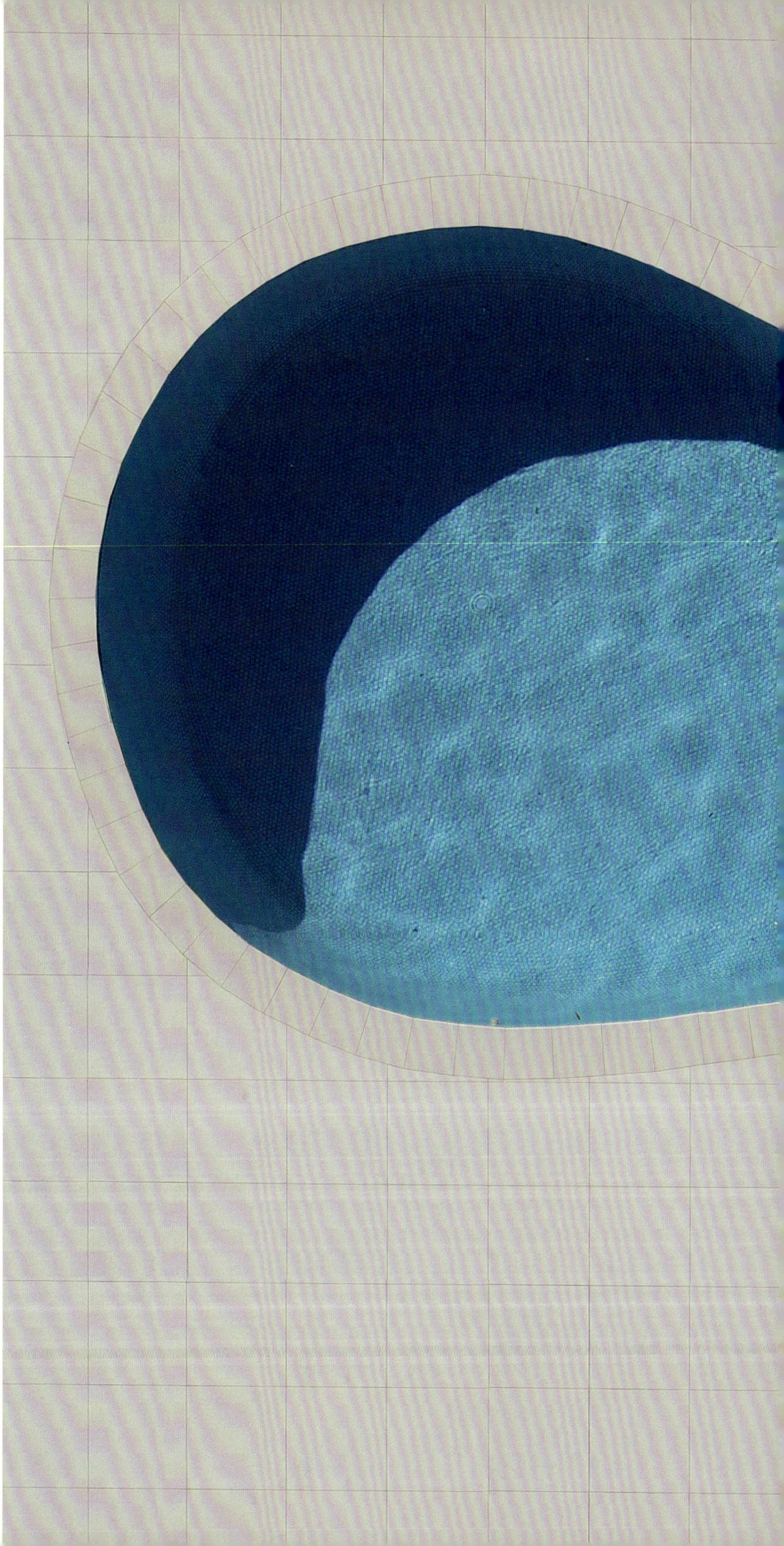

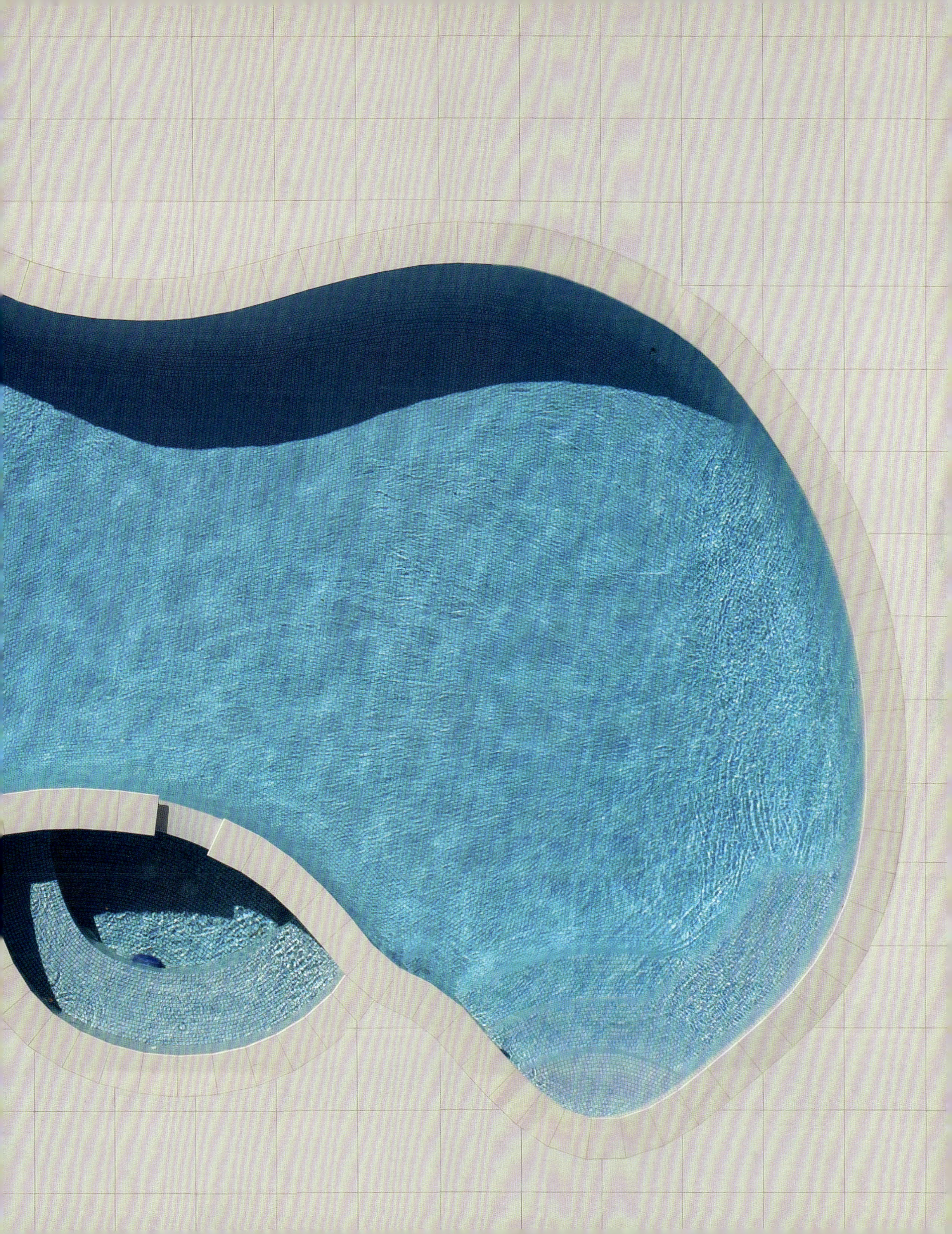

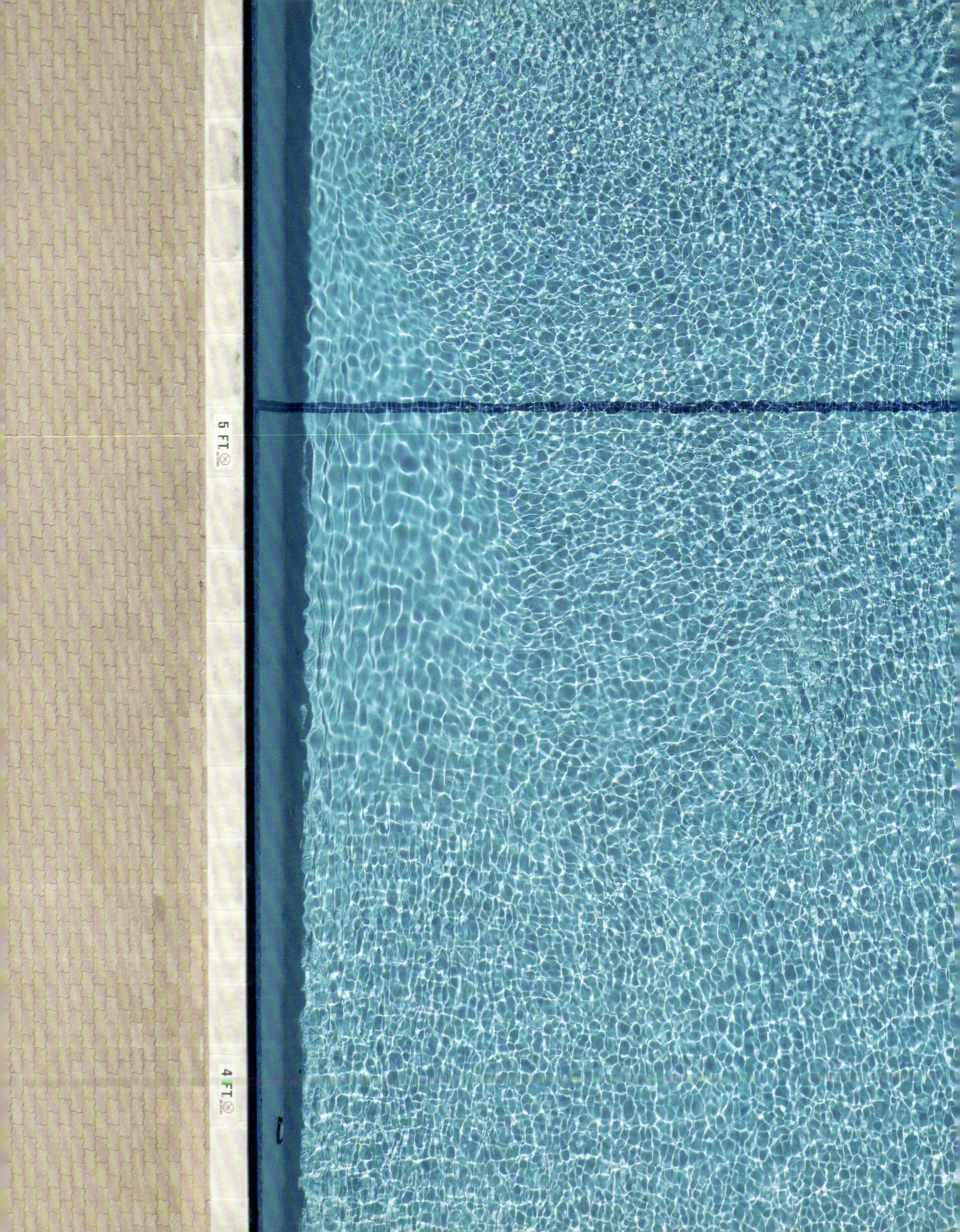
5 FT
4 FT

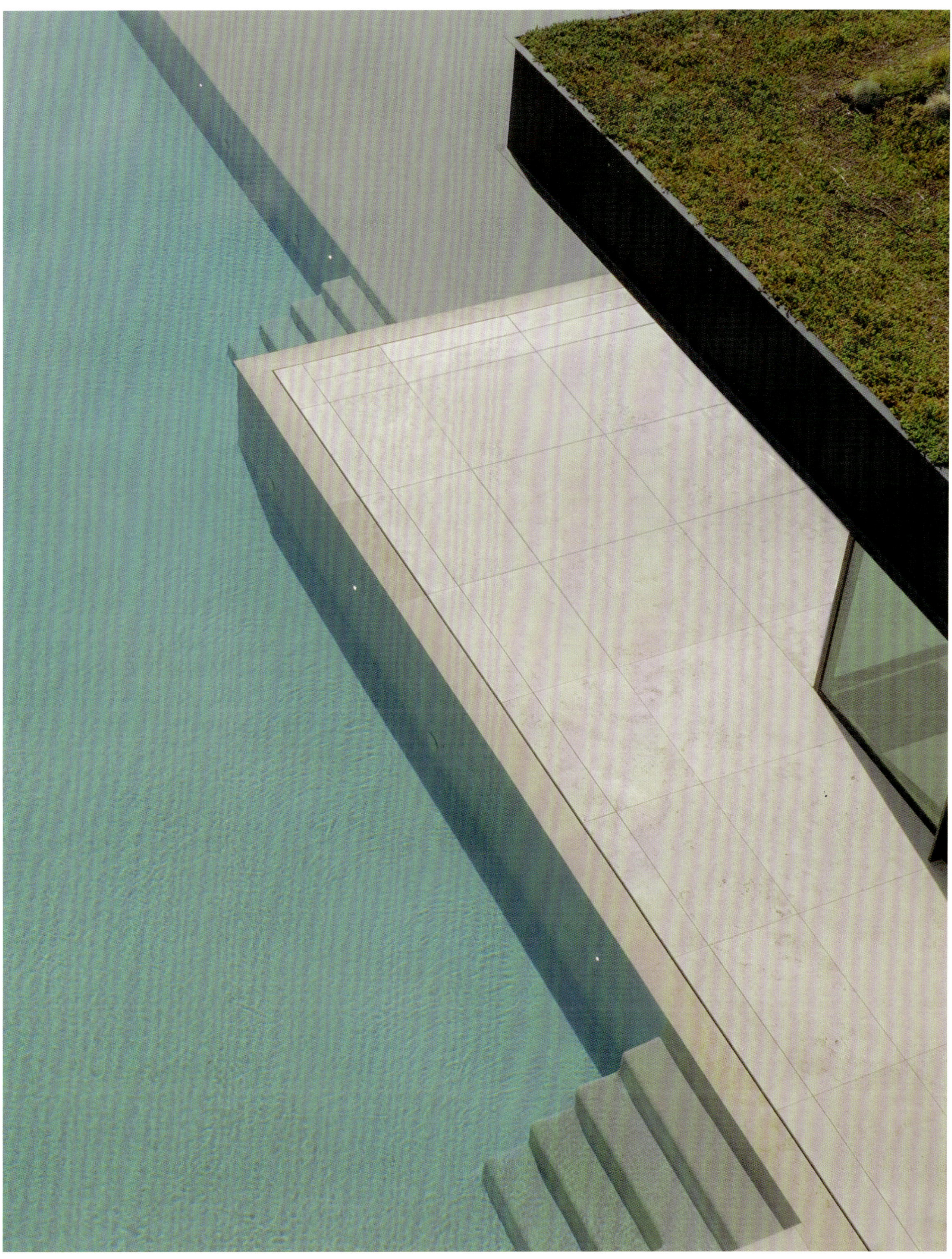

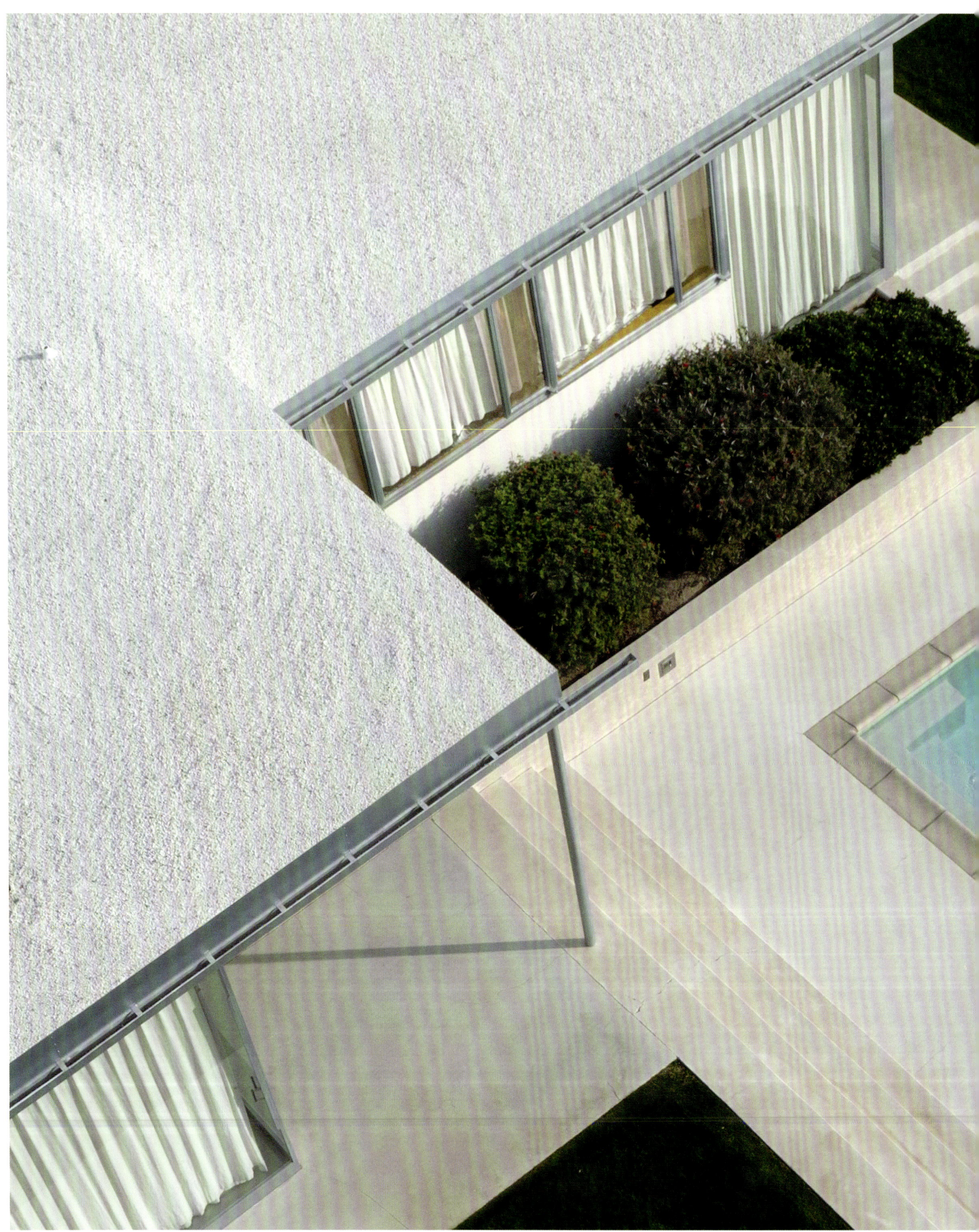

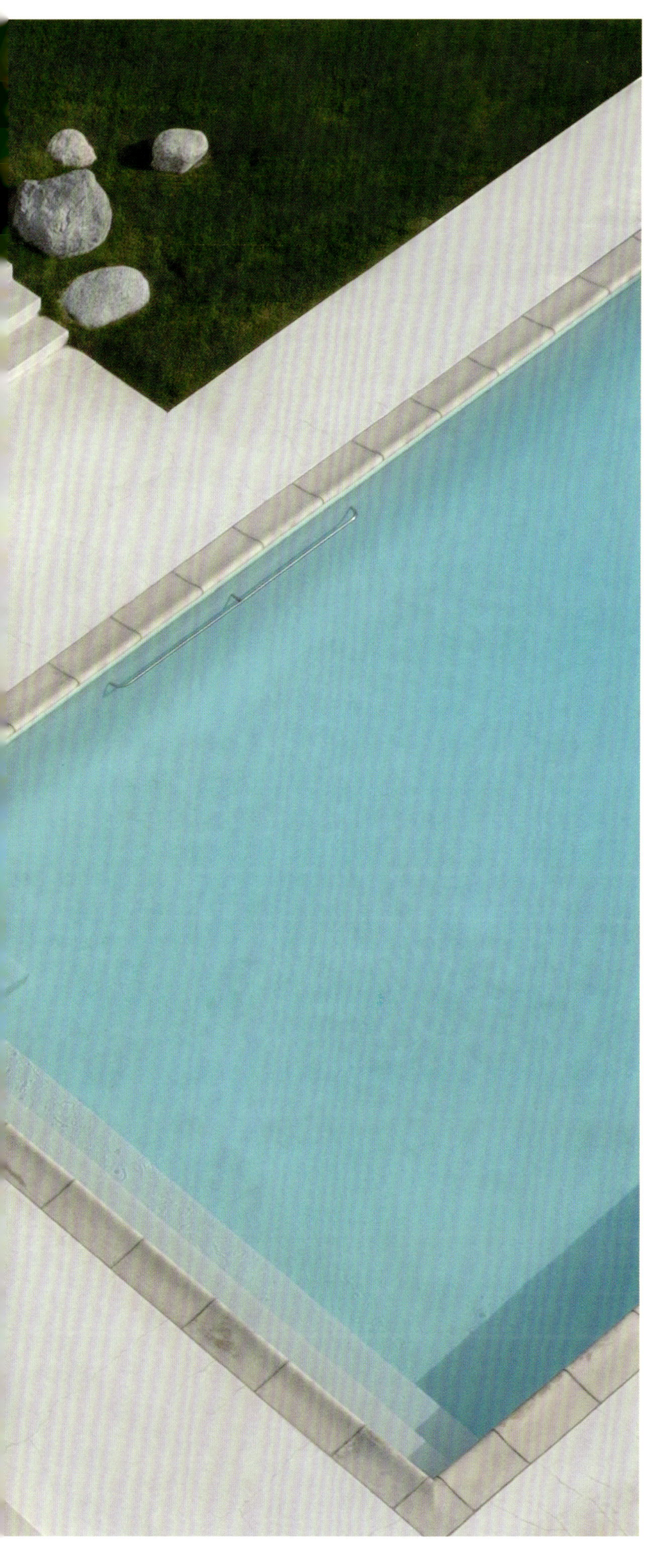

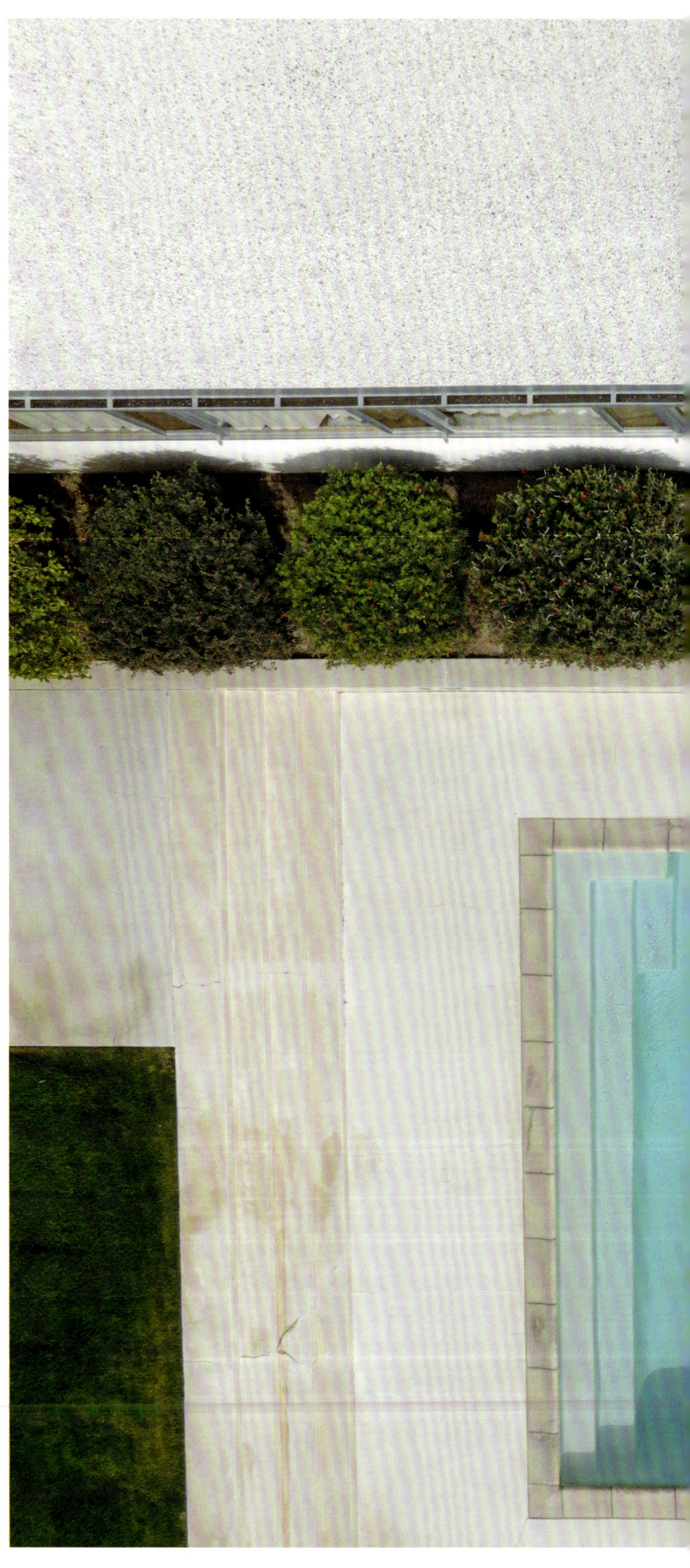

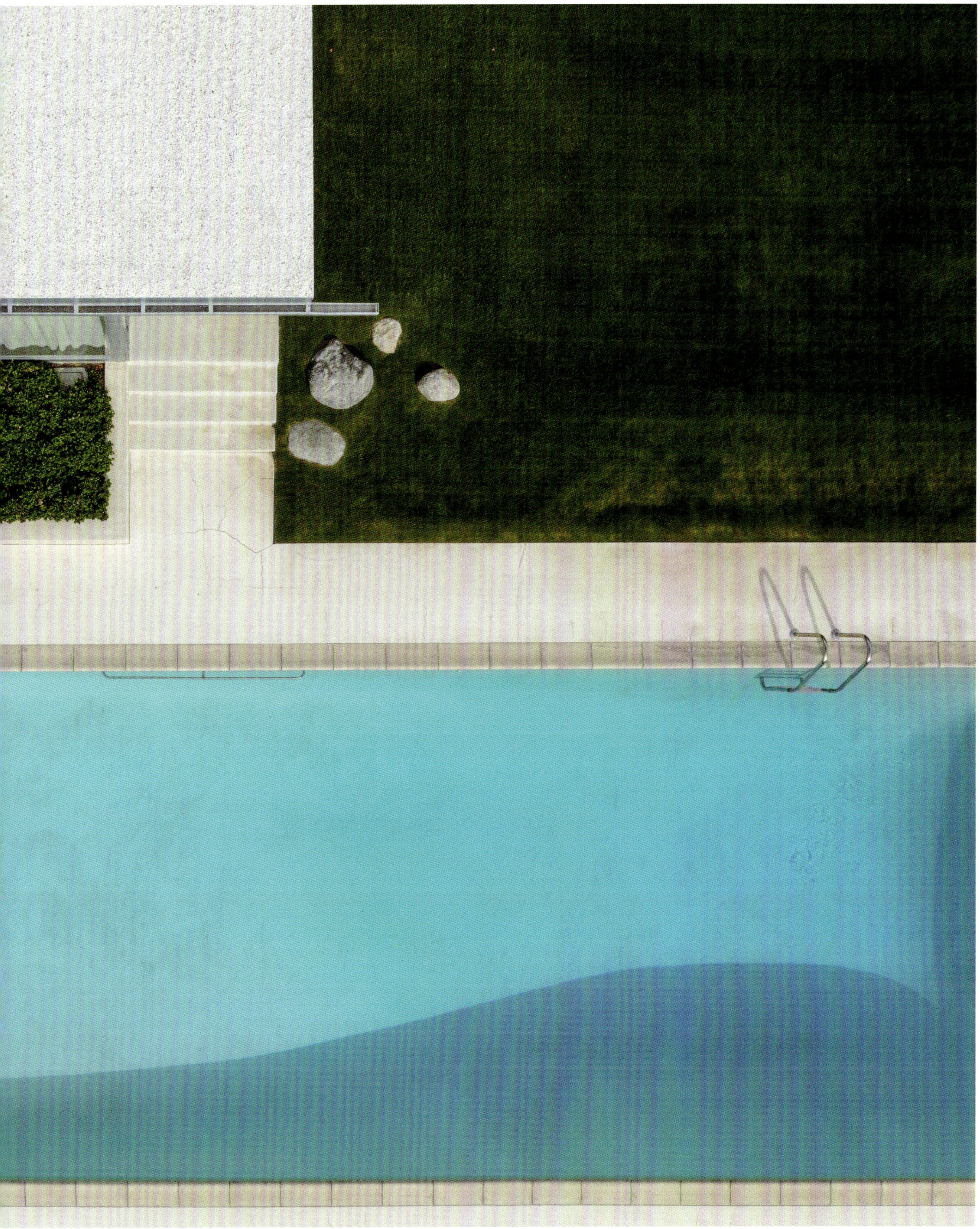

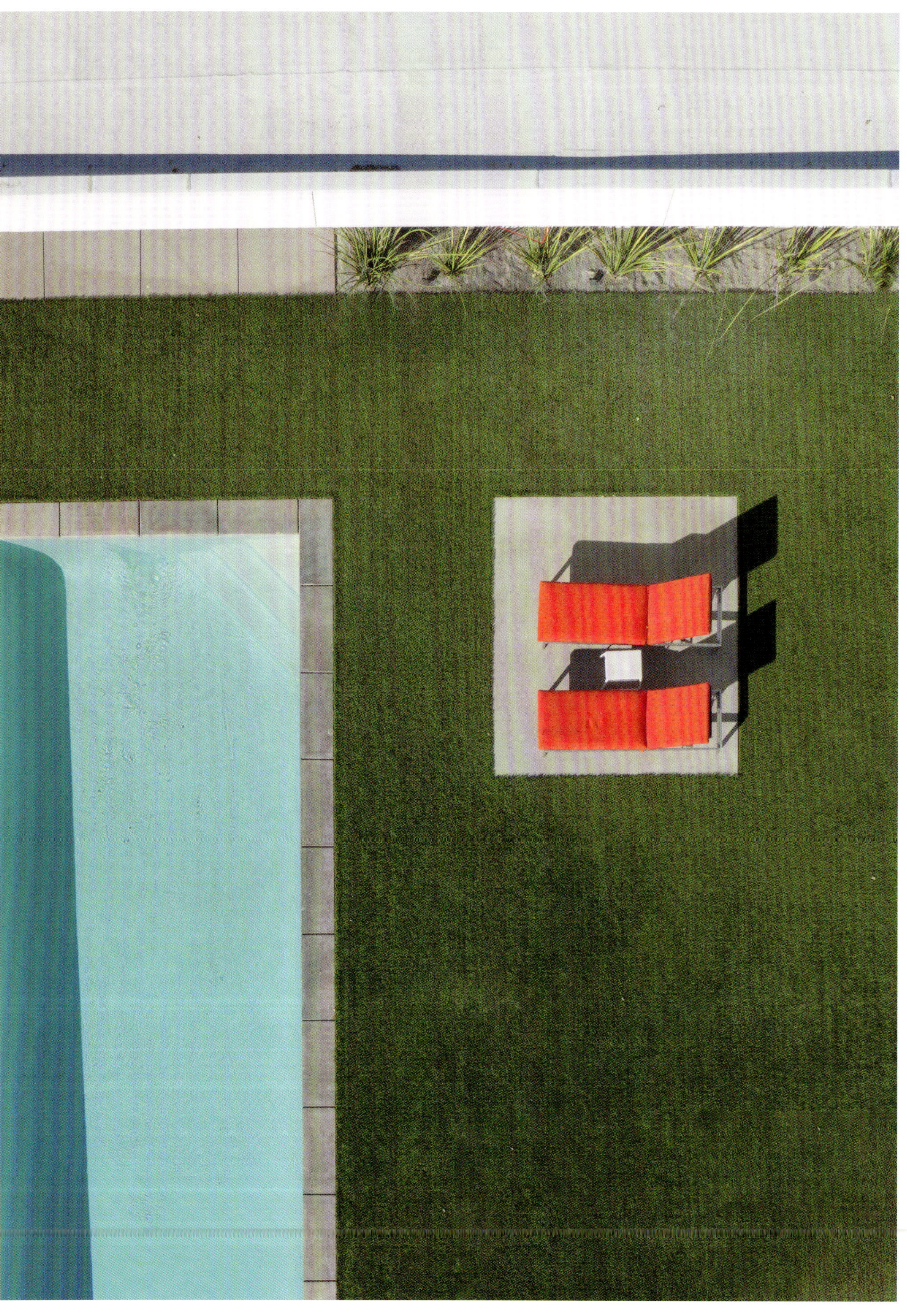

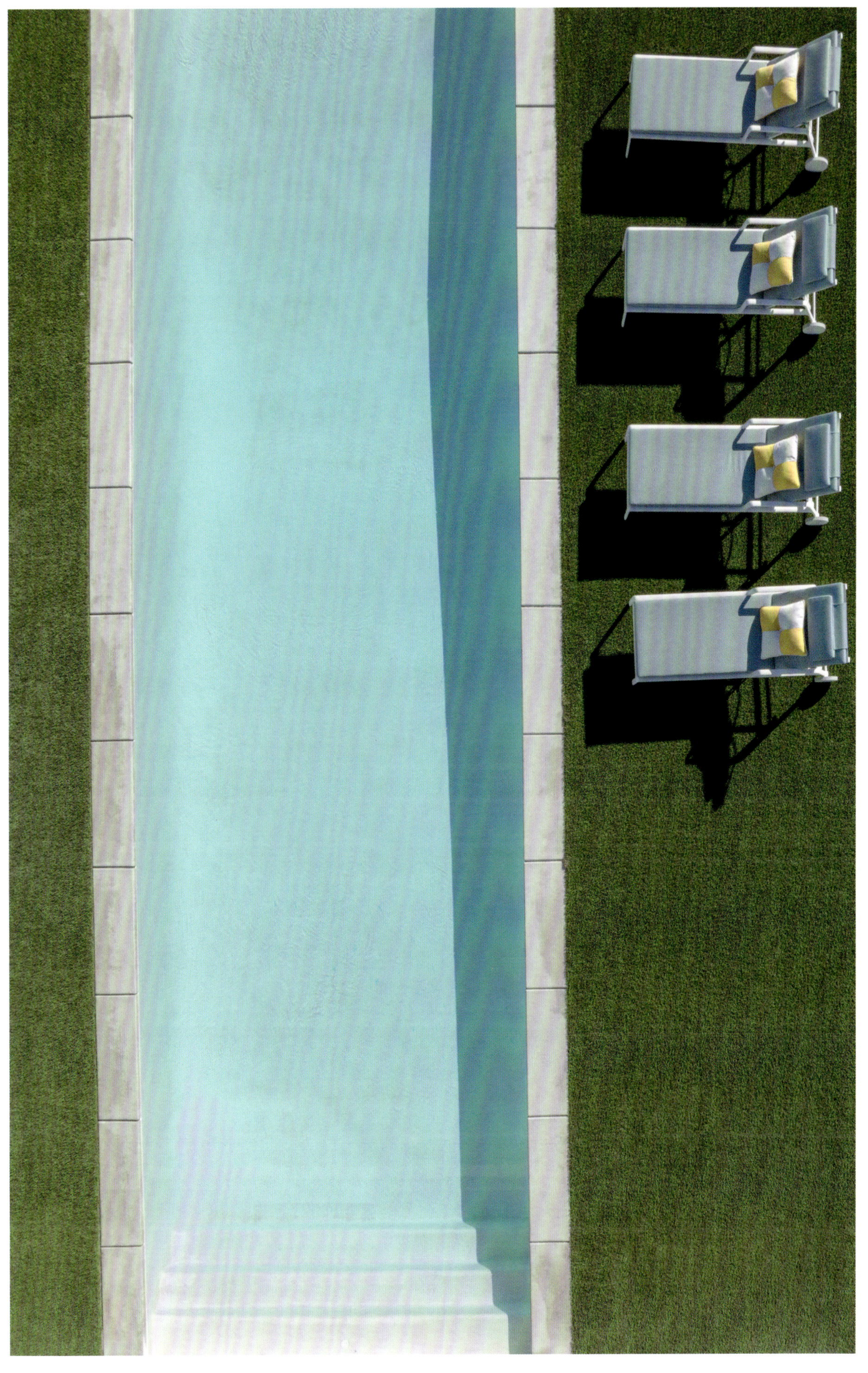

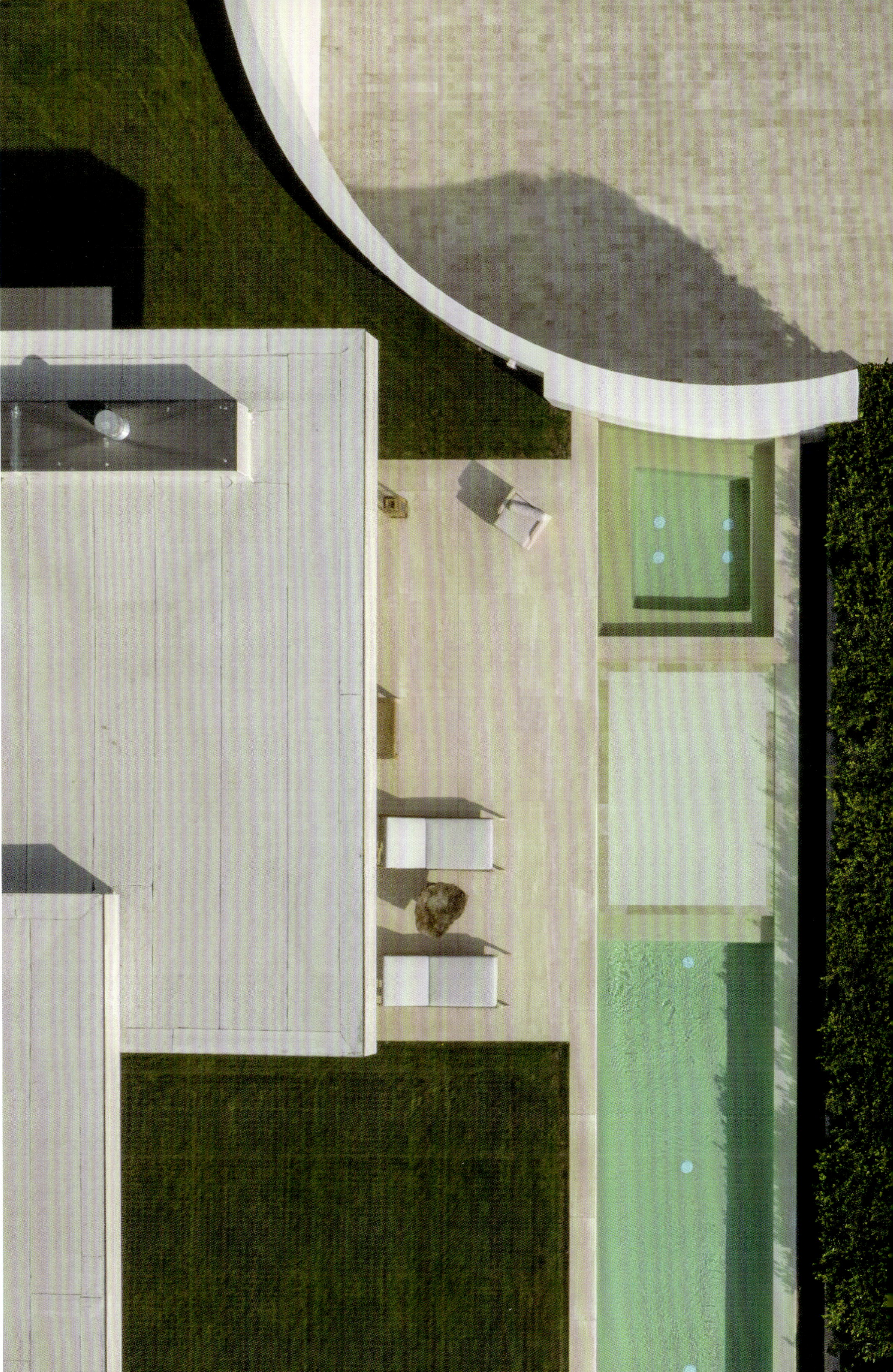

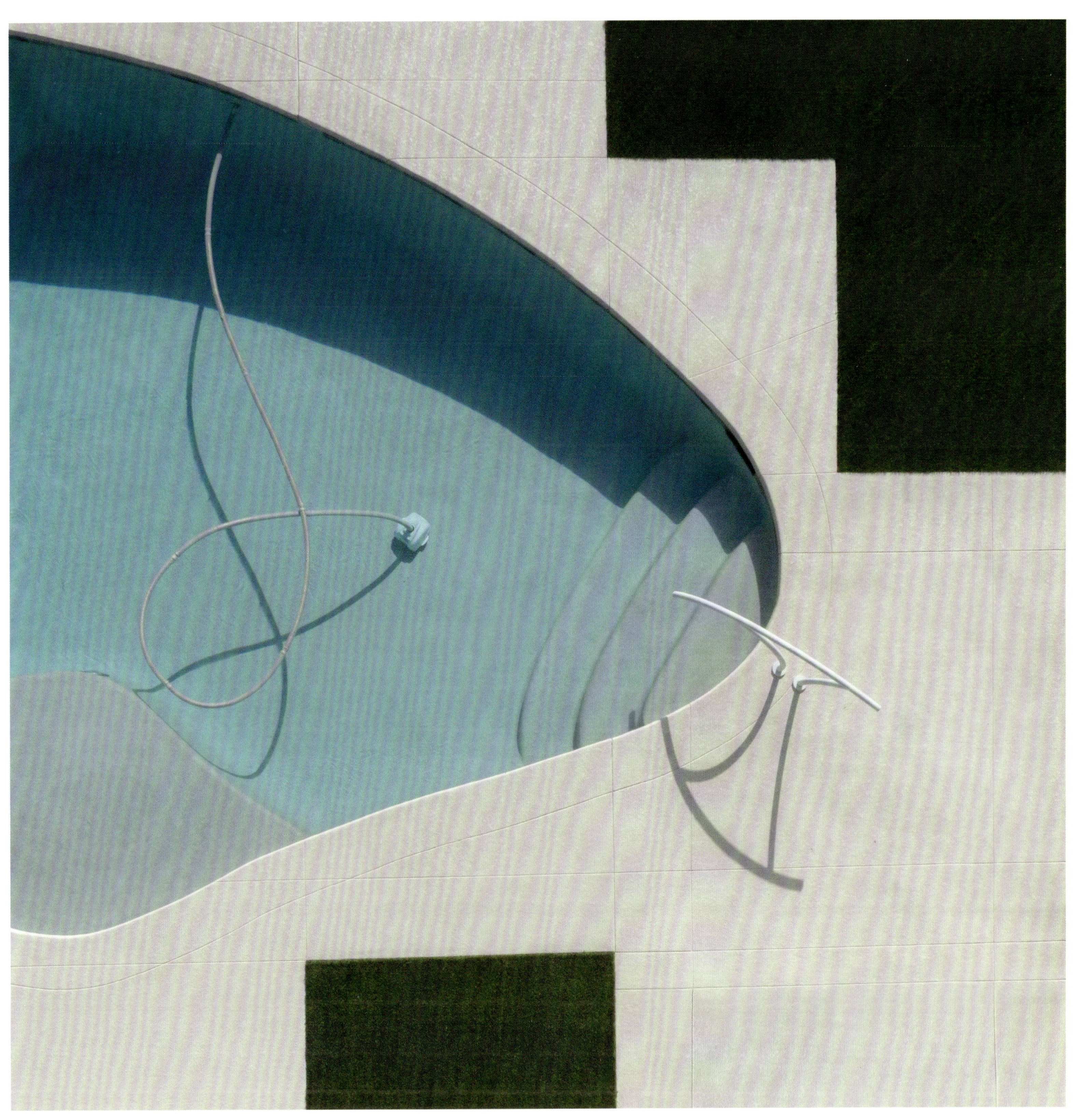

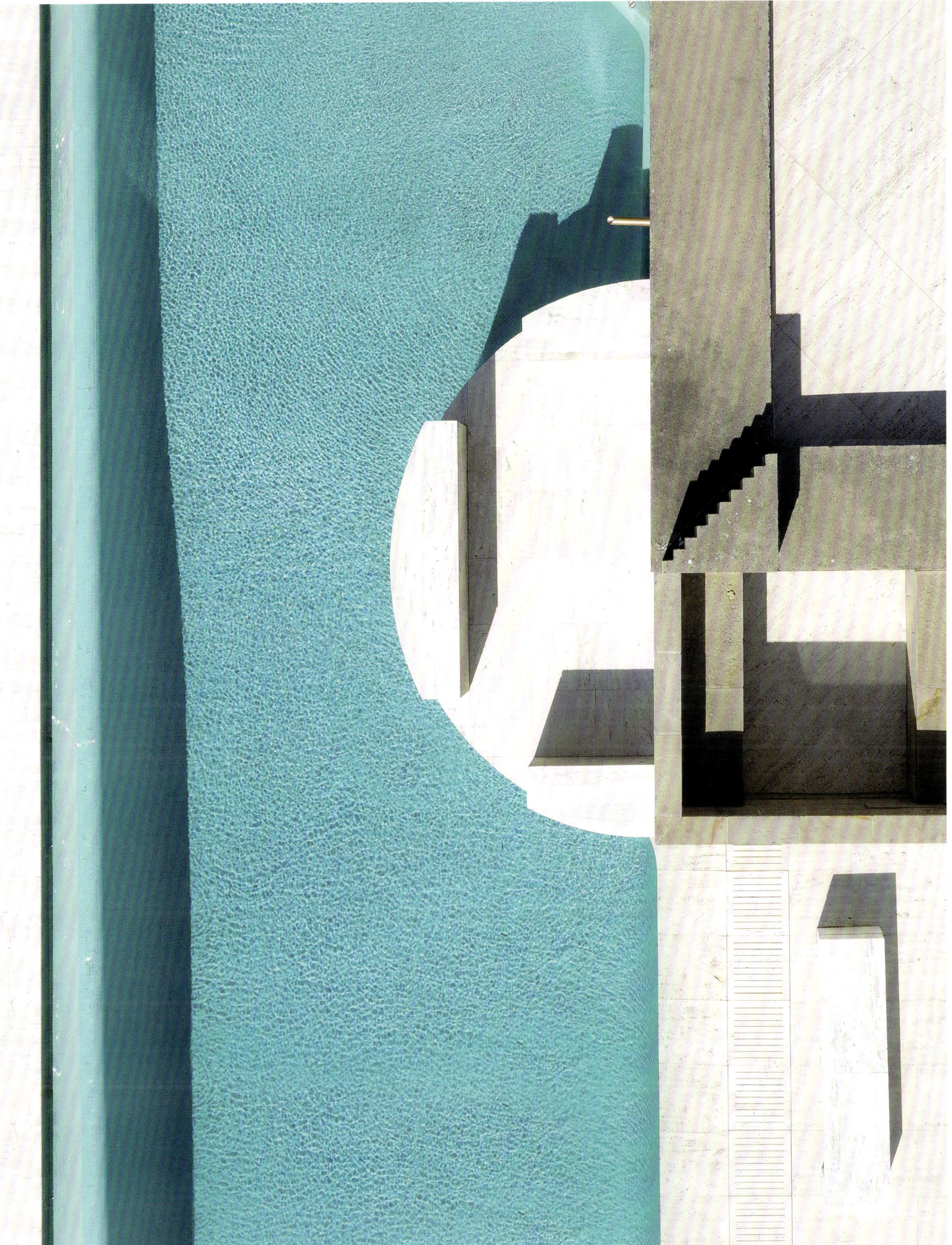

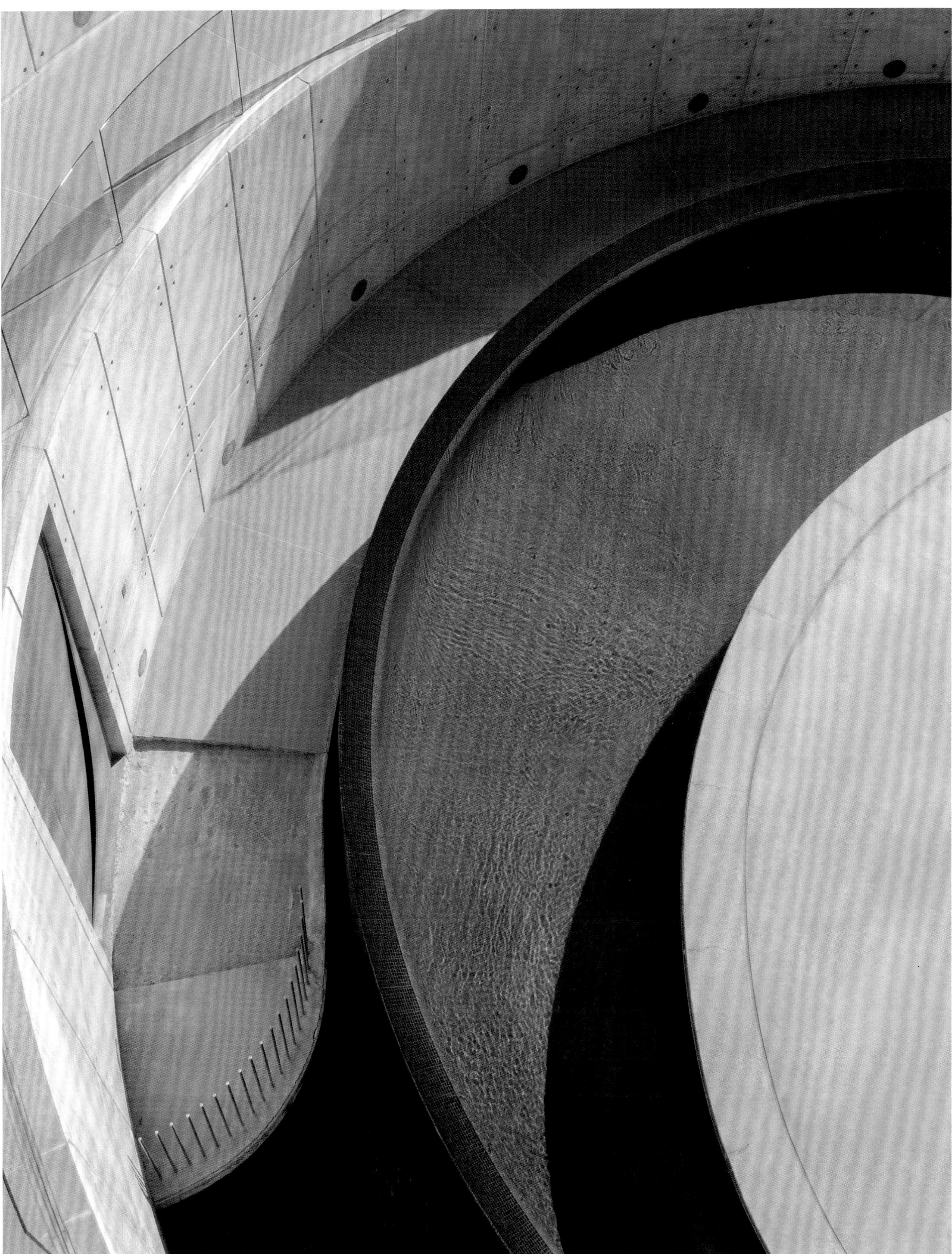

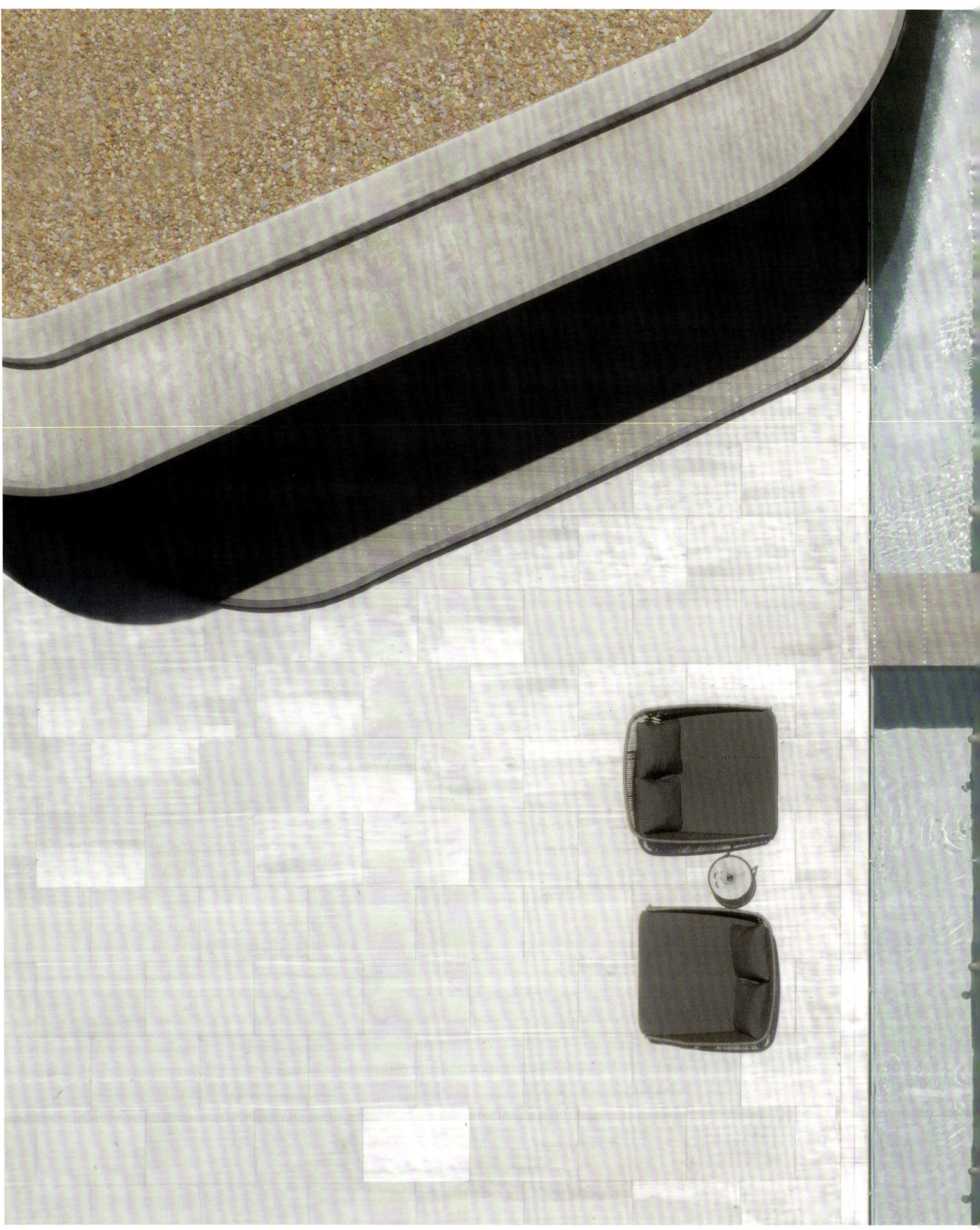

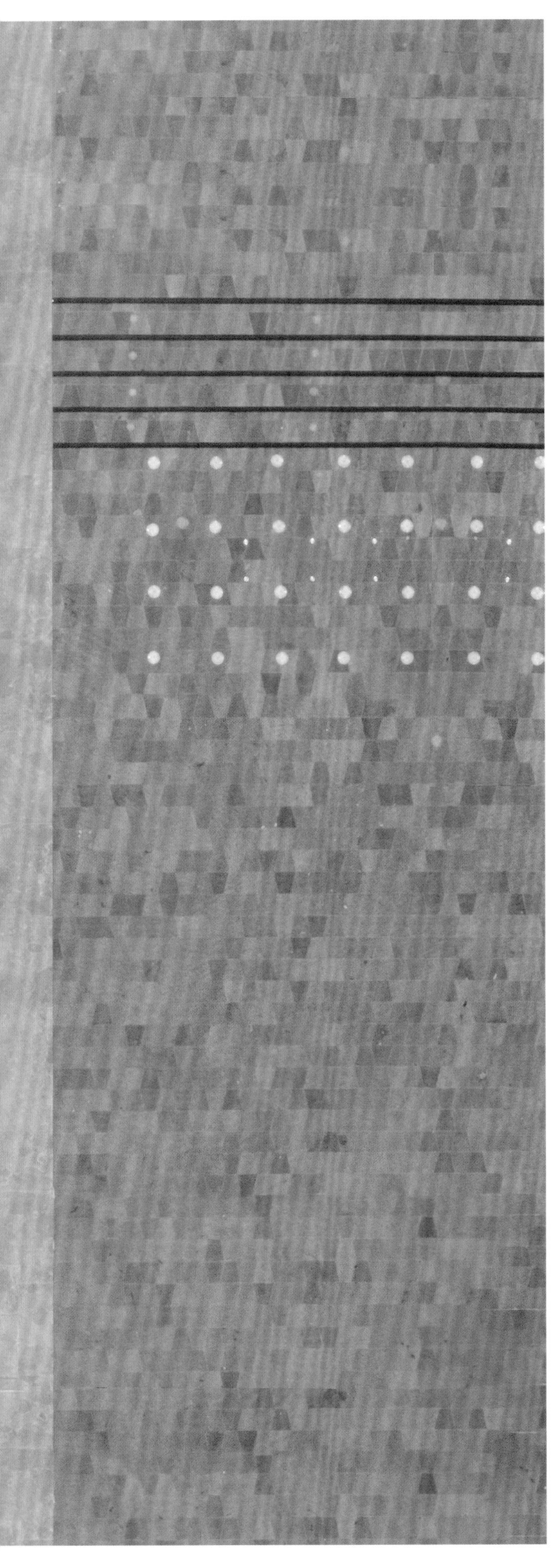

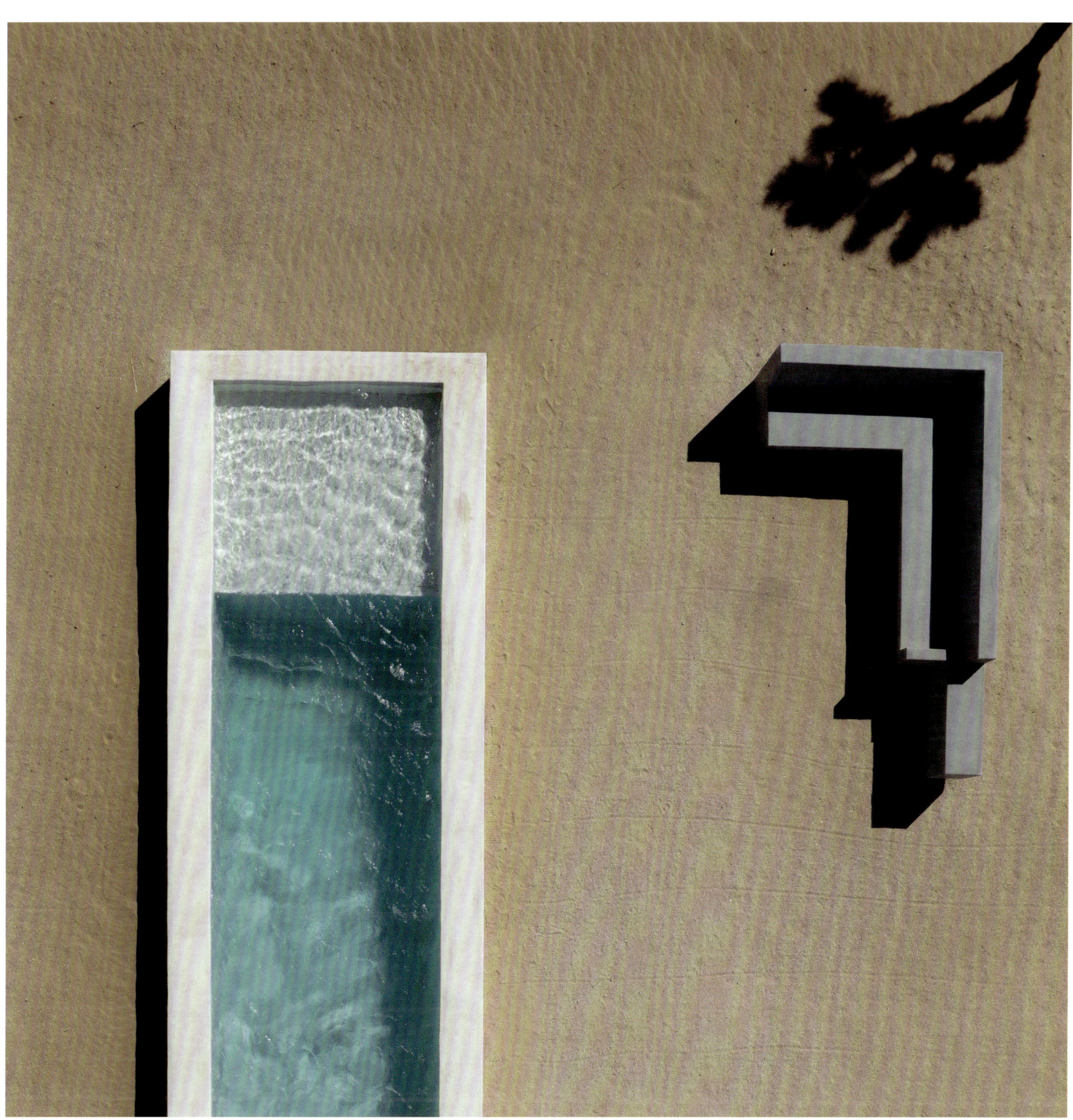

TOORAK, VICTORIA
AUSTRALIA

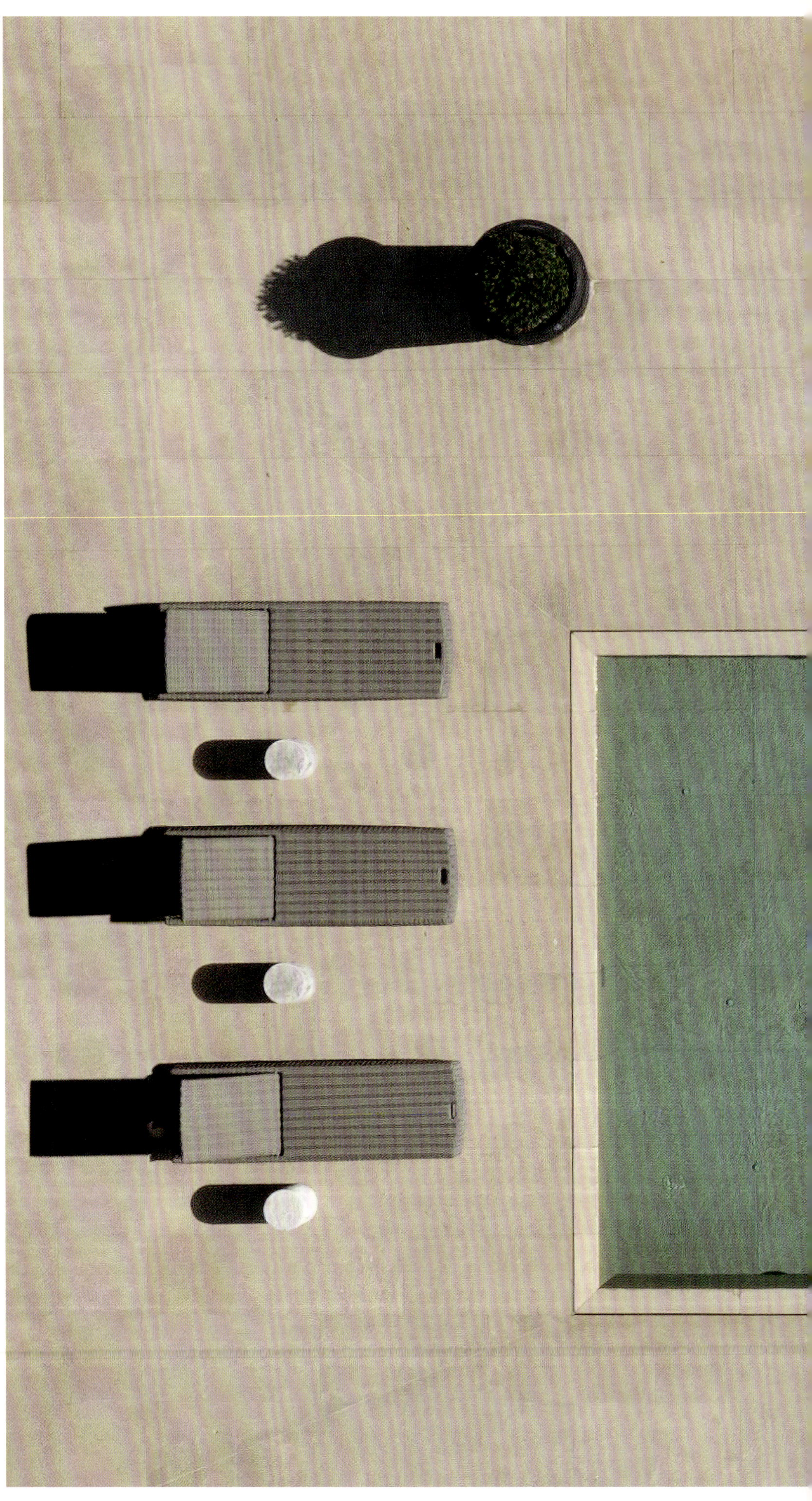

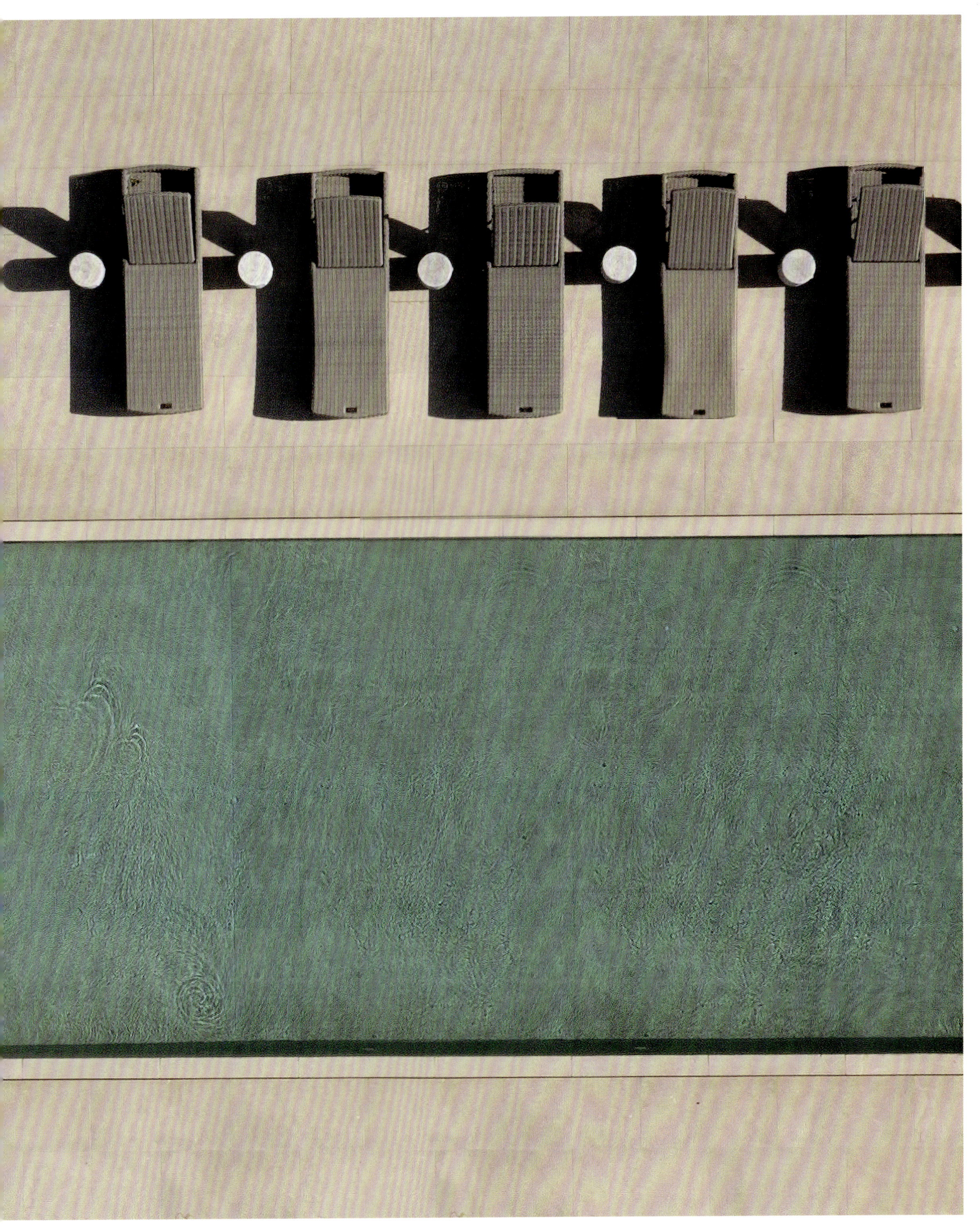

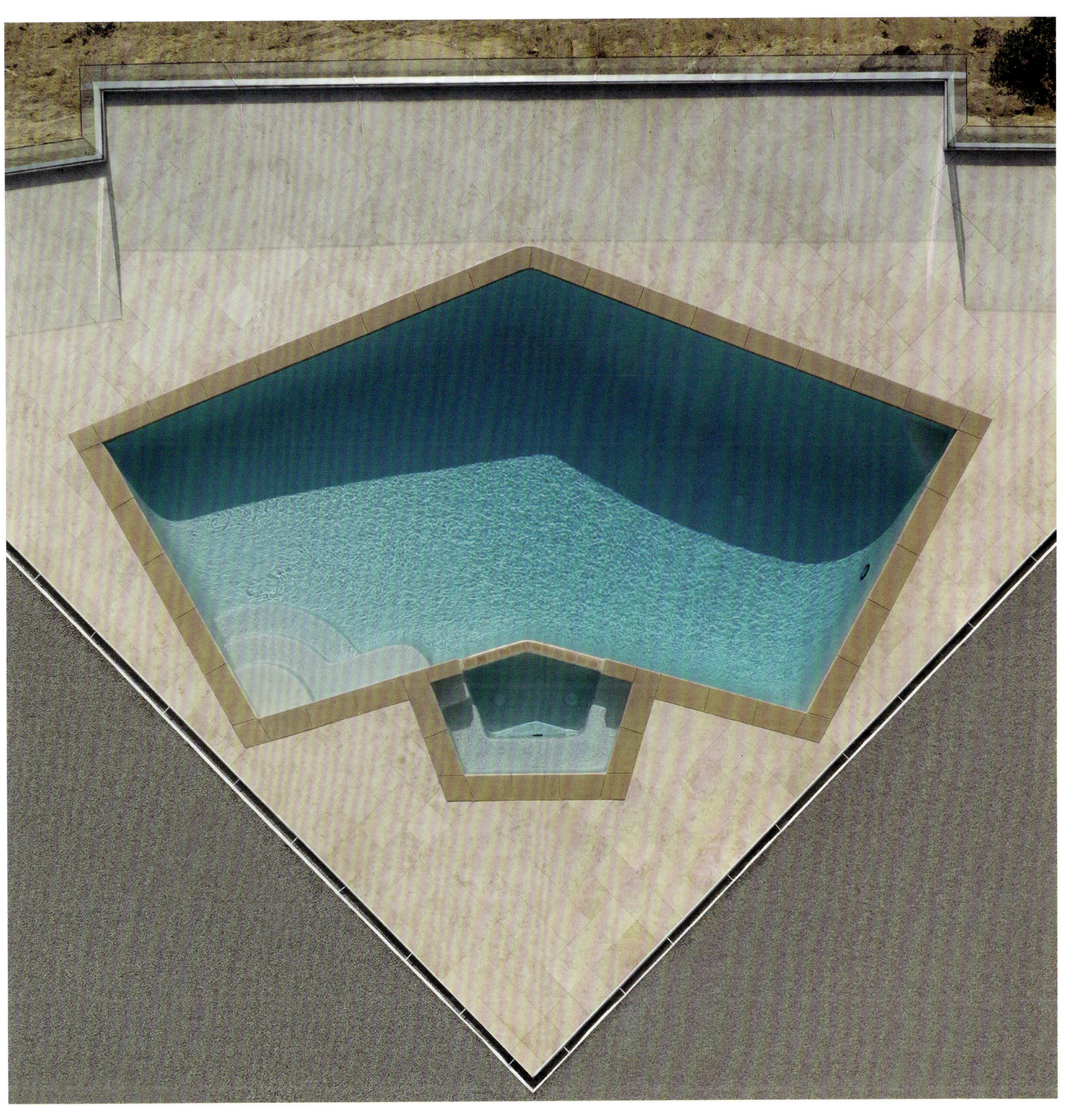

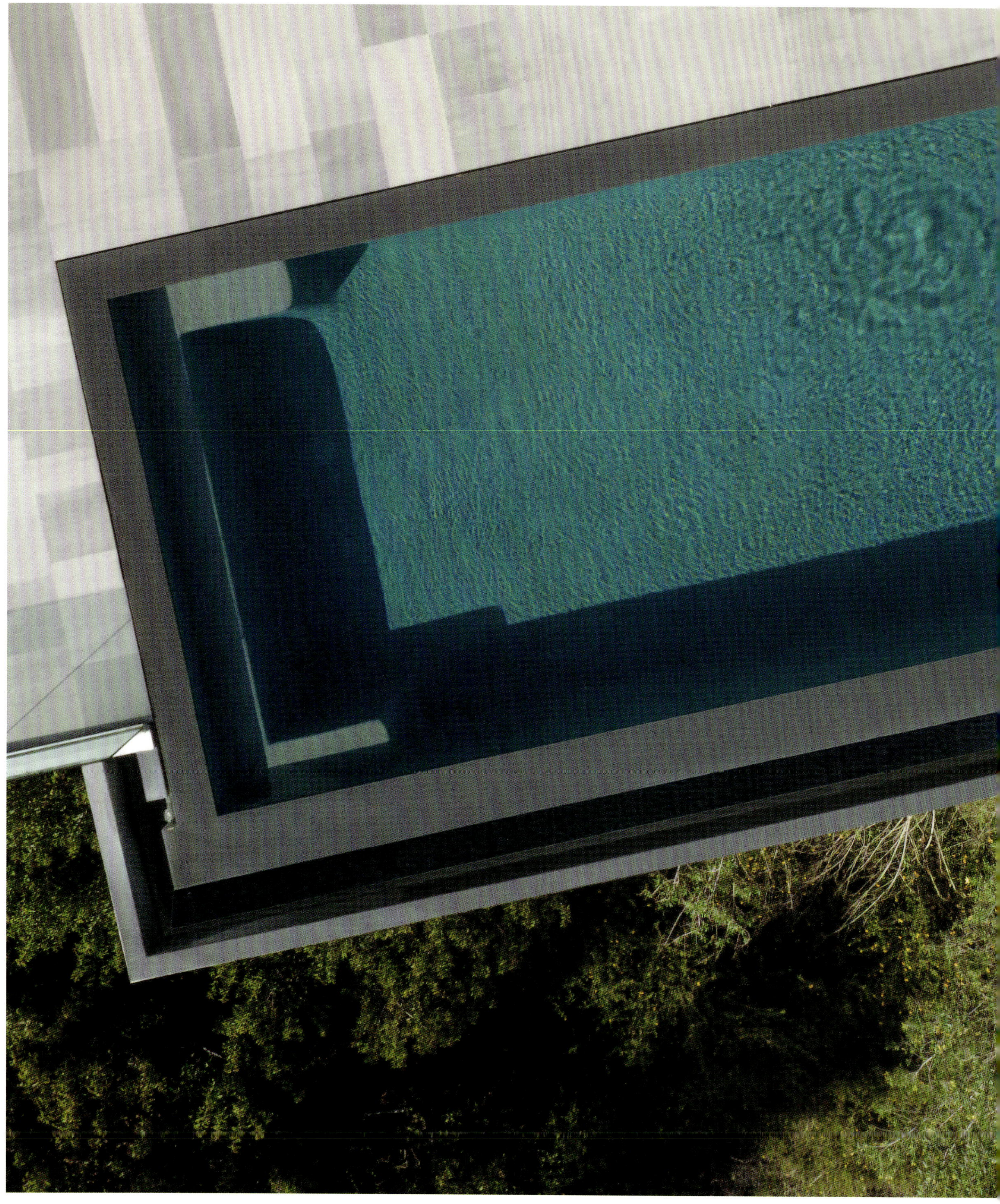

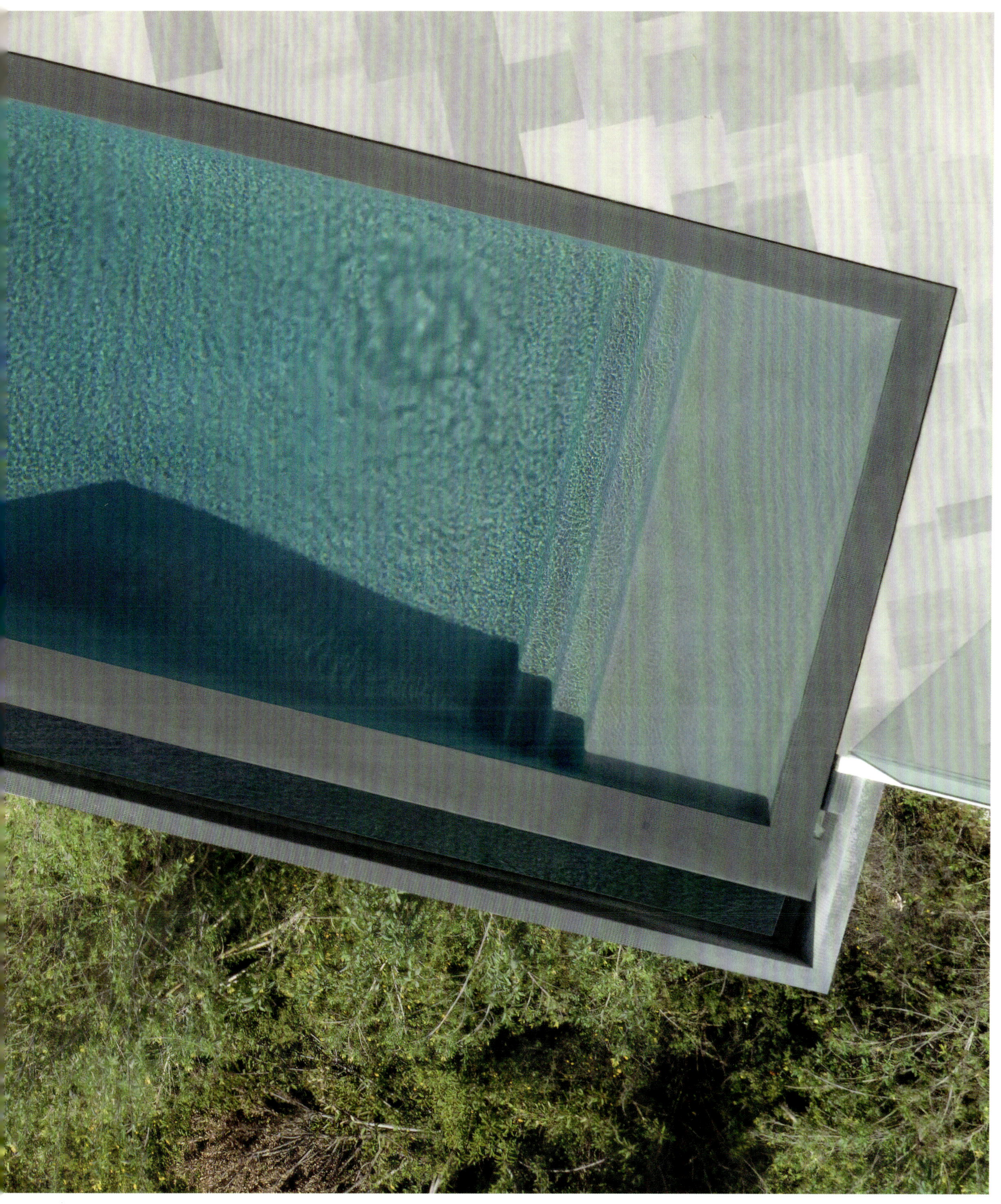

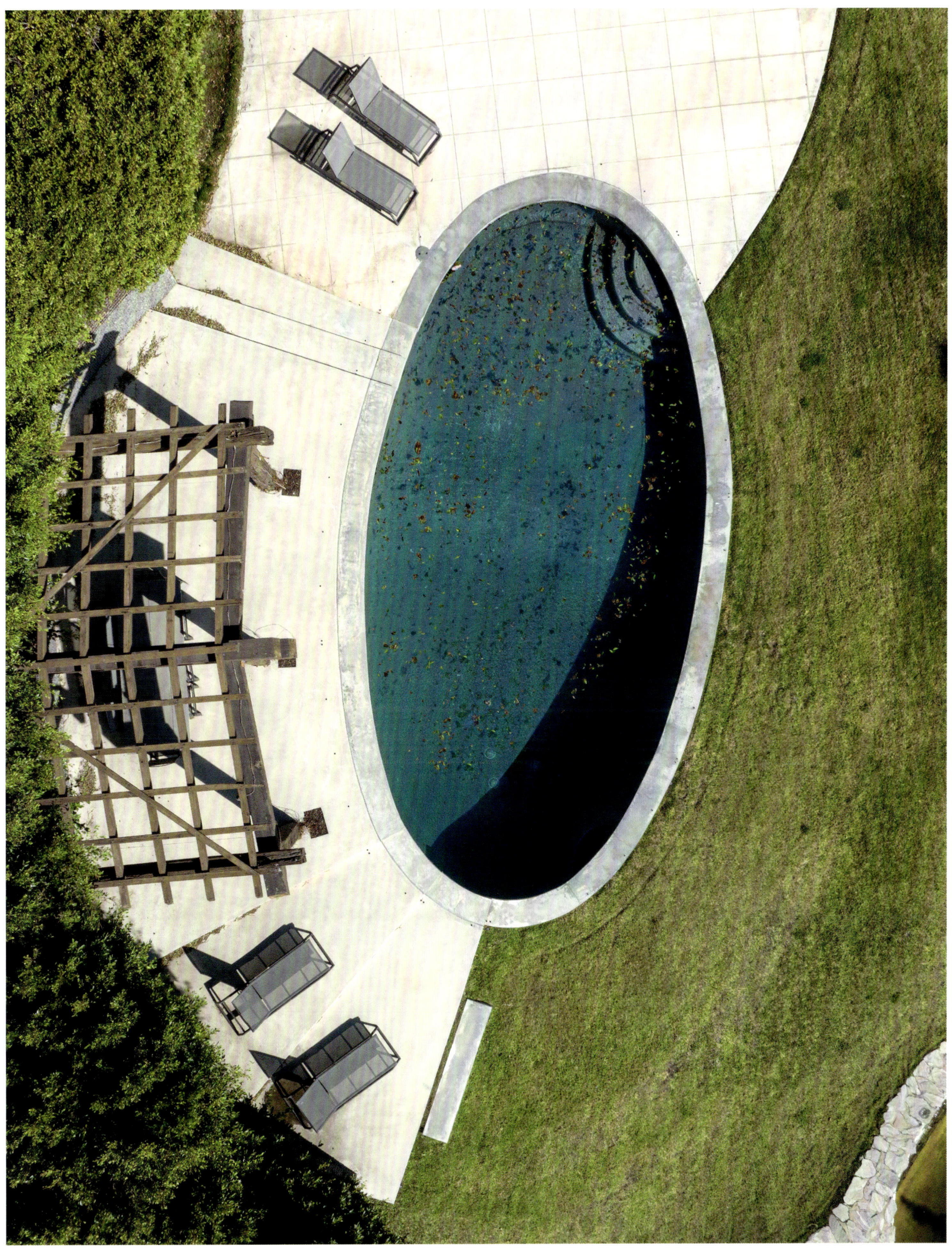

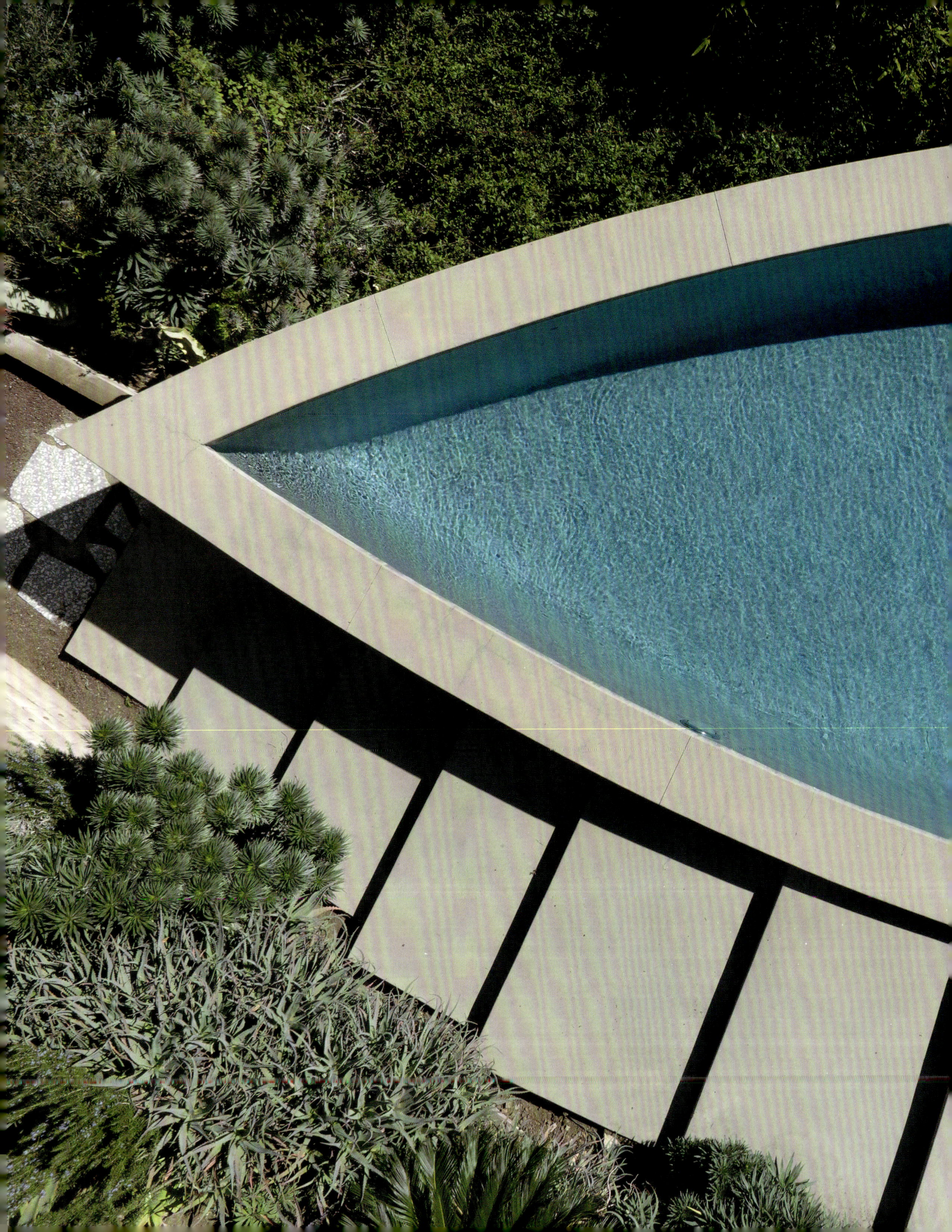

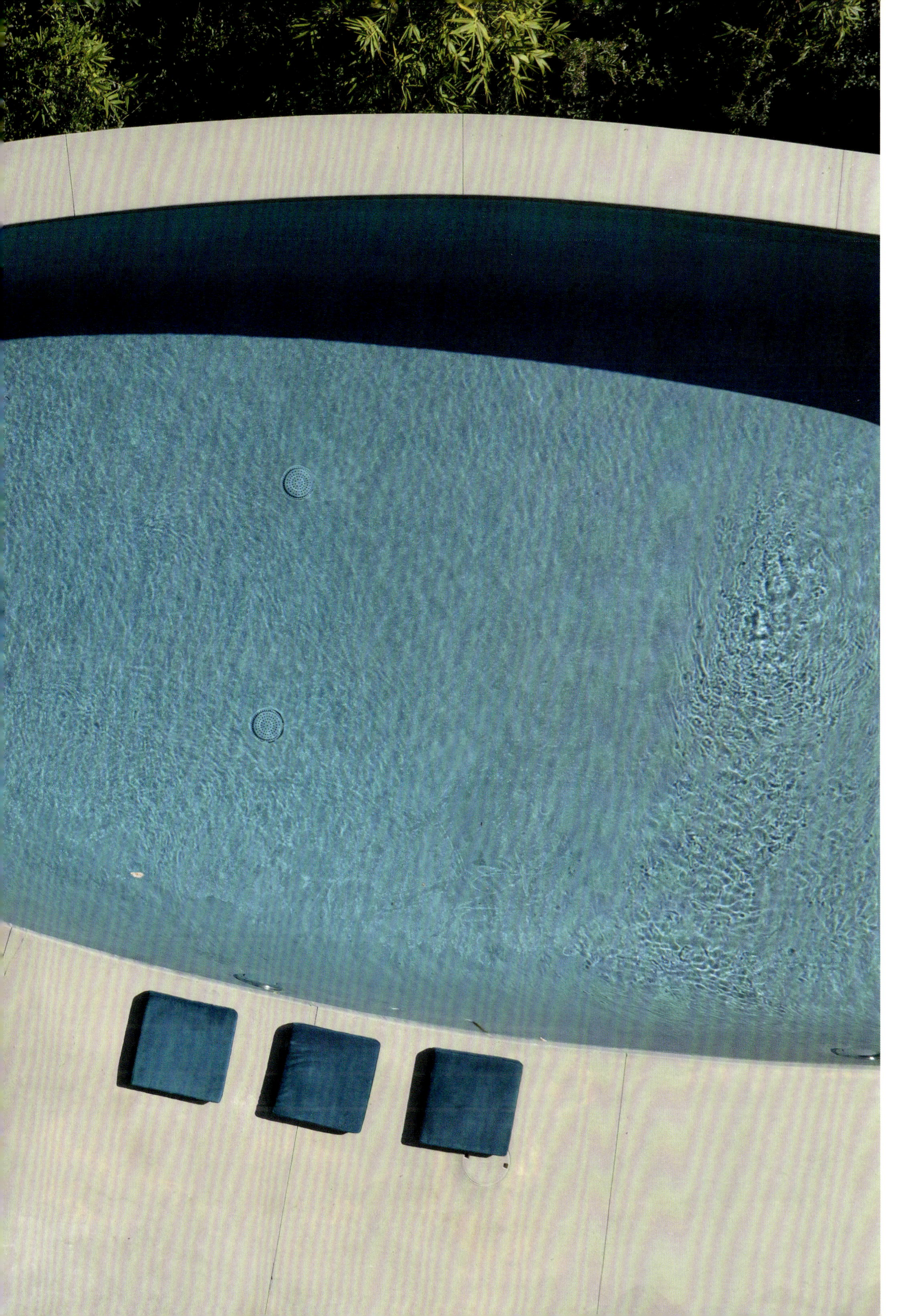

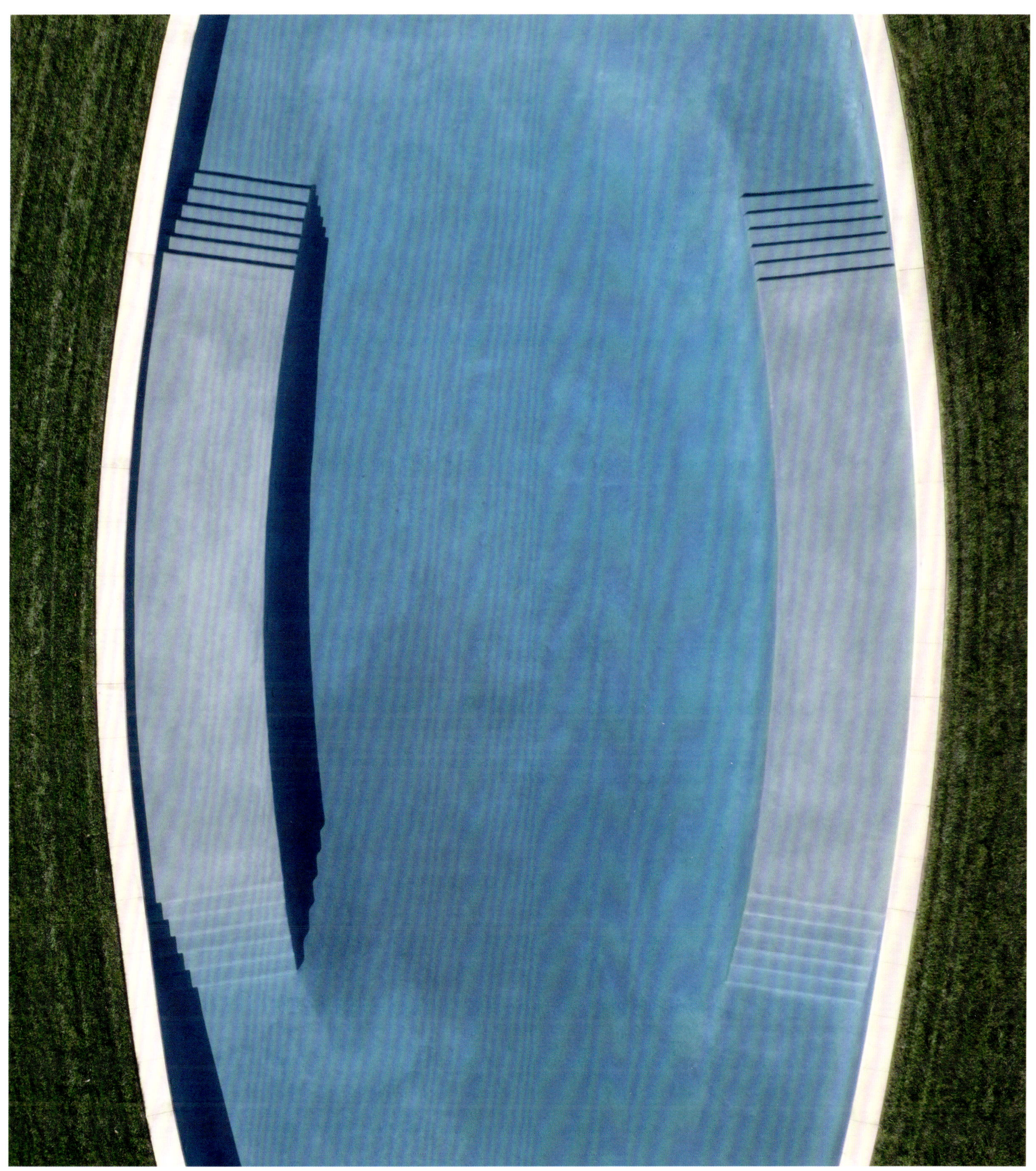

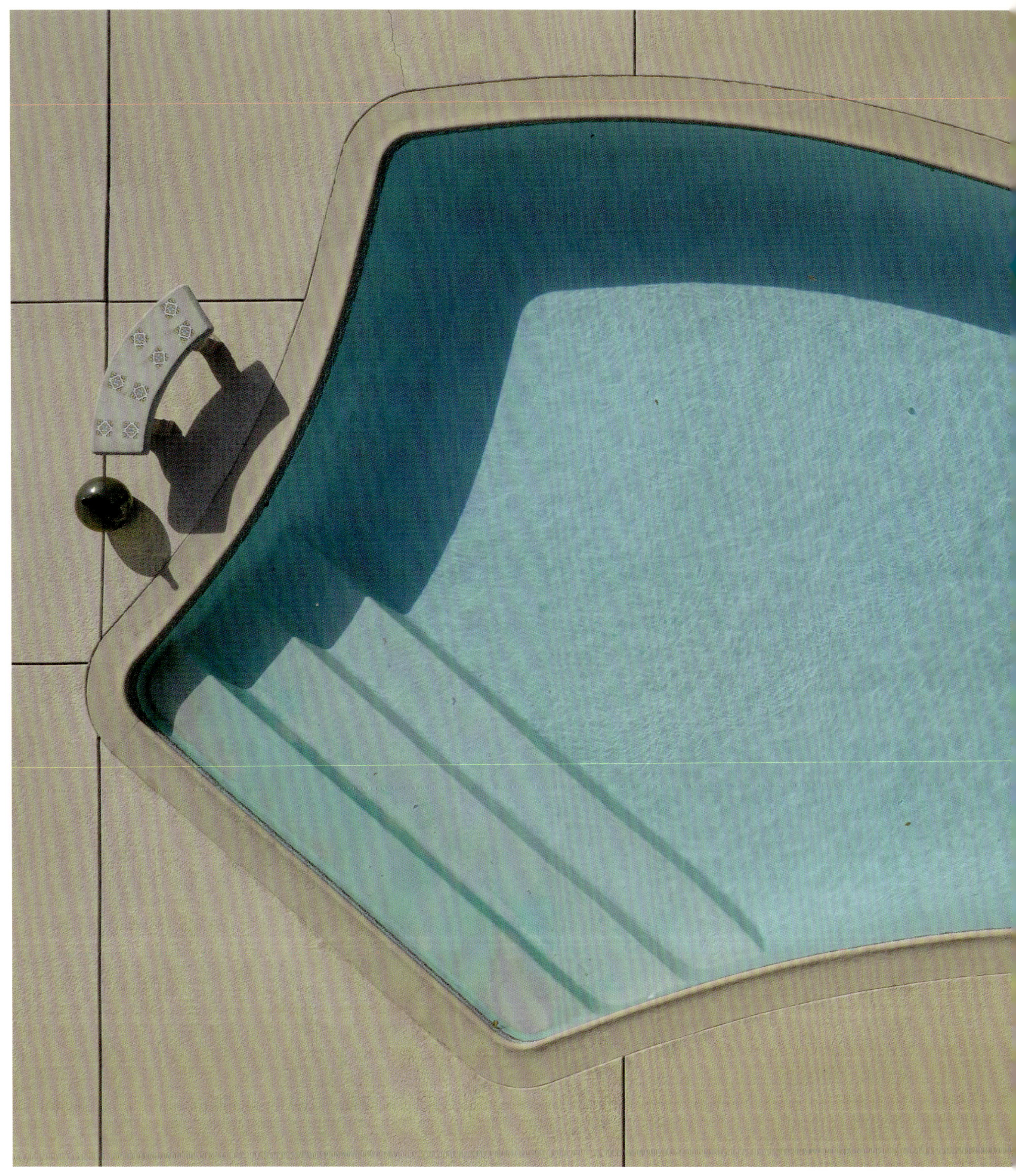

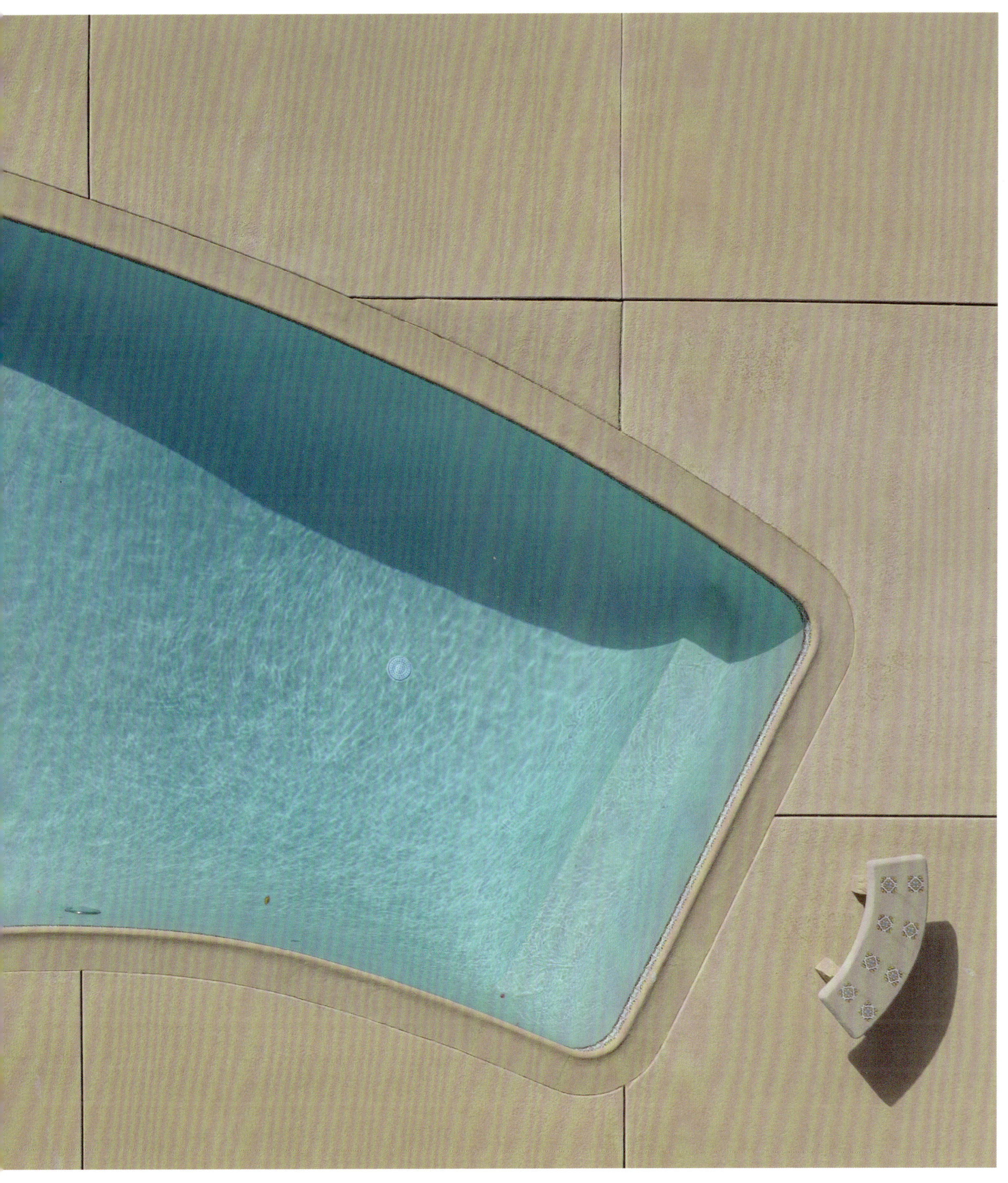

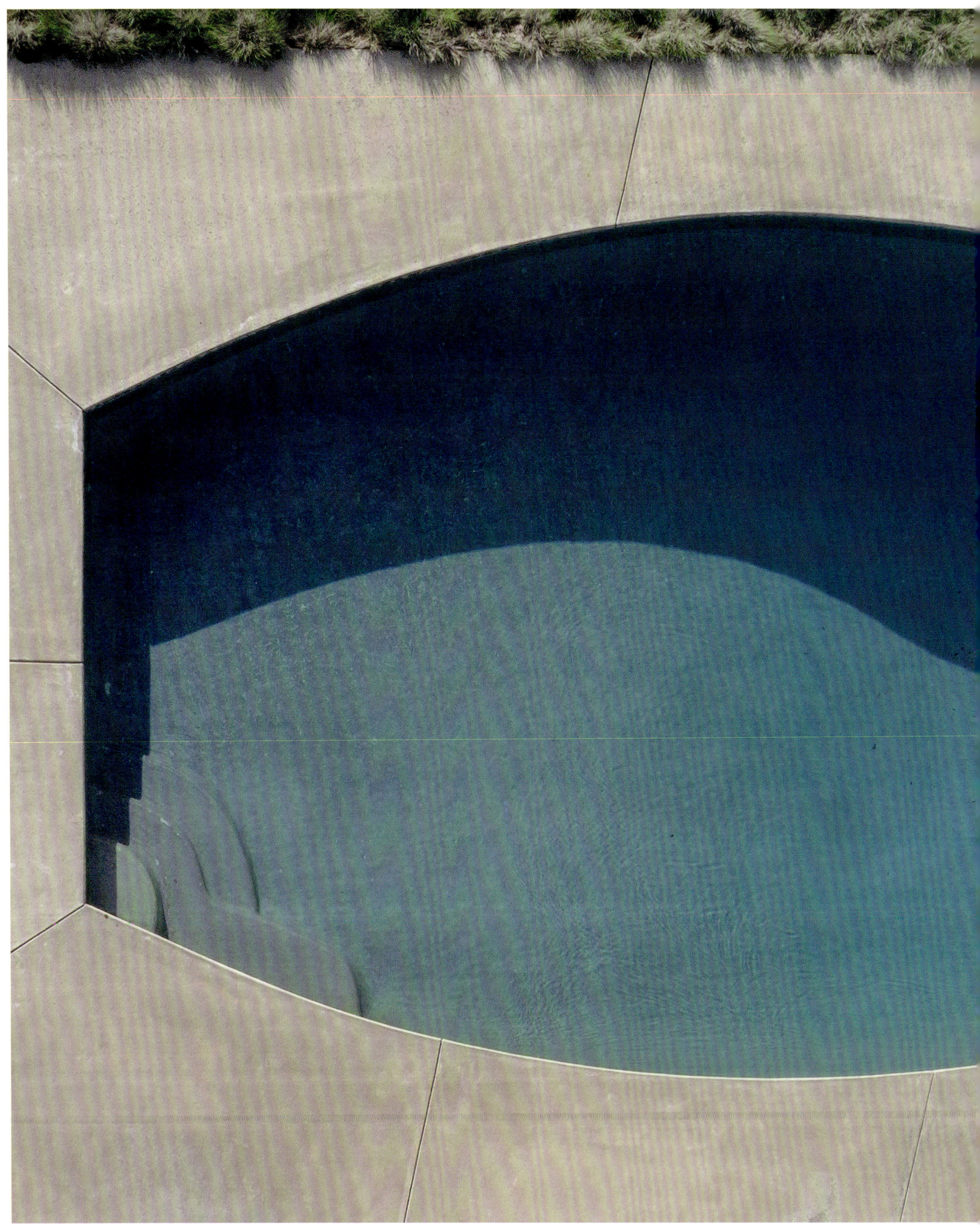

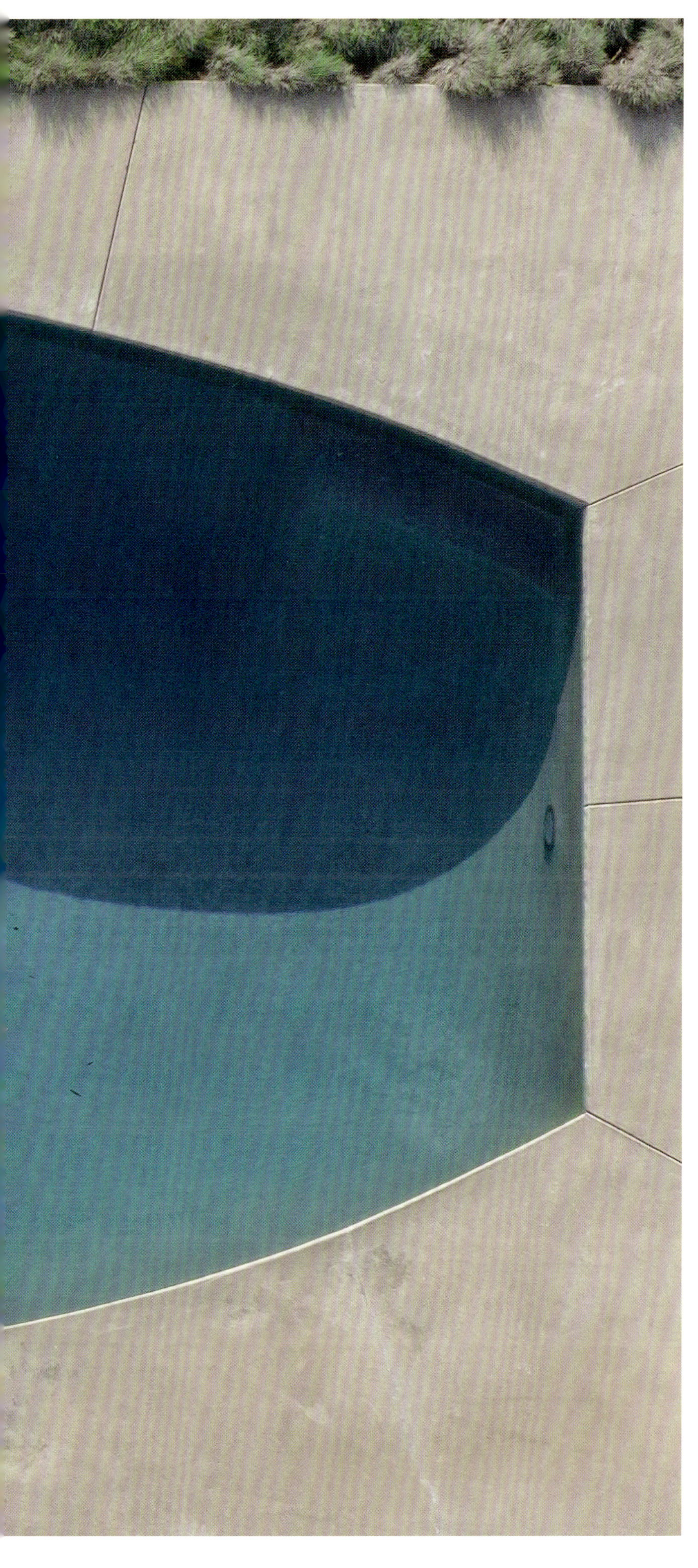

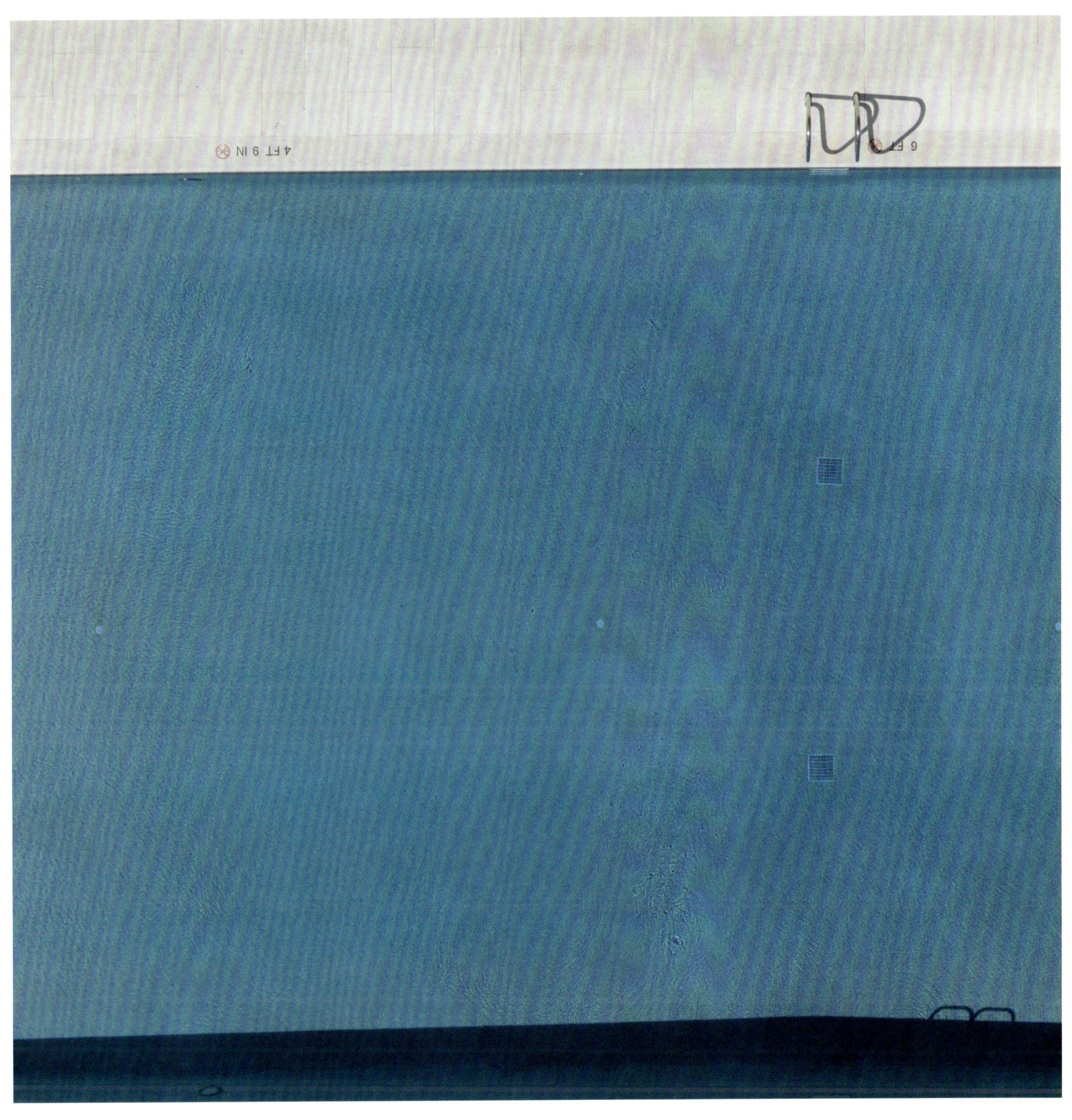
4 FT 9 IN
6 FT

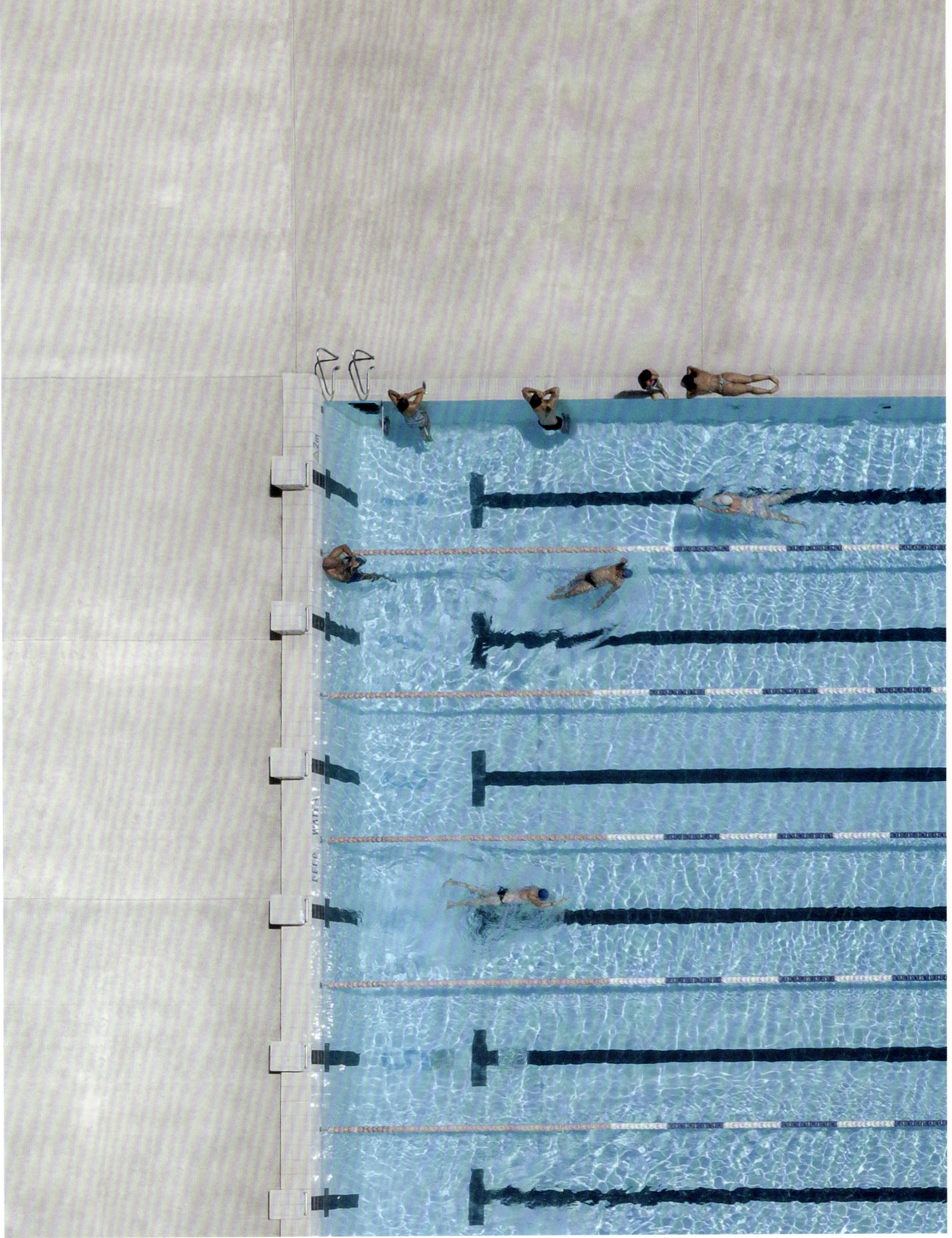

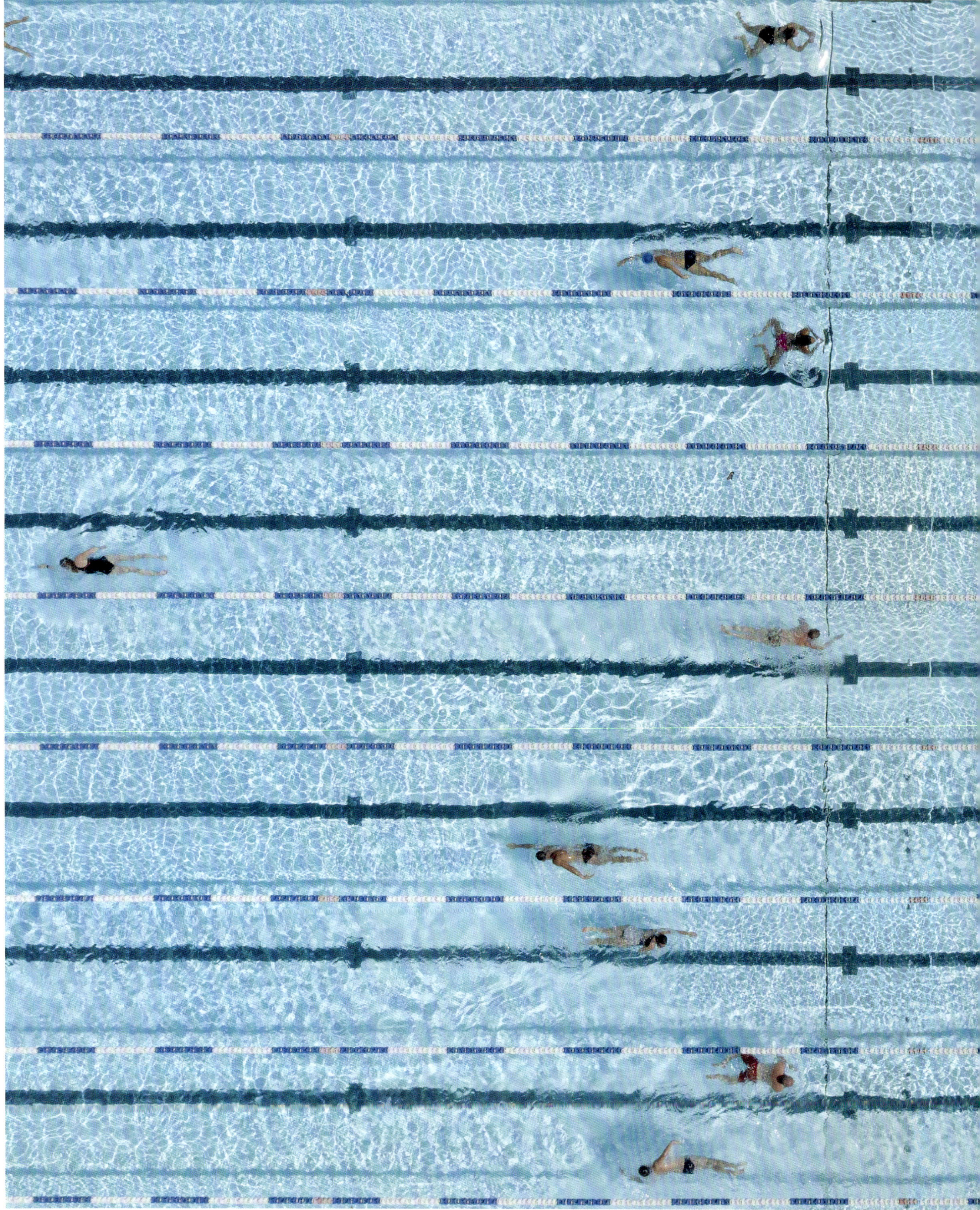

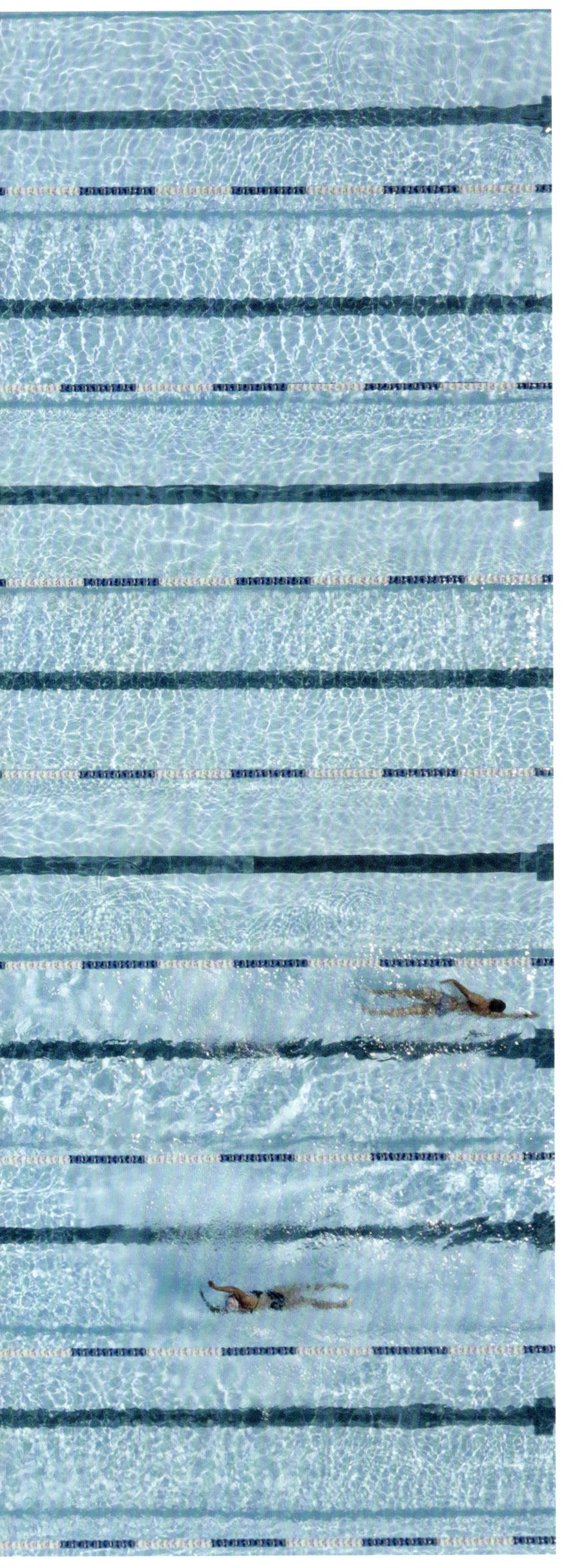

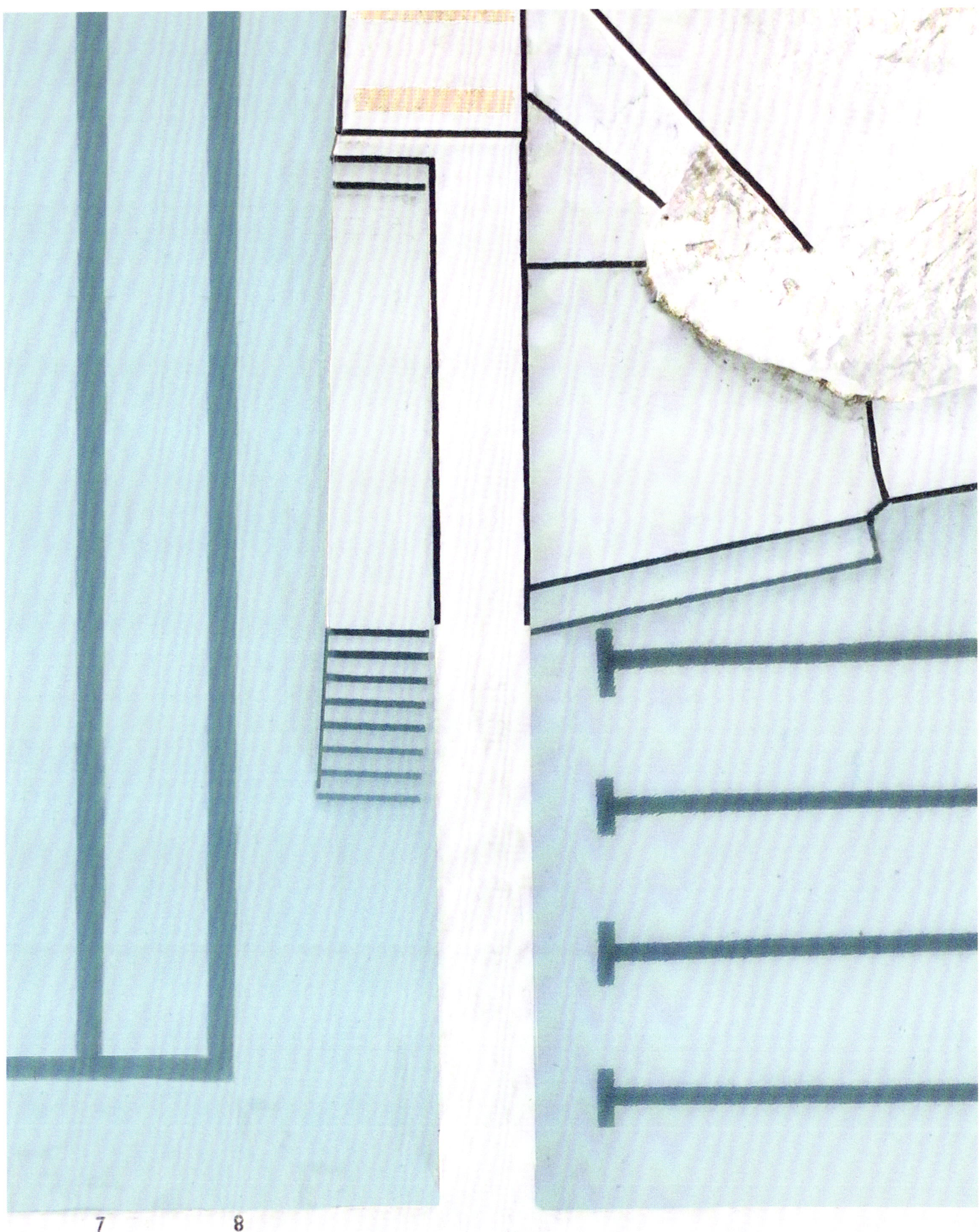

7 8

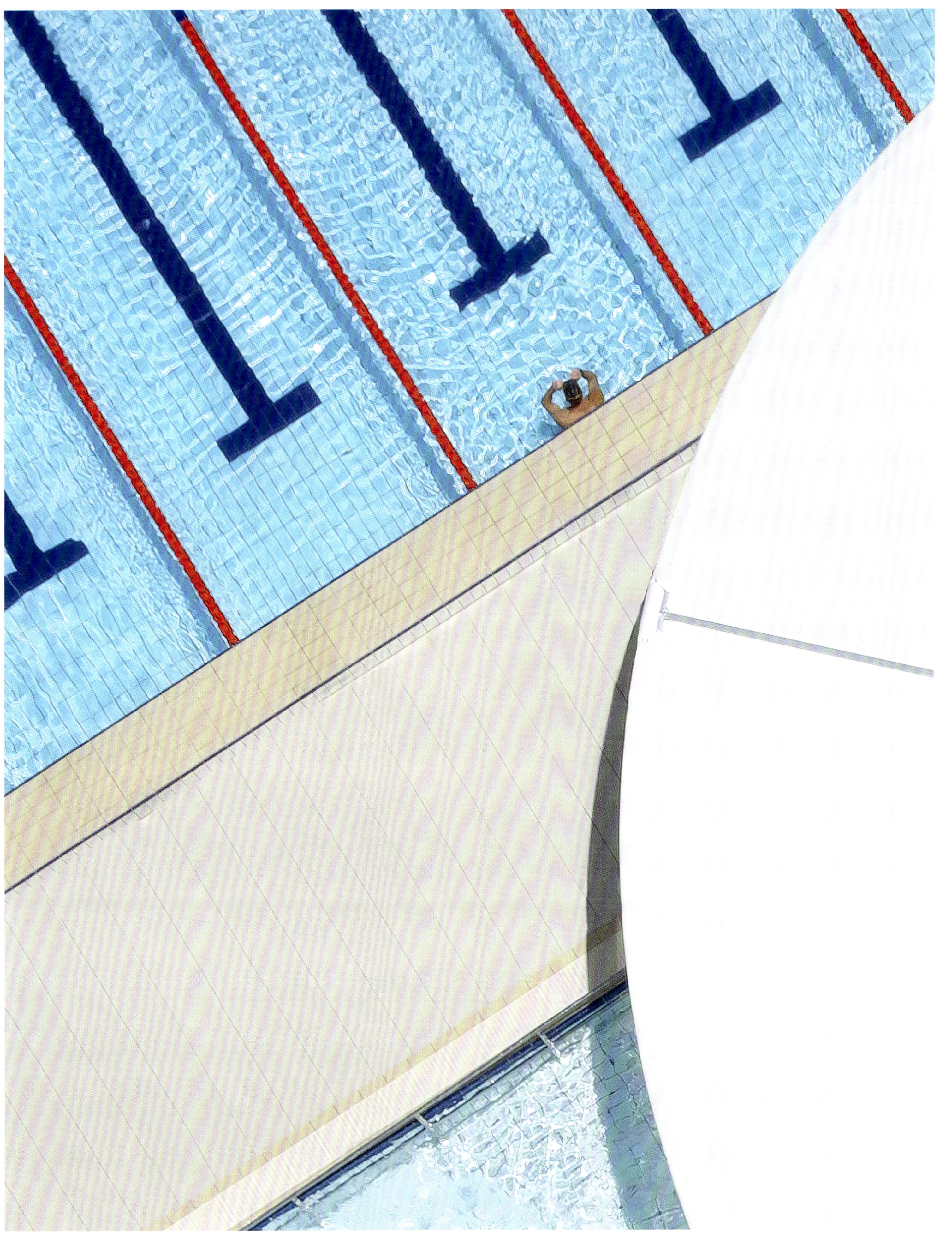

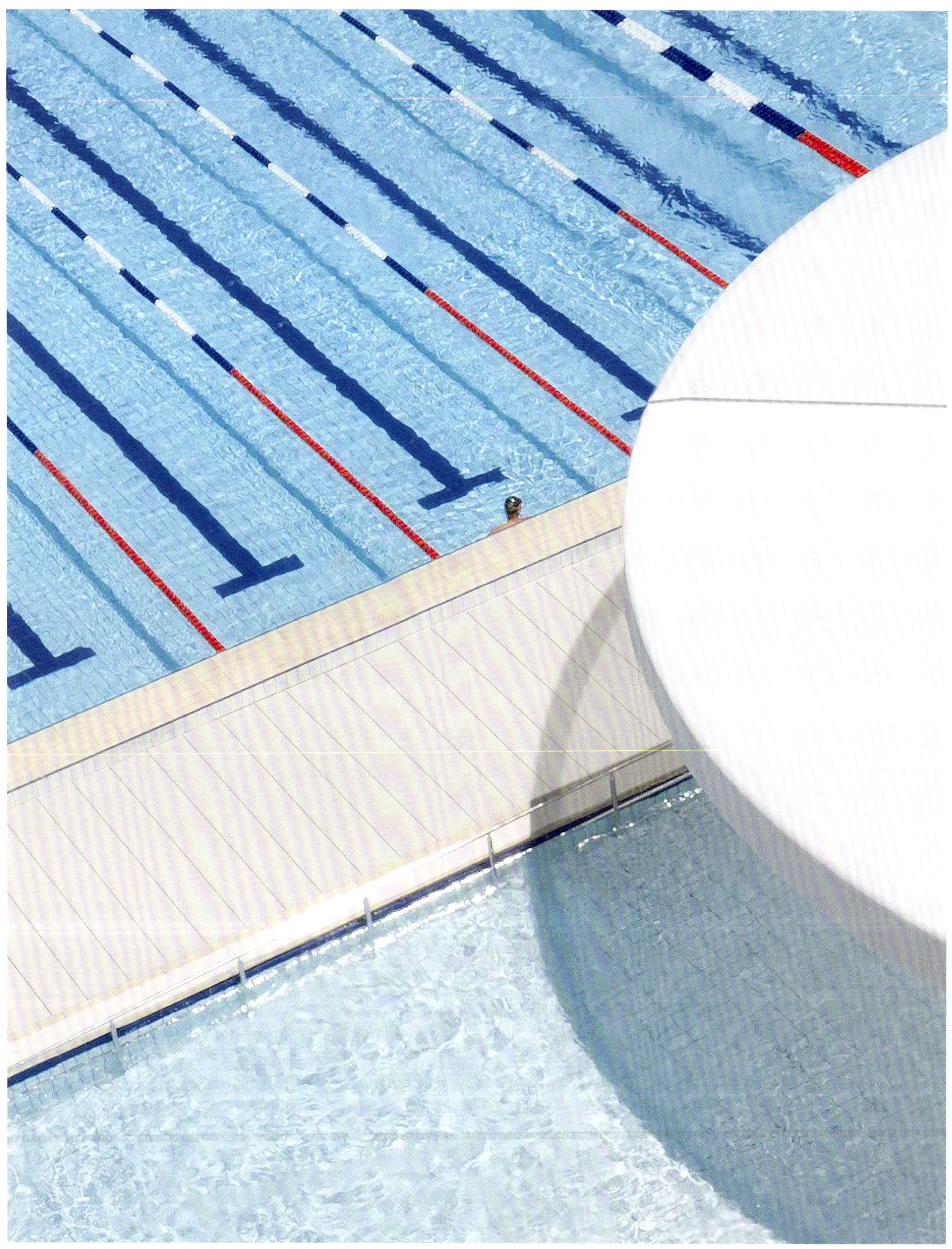

SYDNEY, NSW – AUSTRALIA

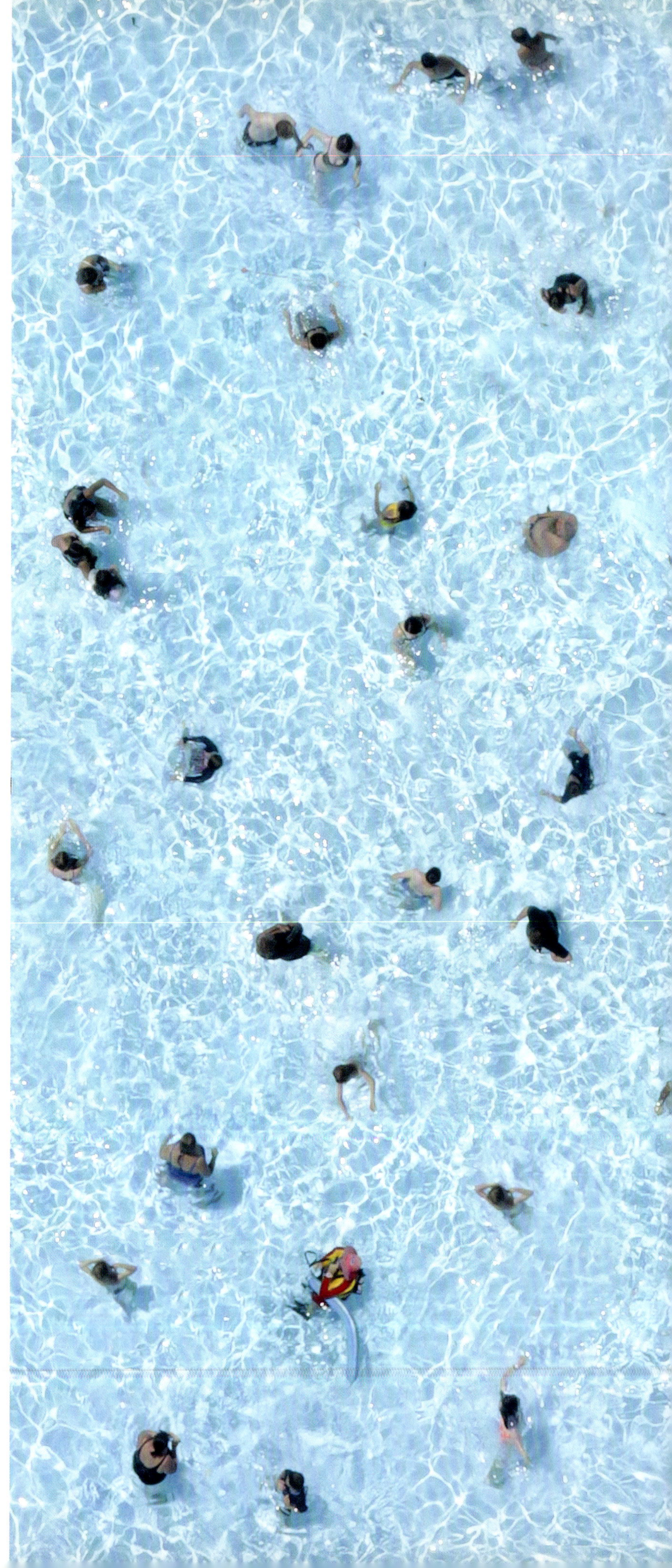

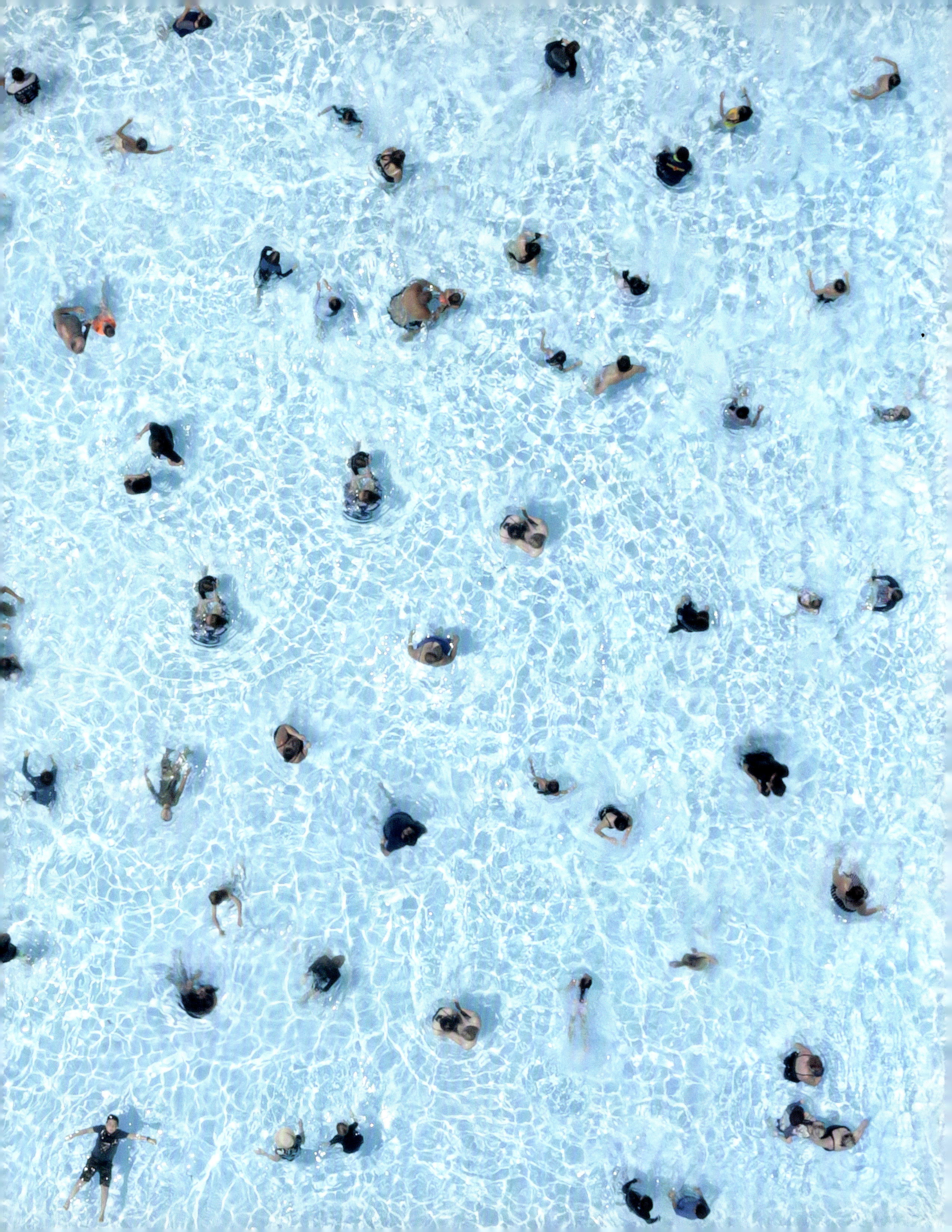

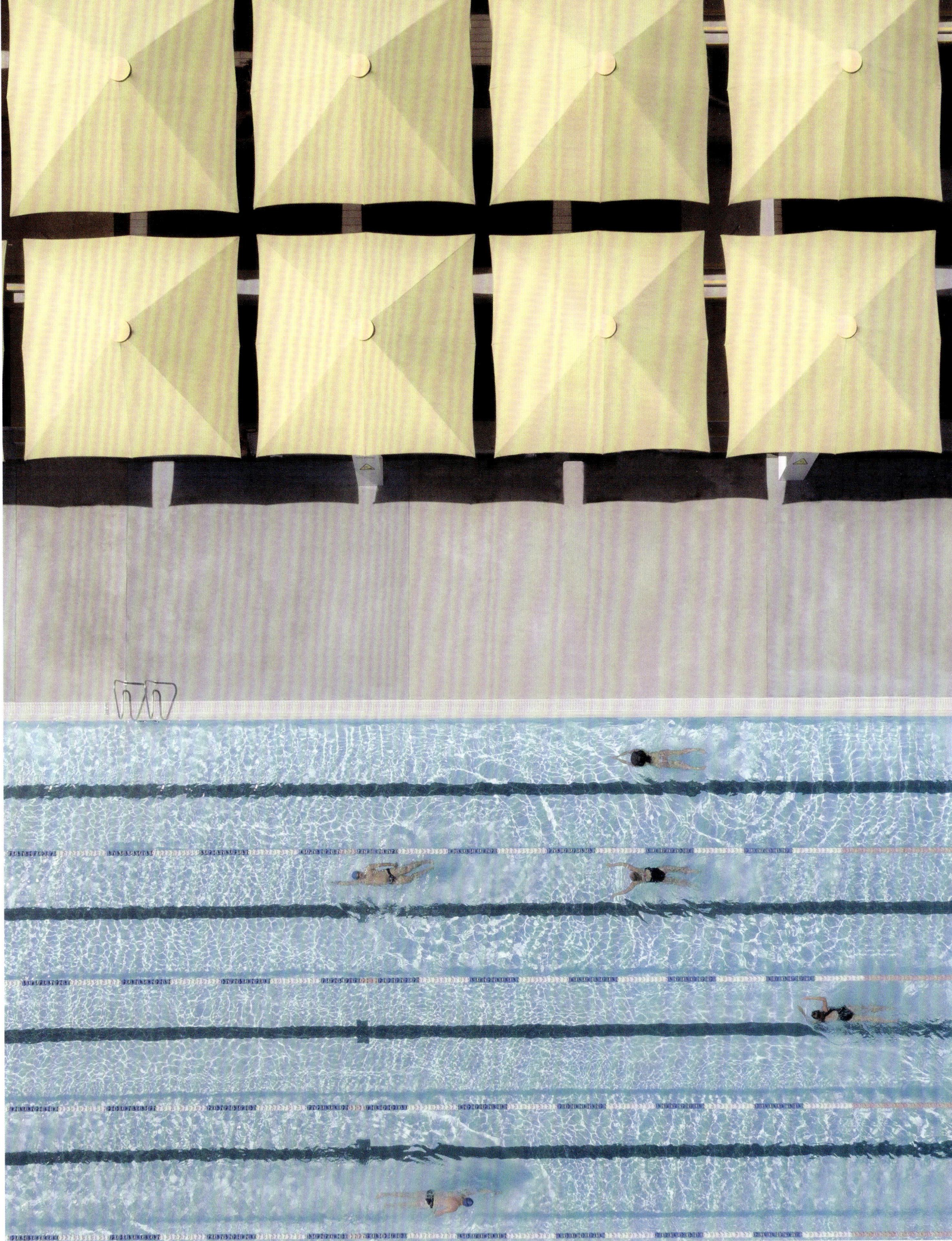

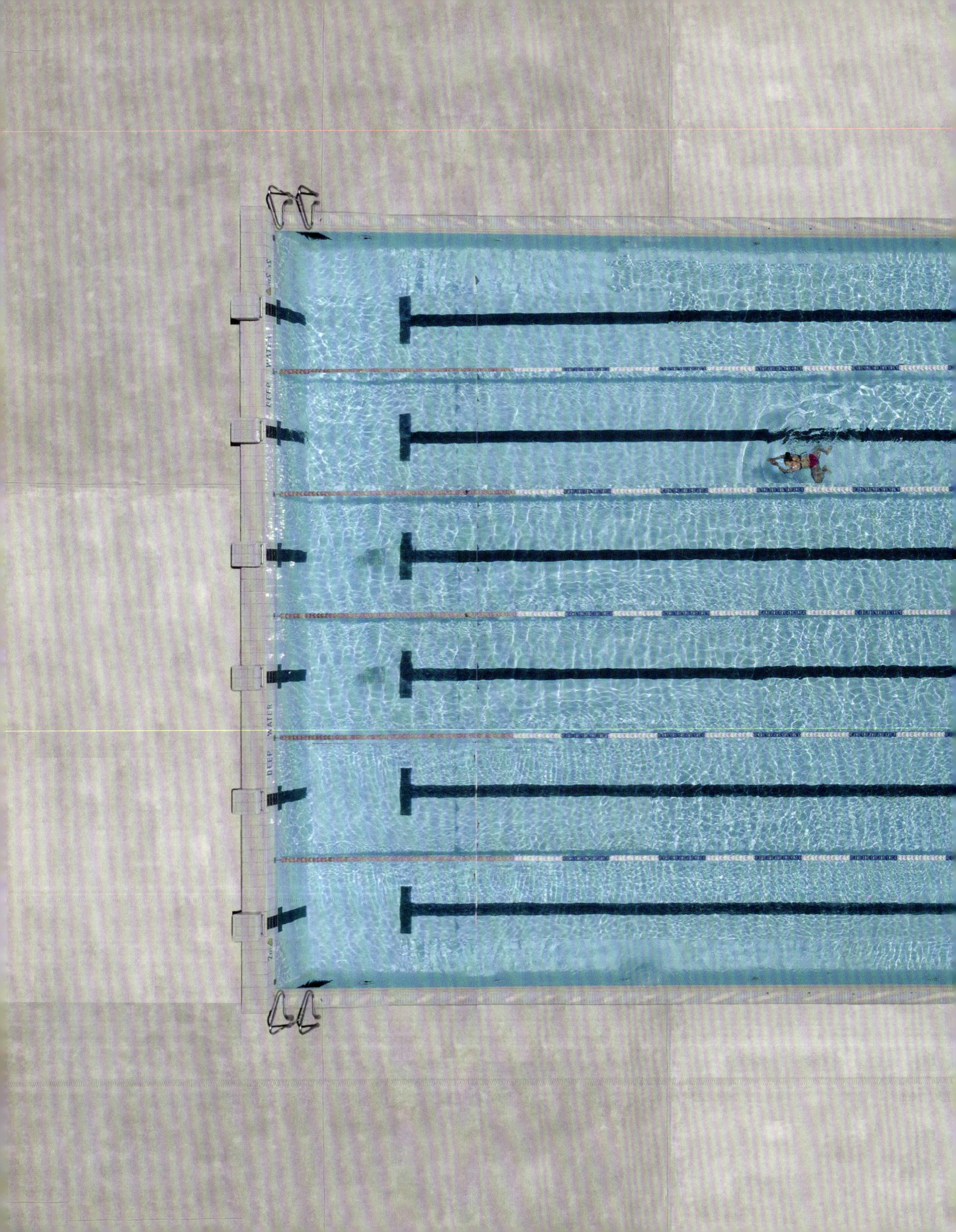
DEEP WATER
DEEP WATER

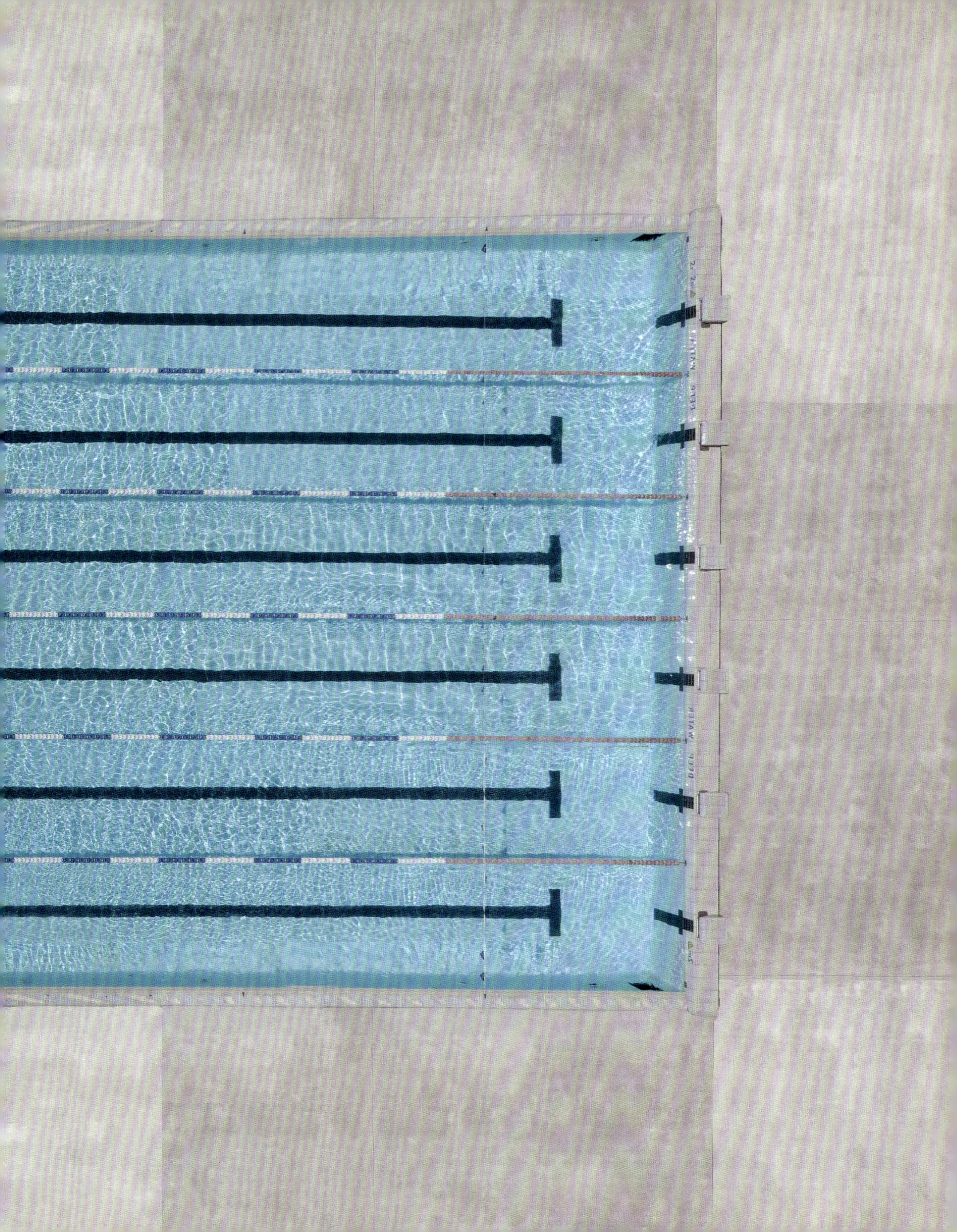
DEEP WATER
DEEP WATER

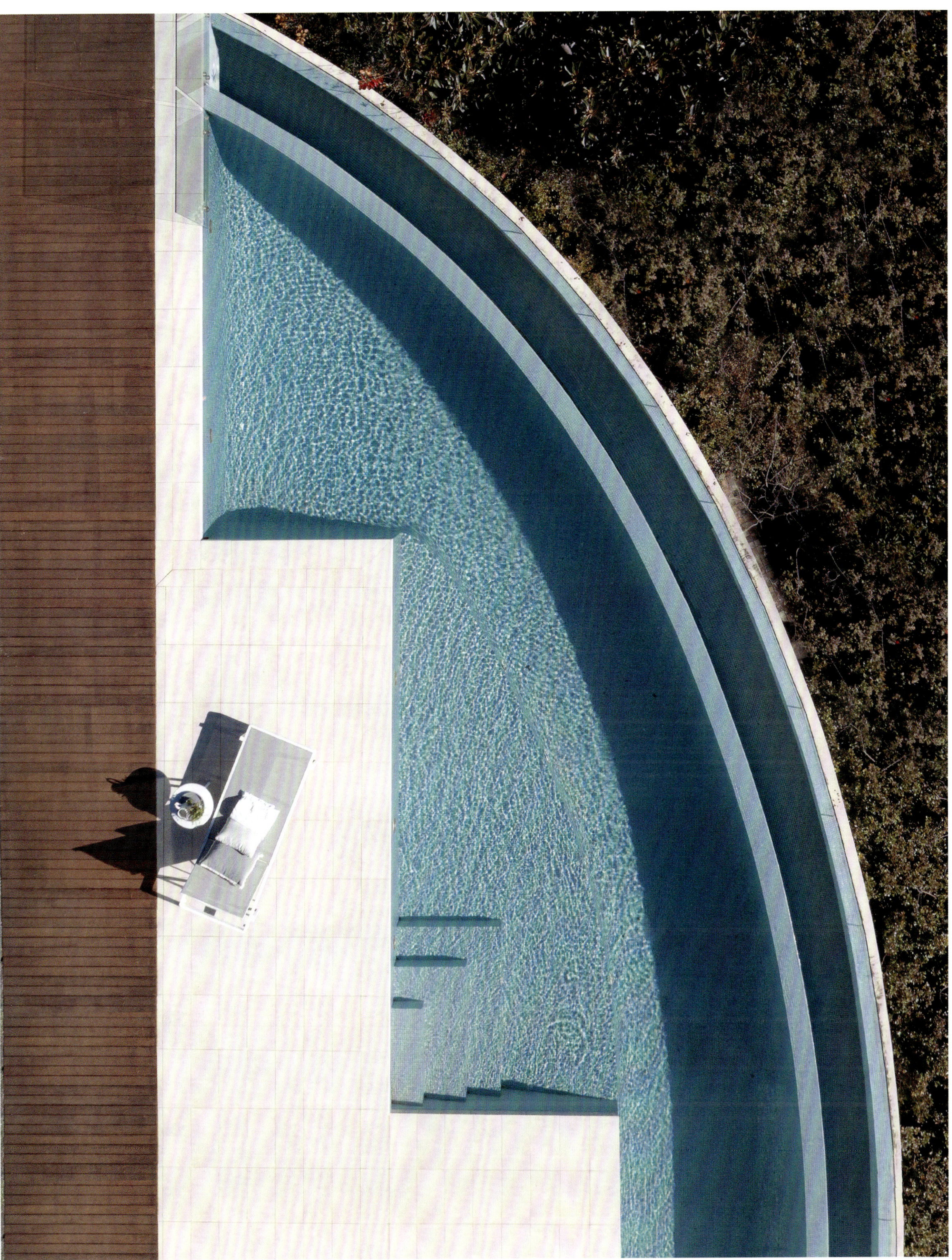

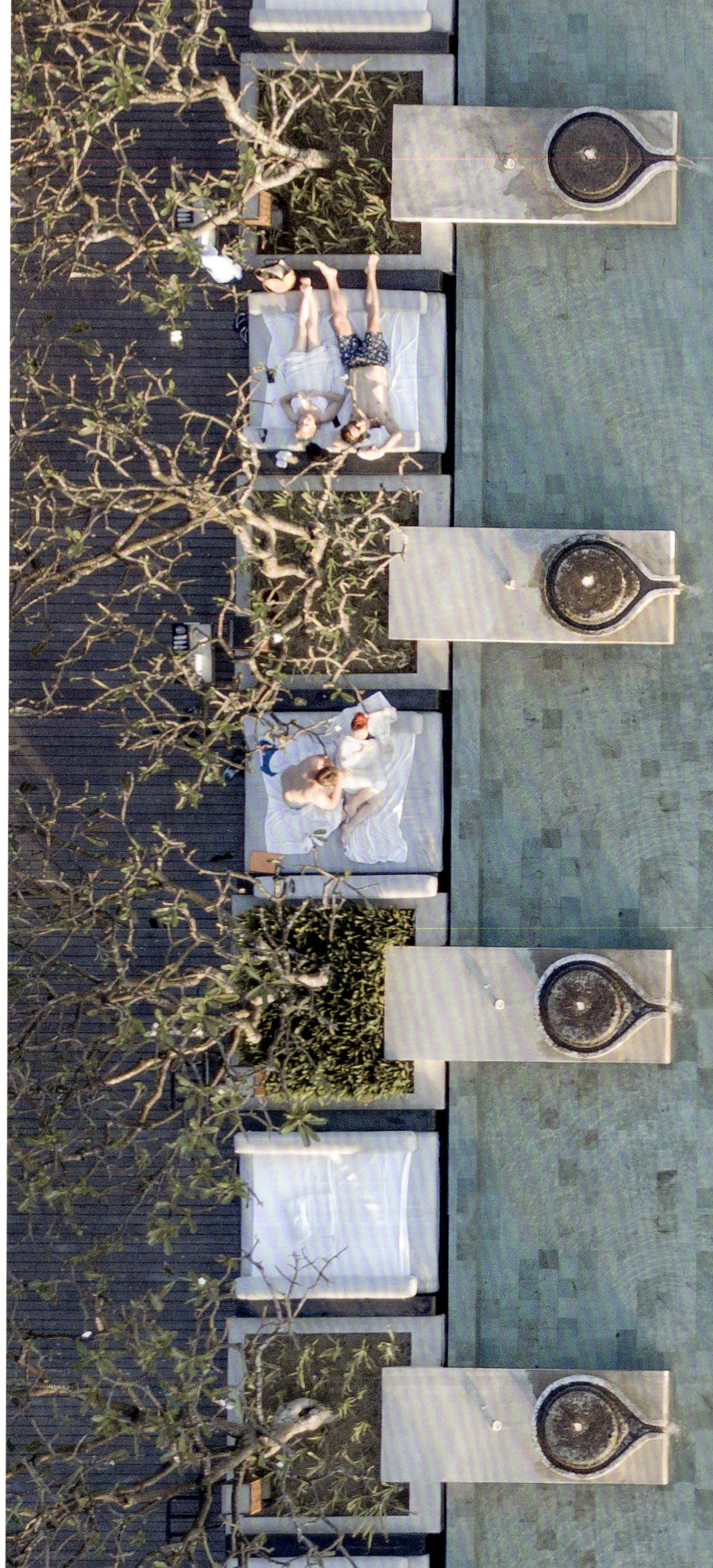

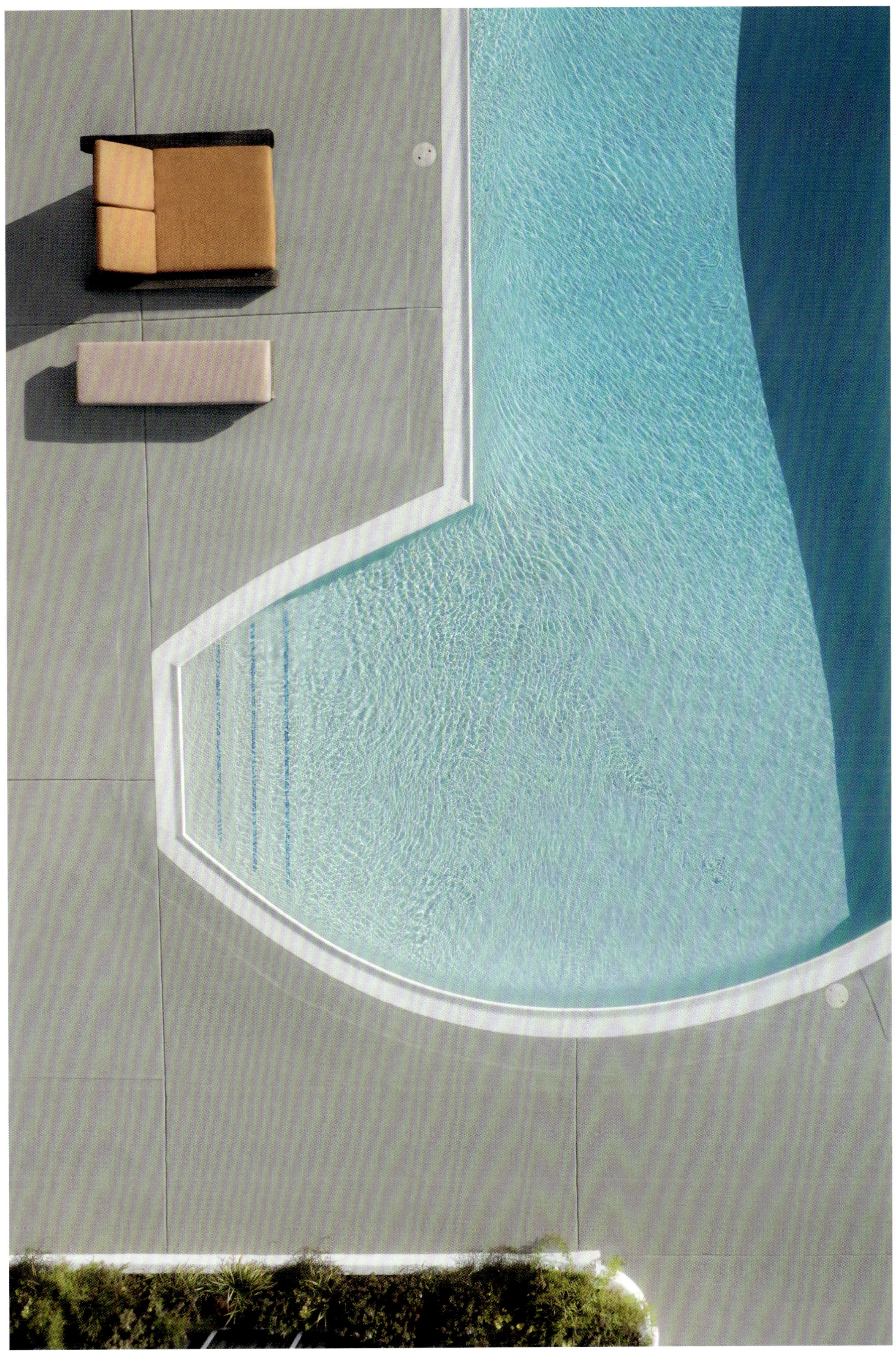

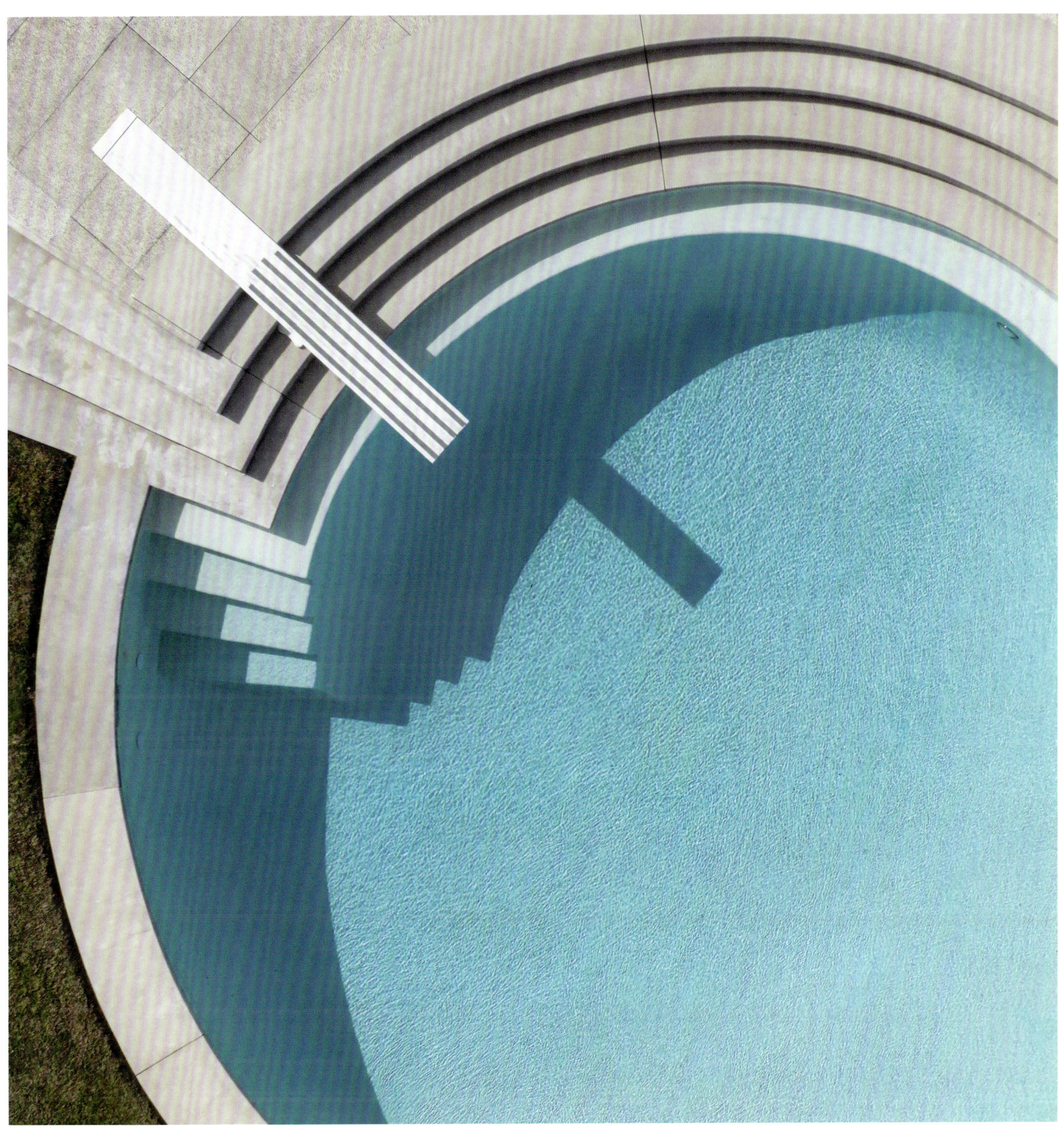

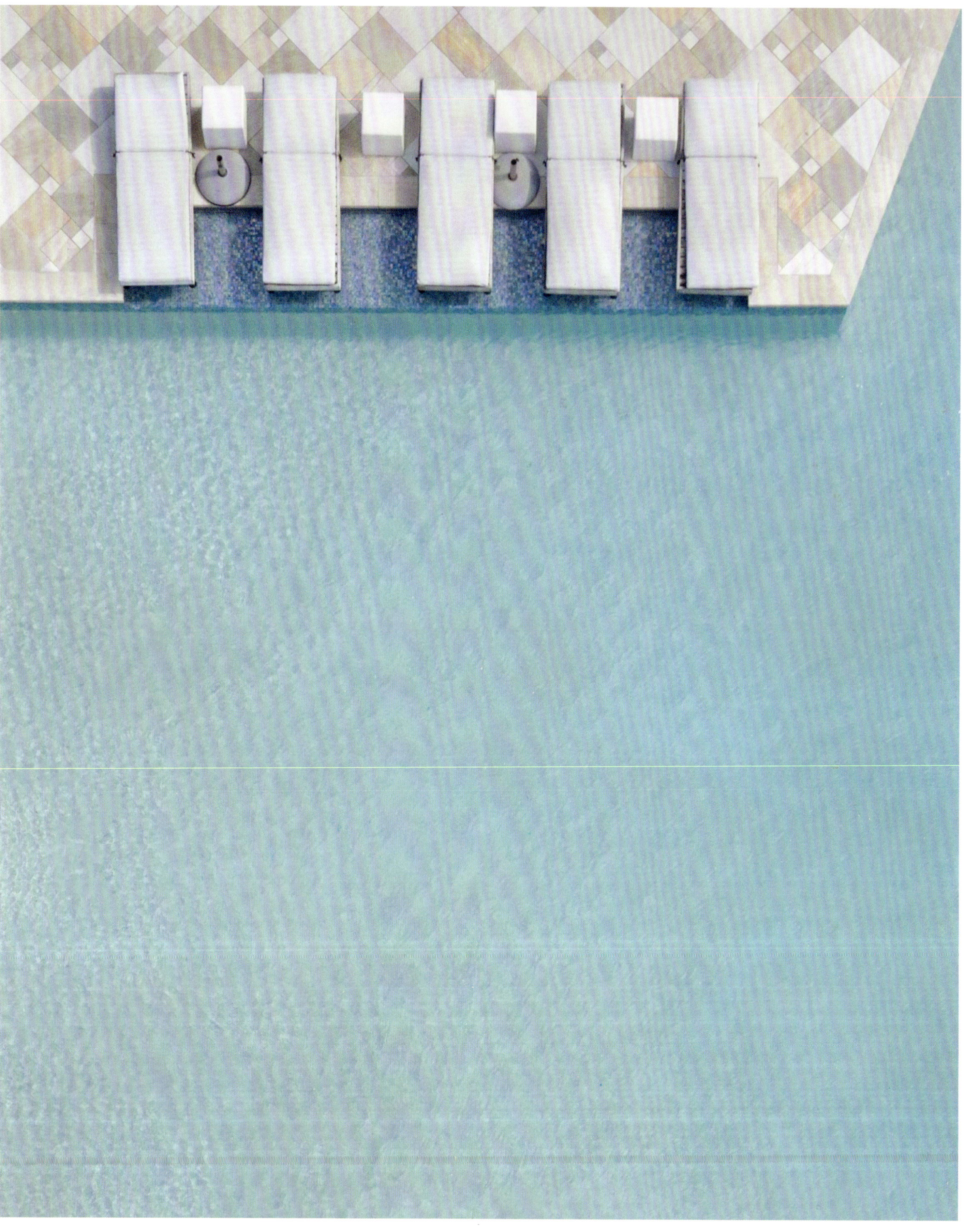

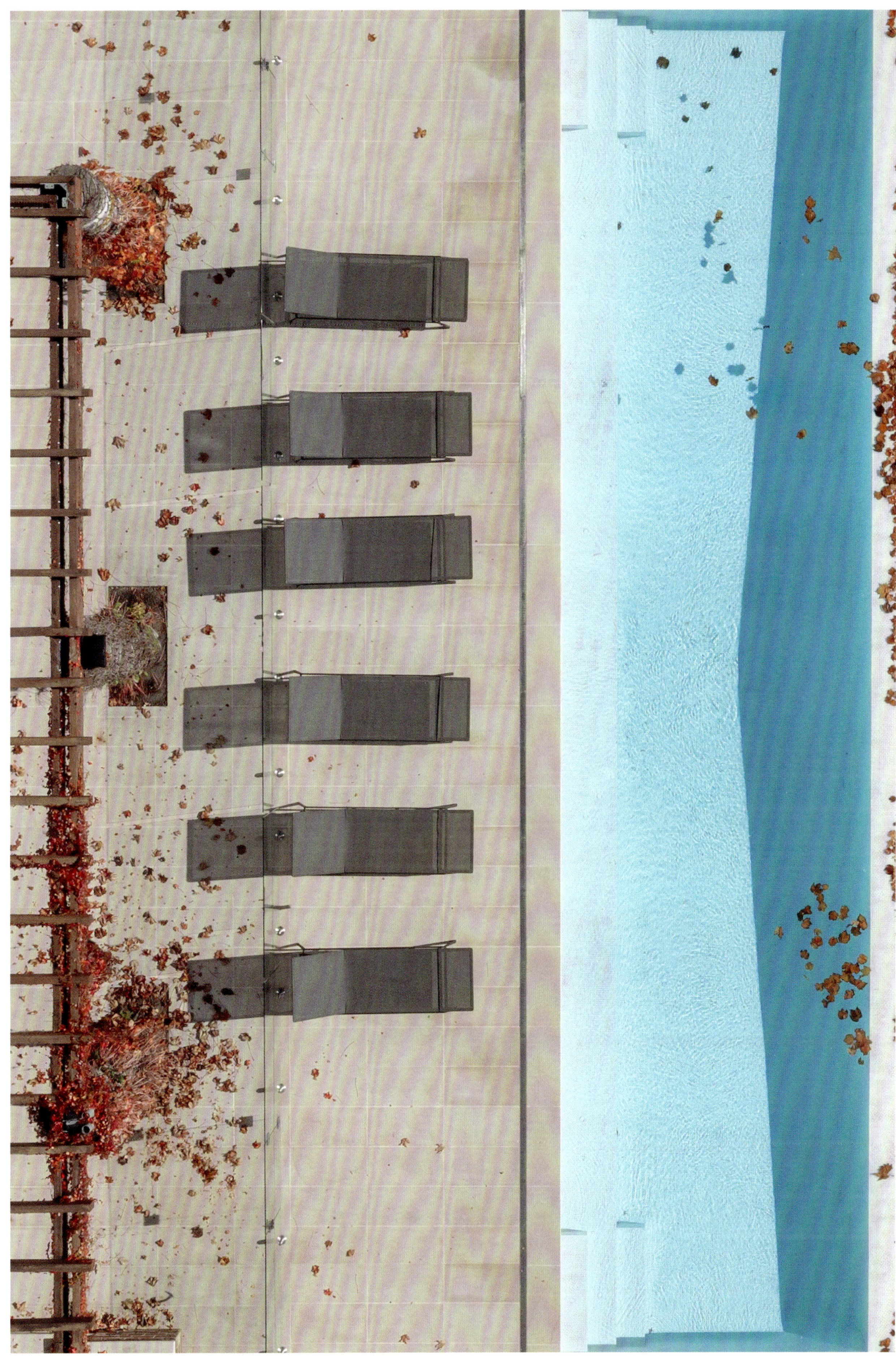

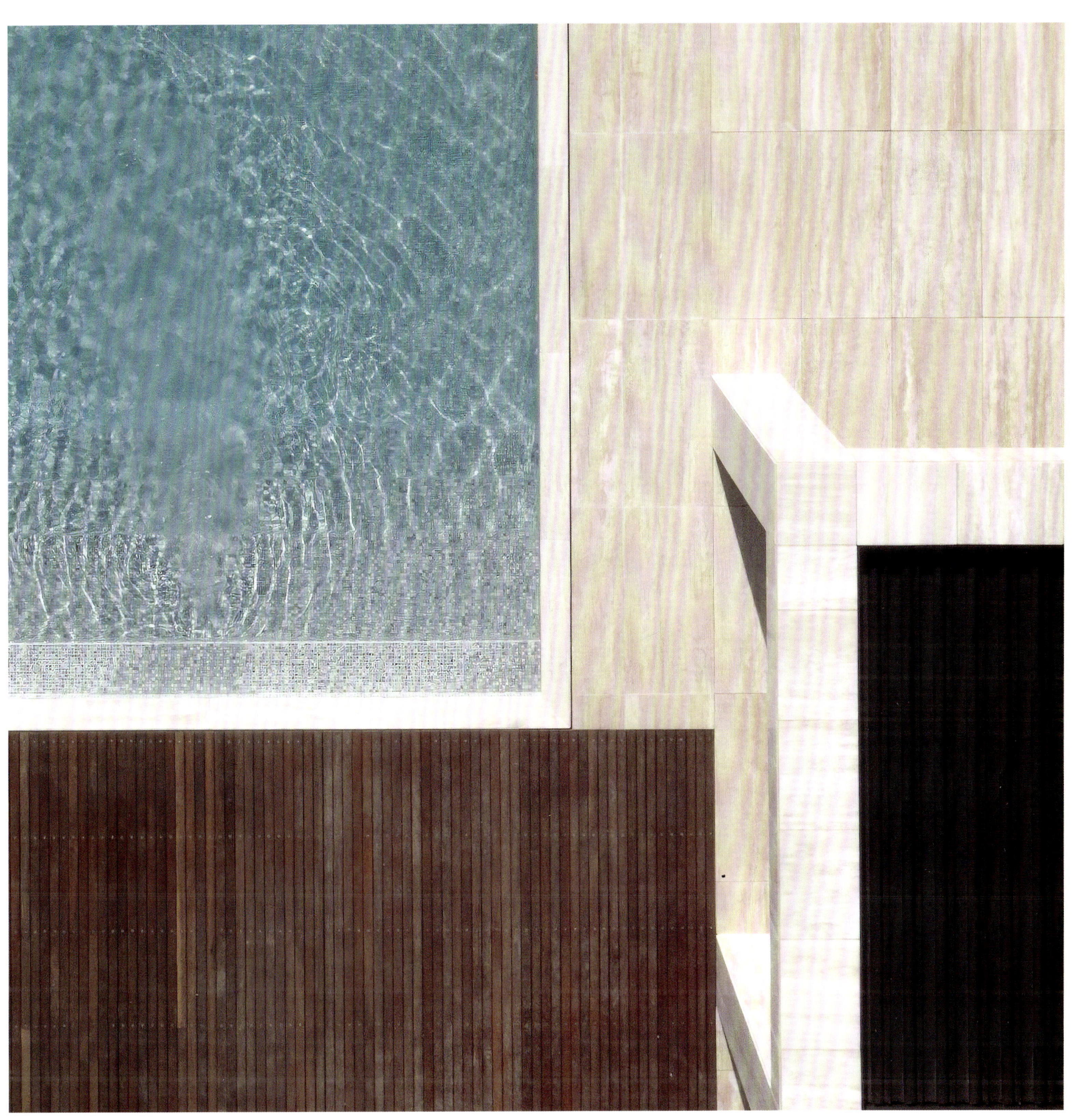

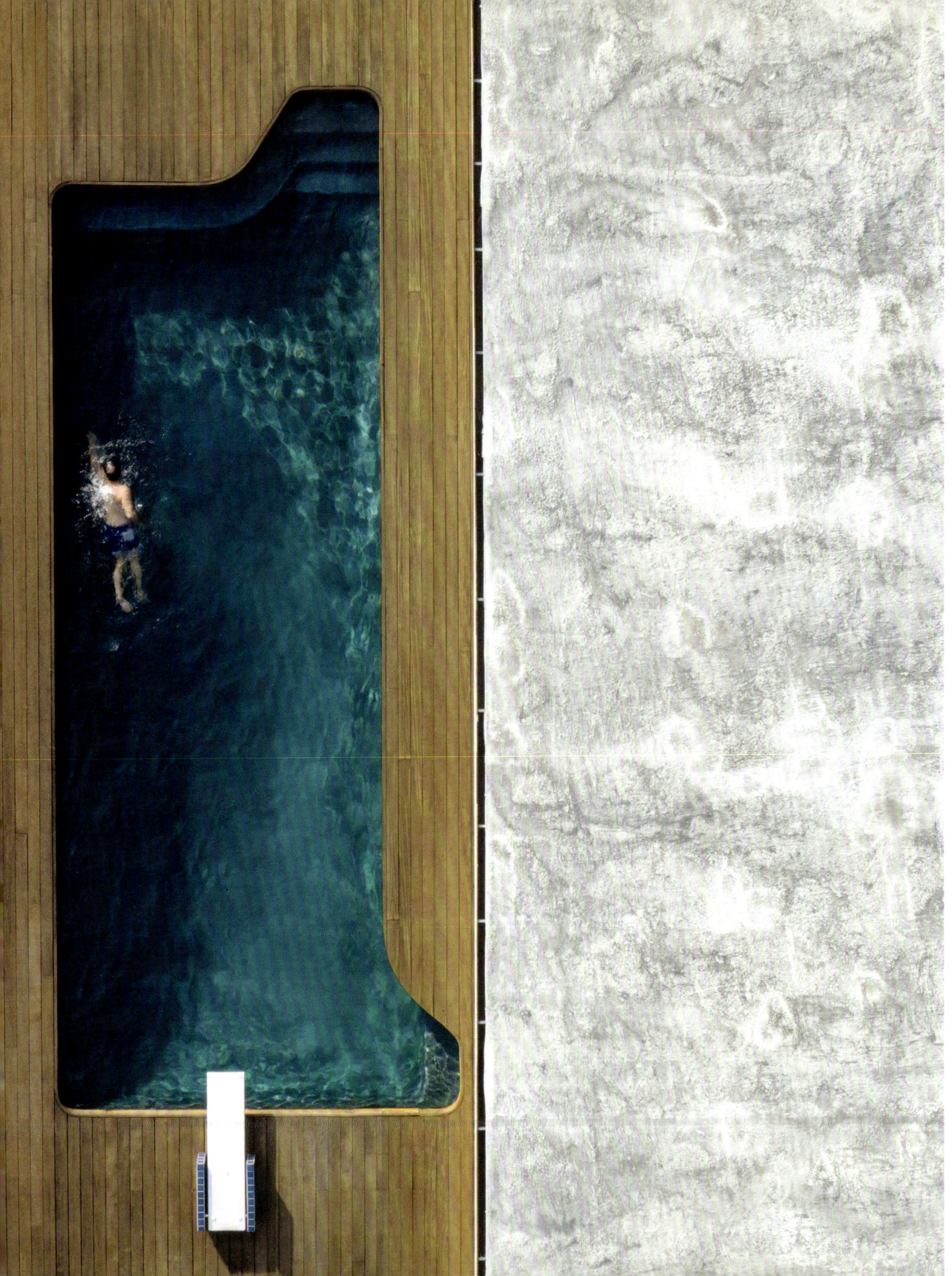

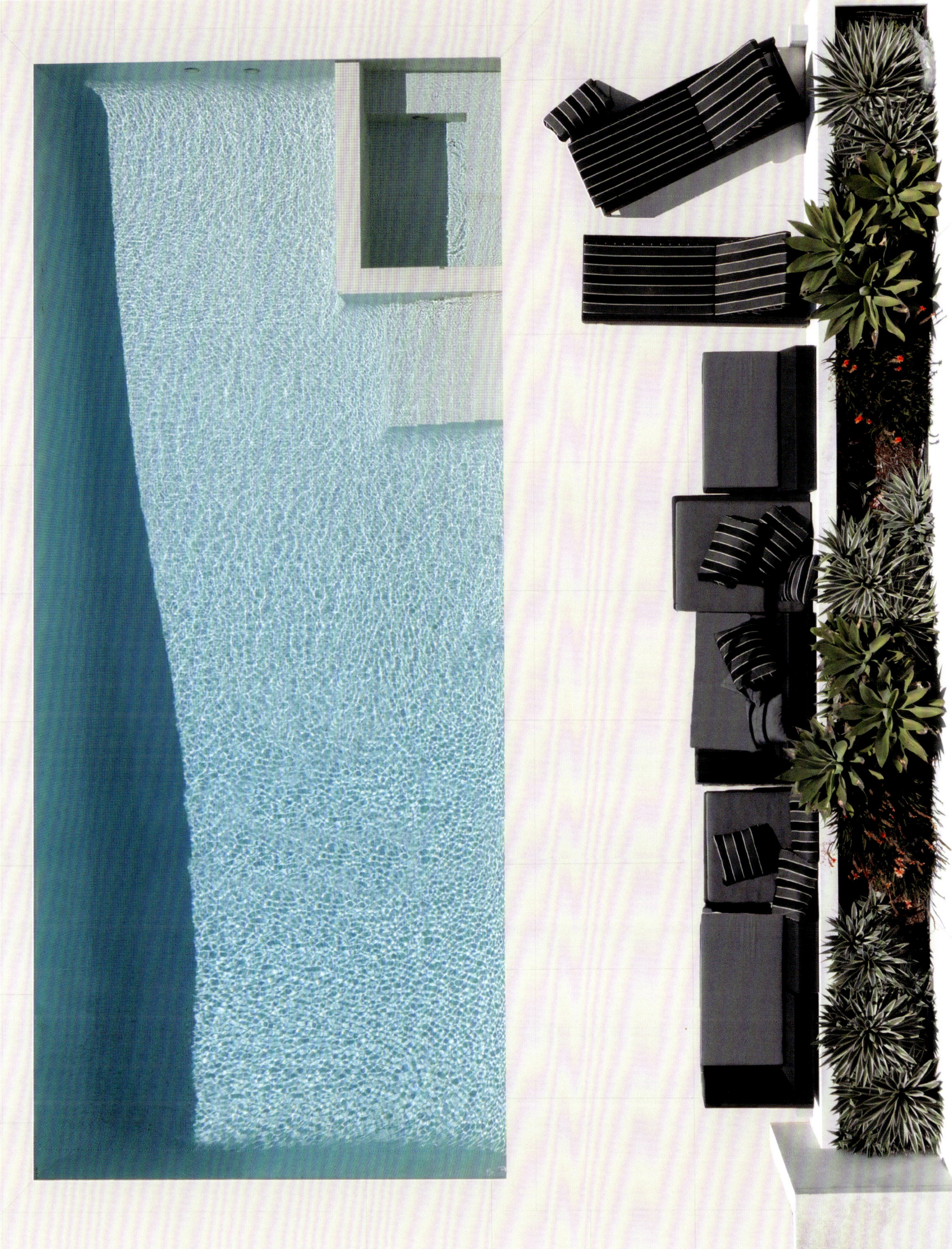

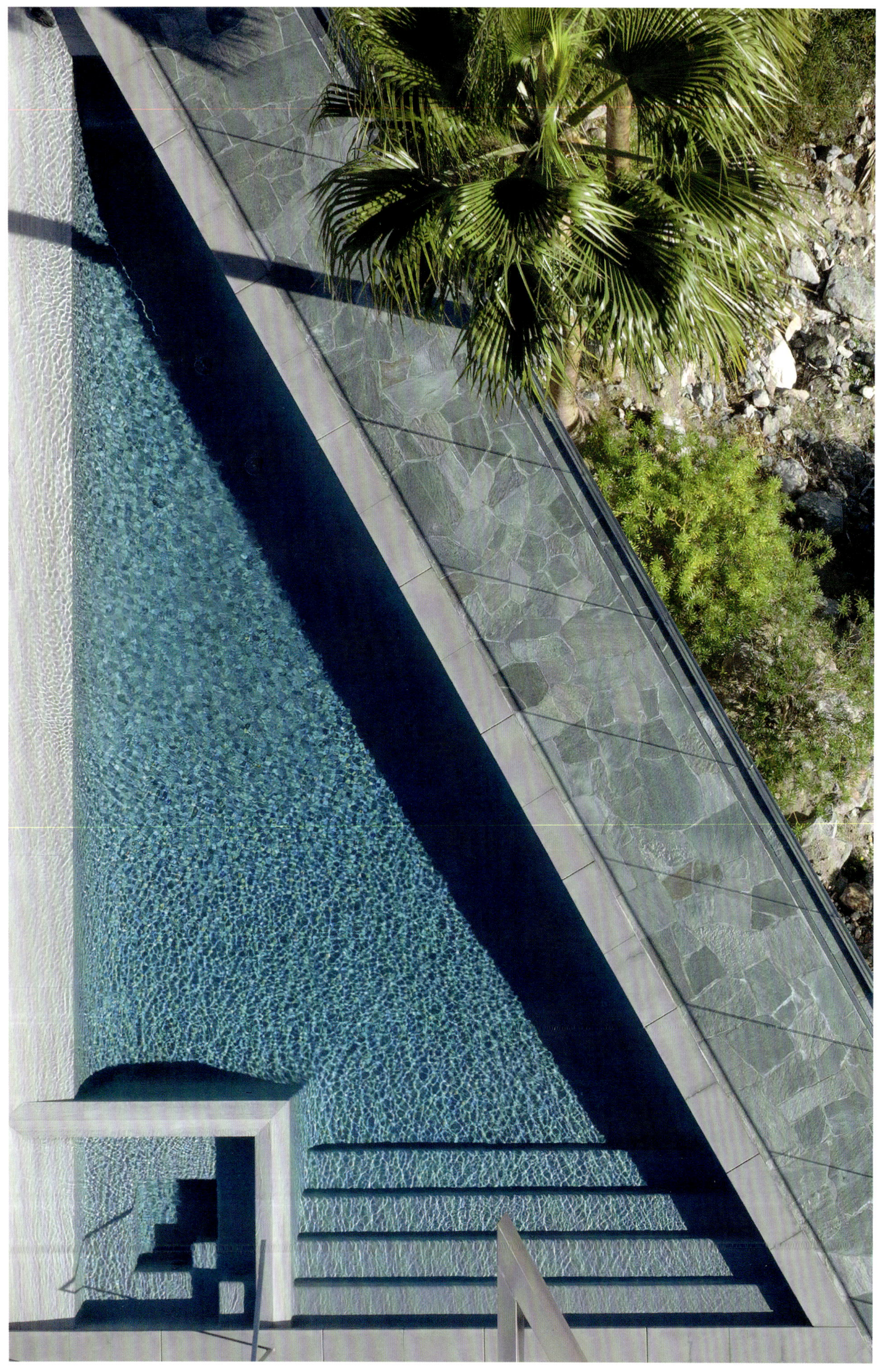

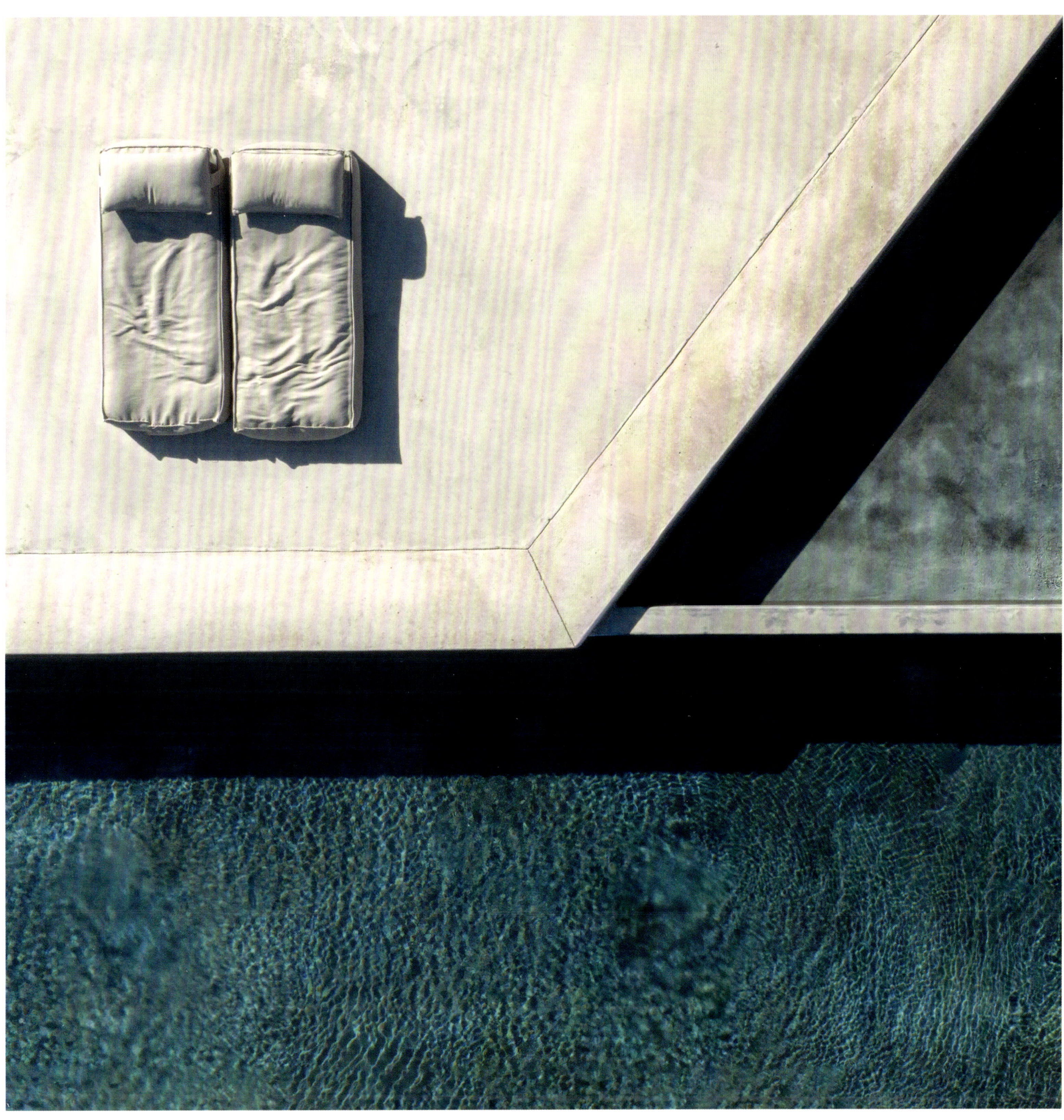

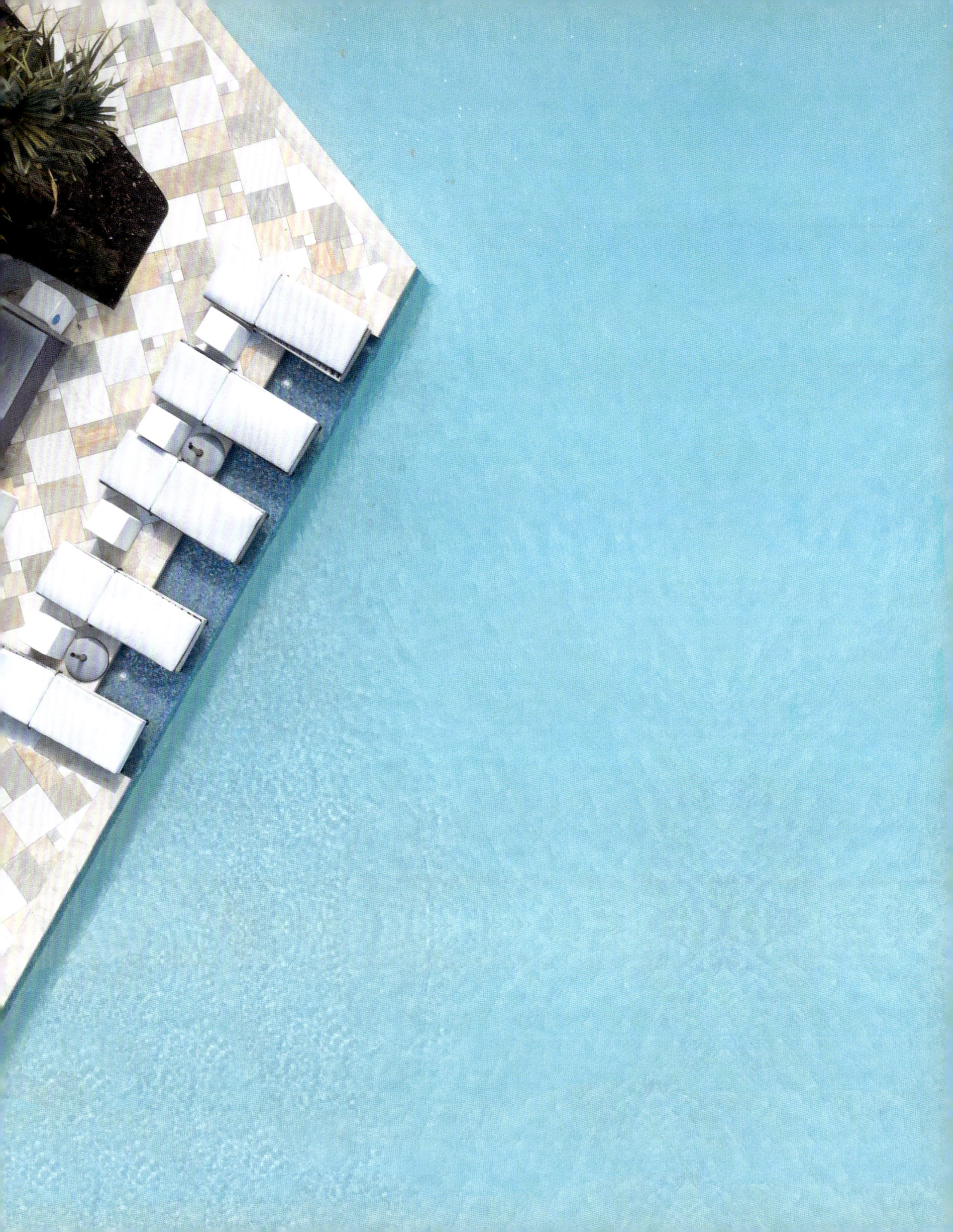

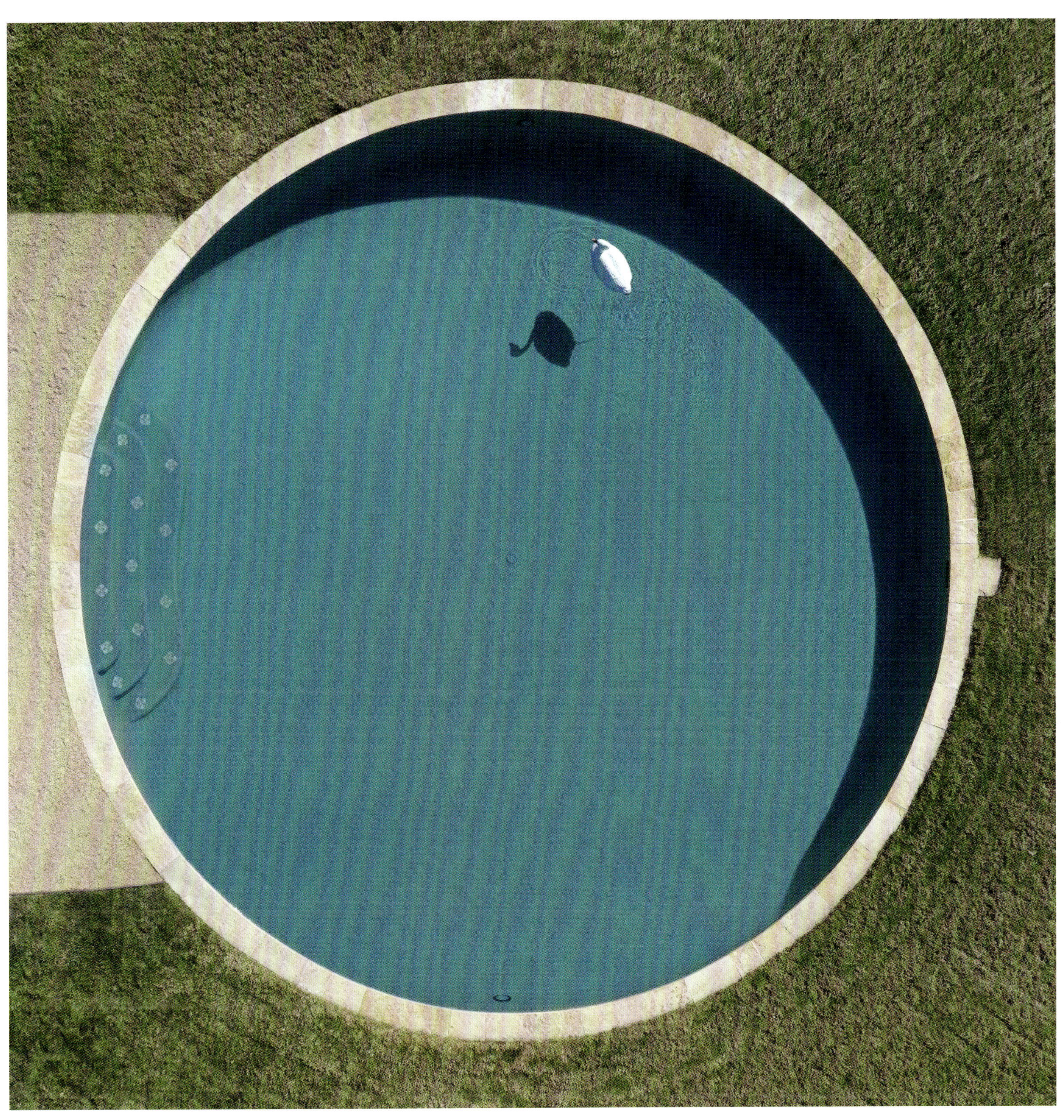

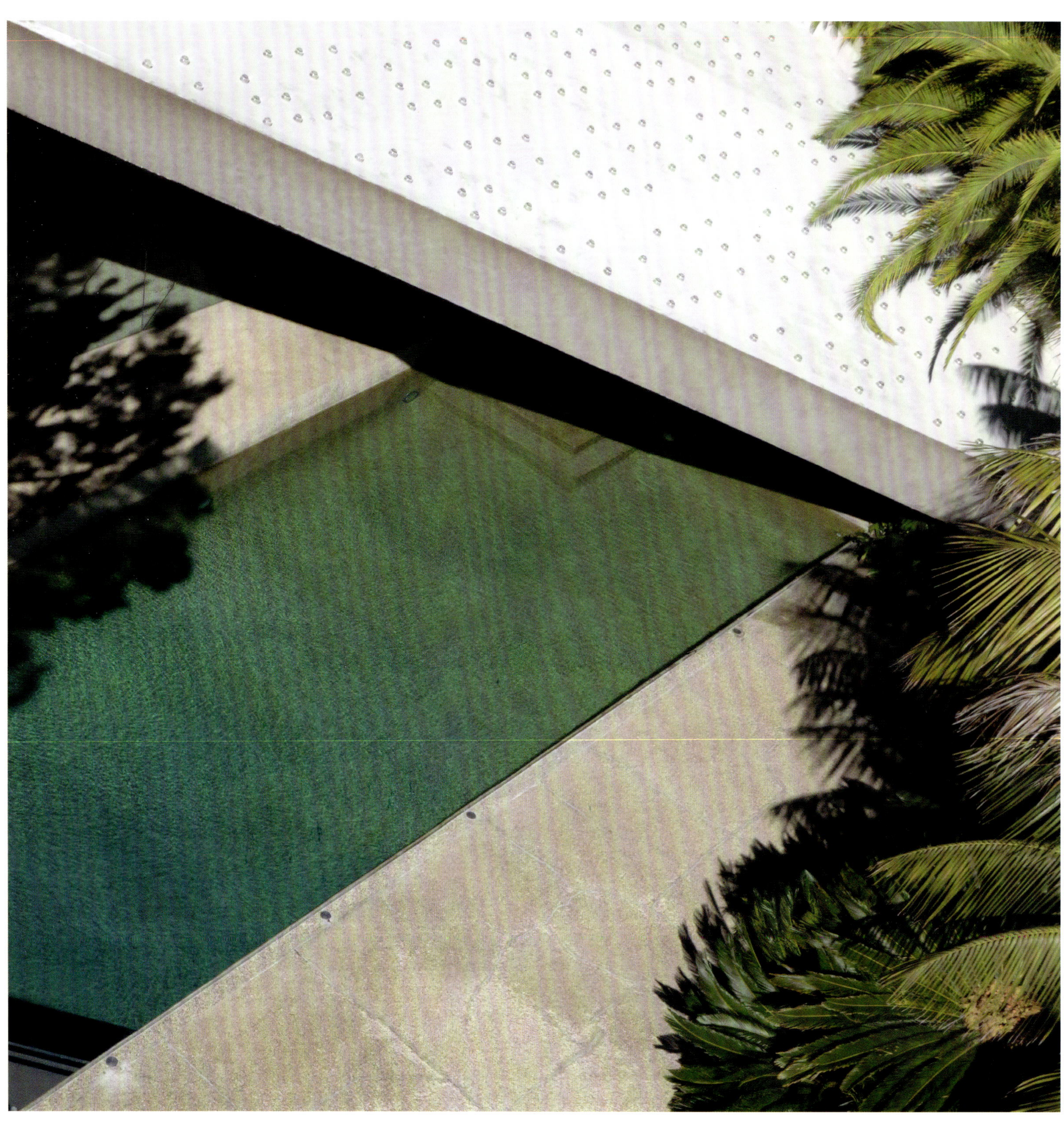

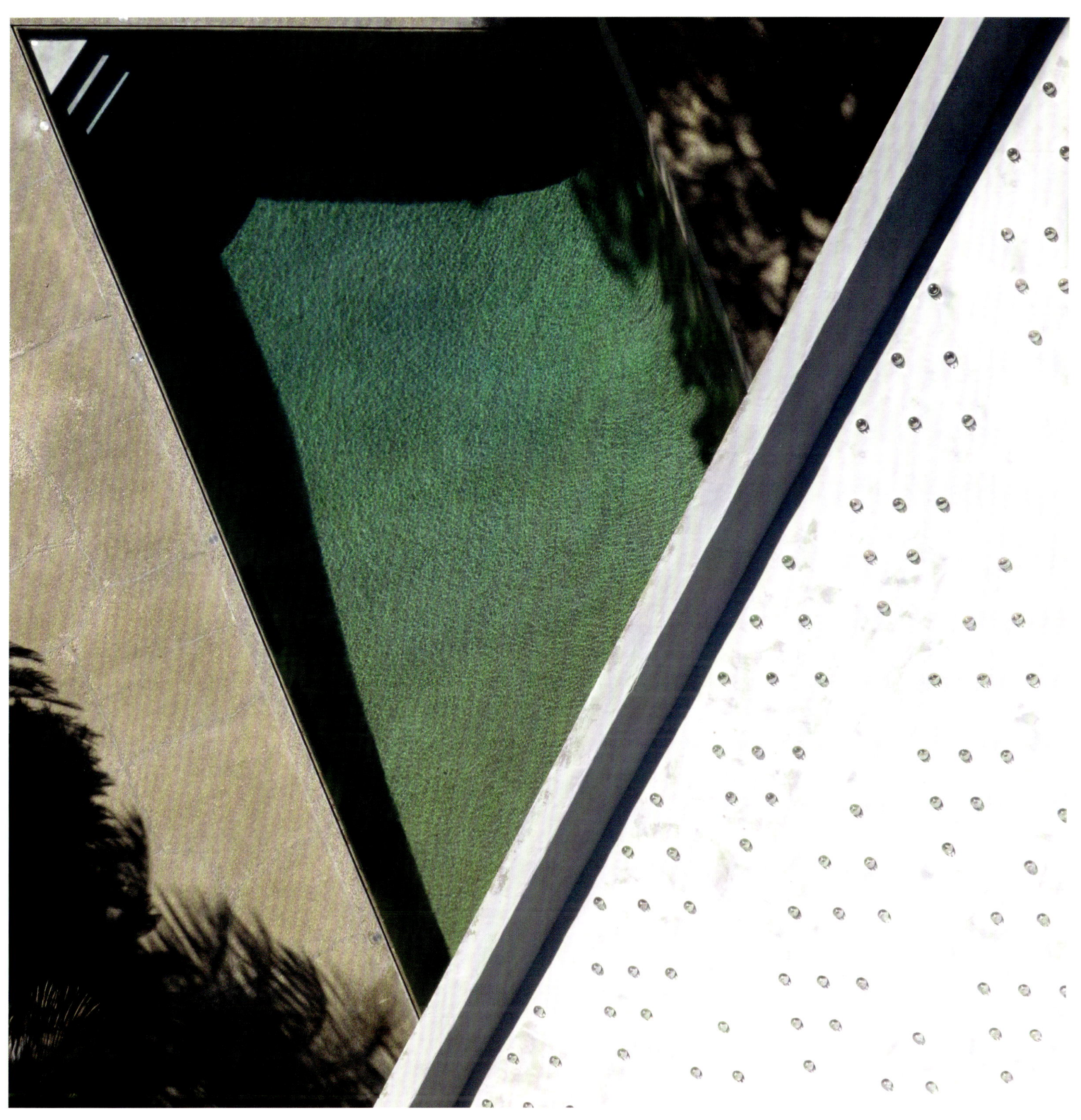

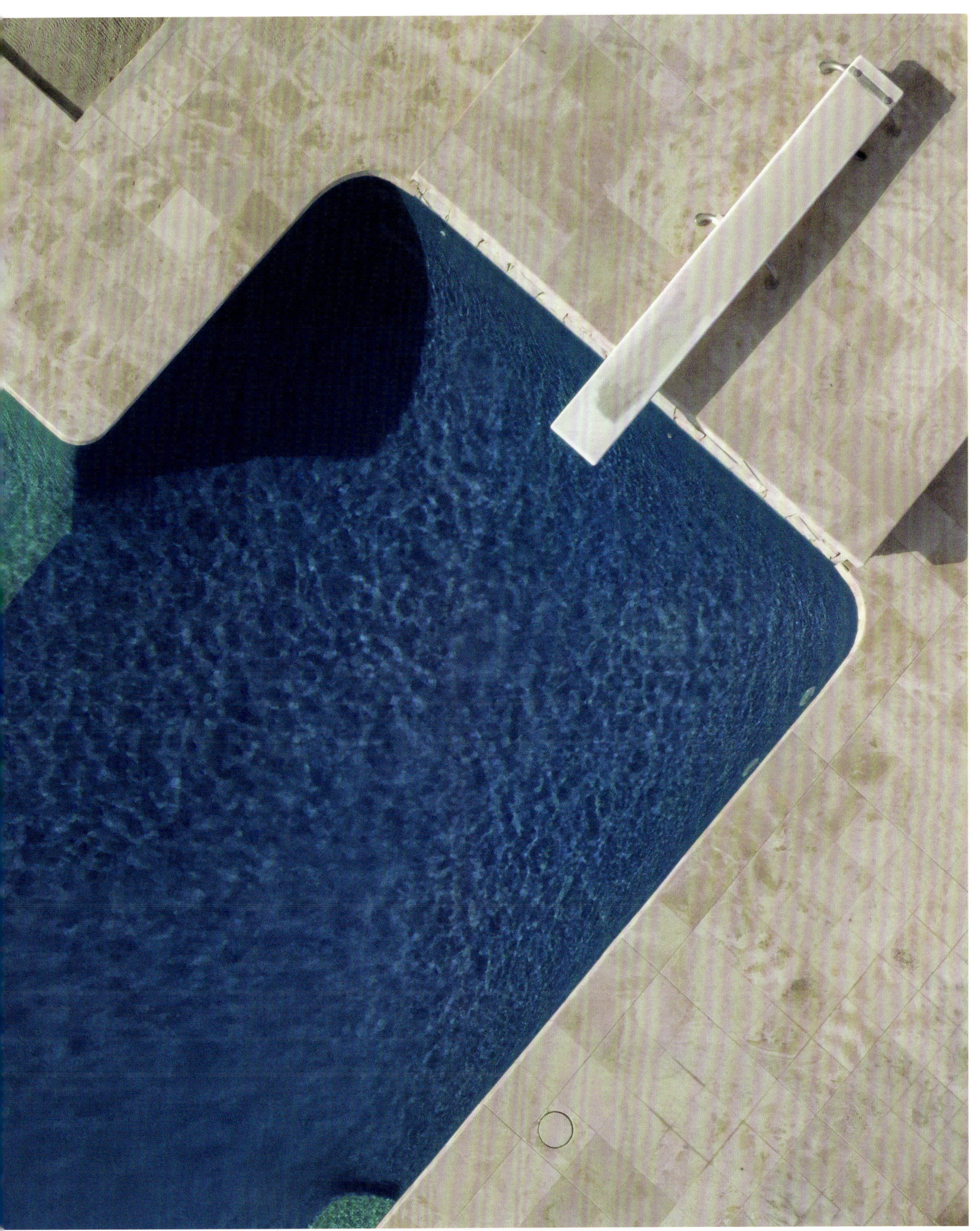

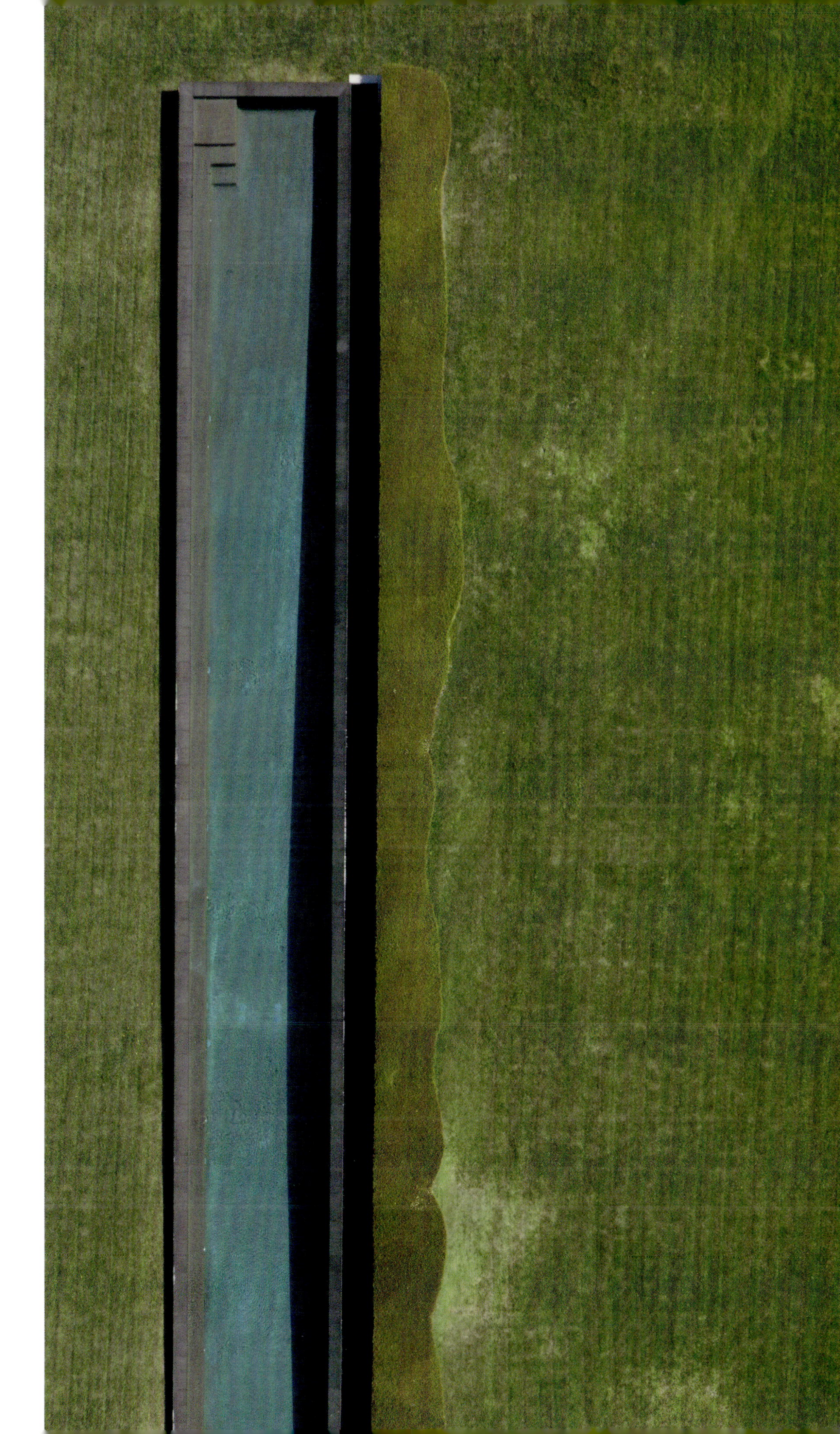

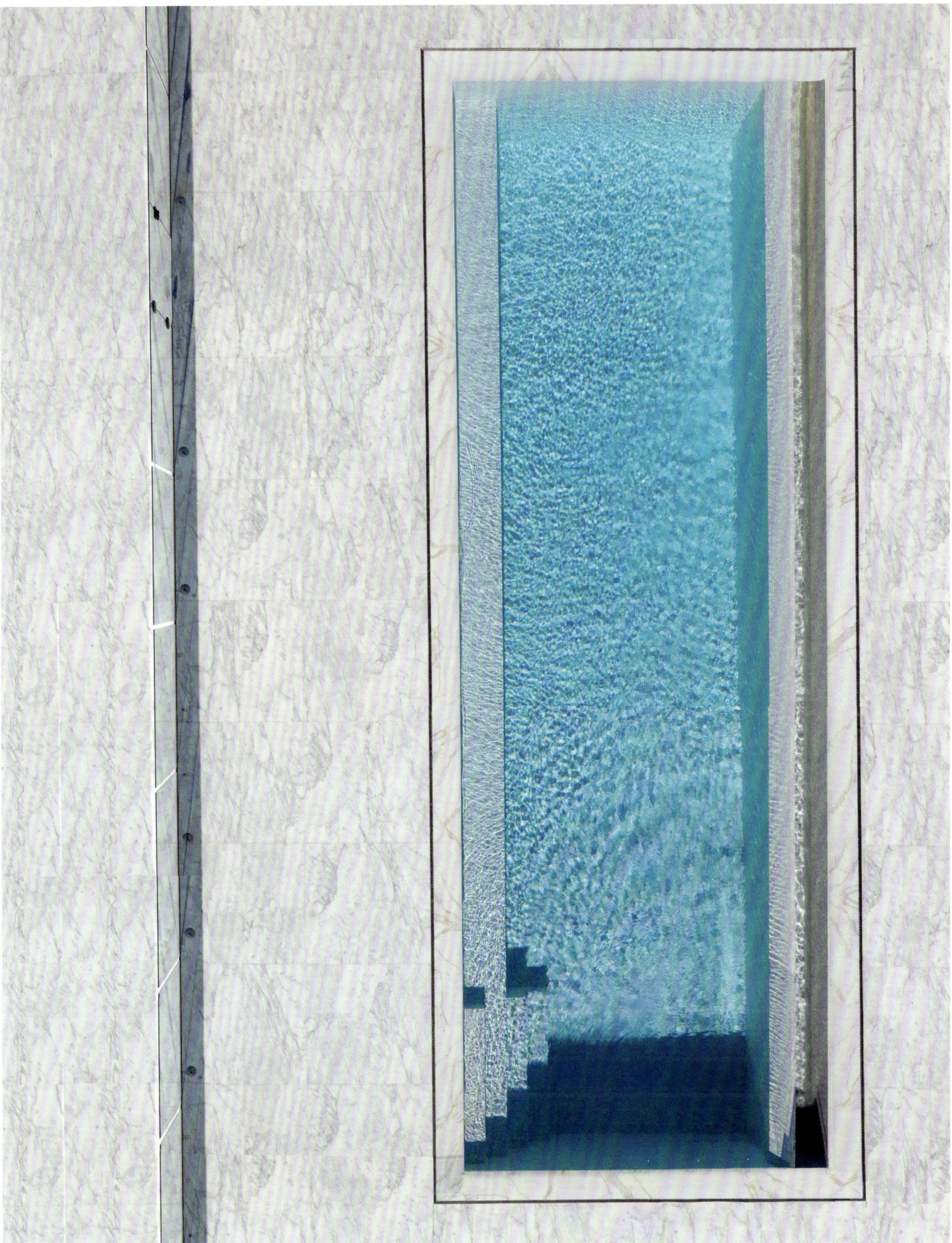

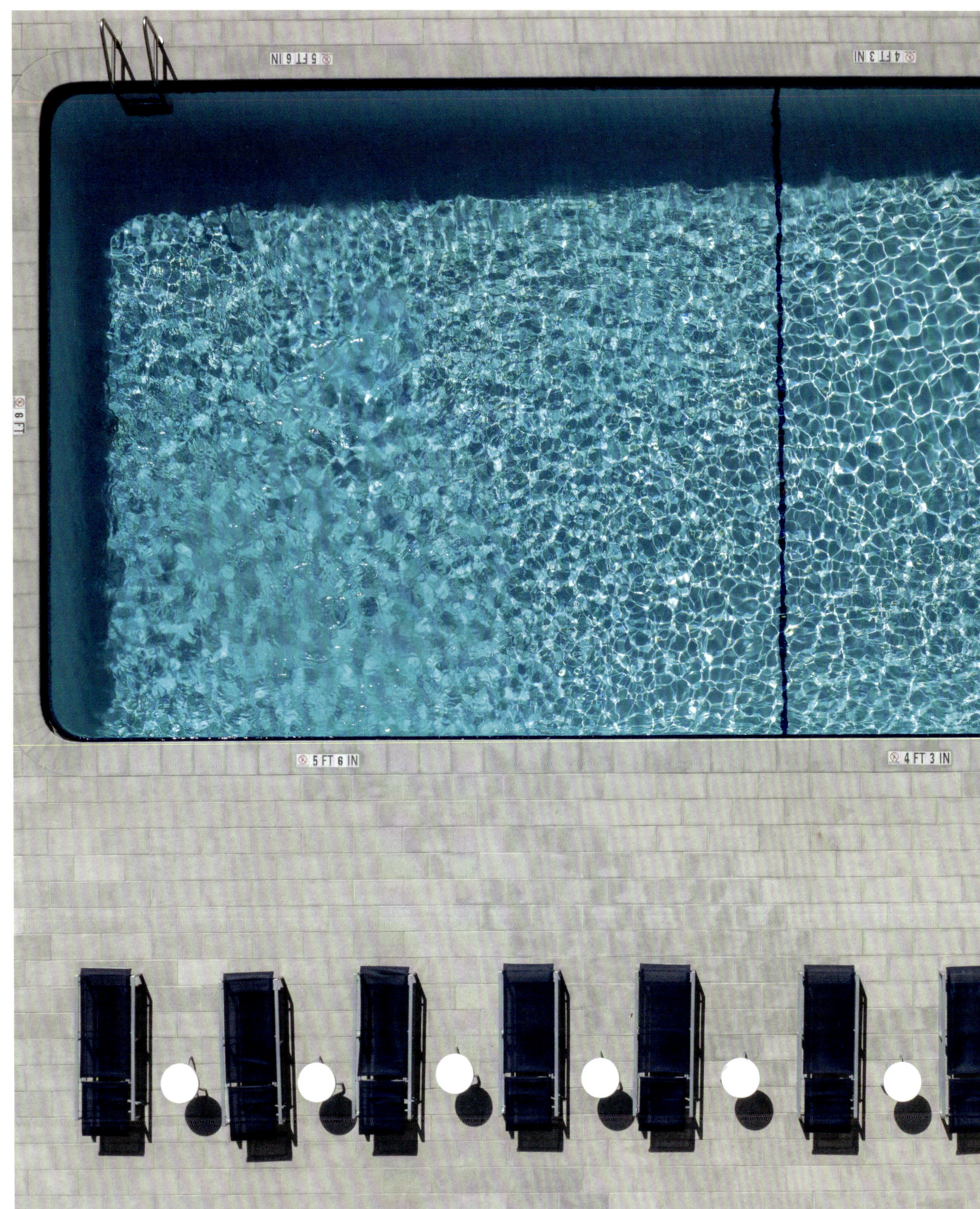
5 FT 6 IN
4 FT 3 IN
6 FT

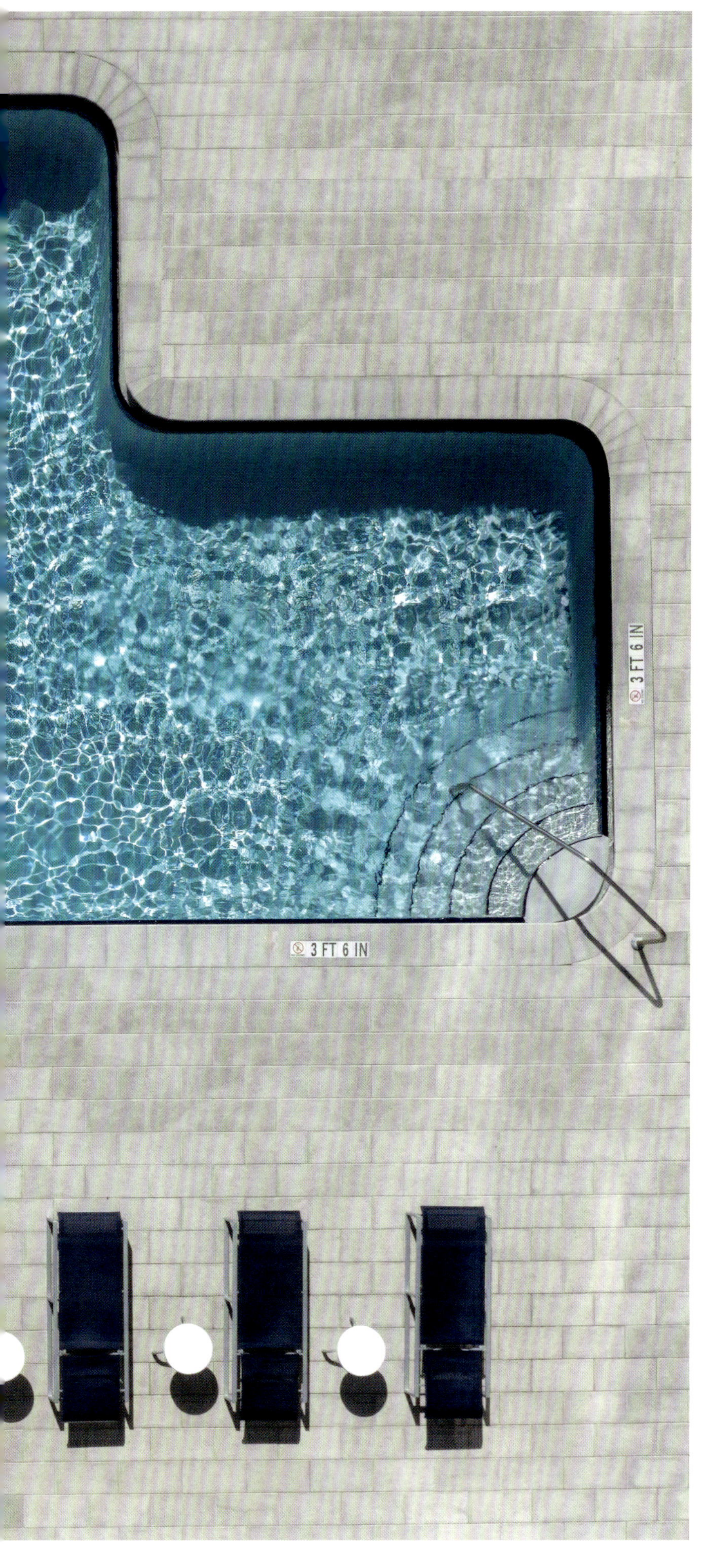

MIAMI BEACH, FLORIDA — USA

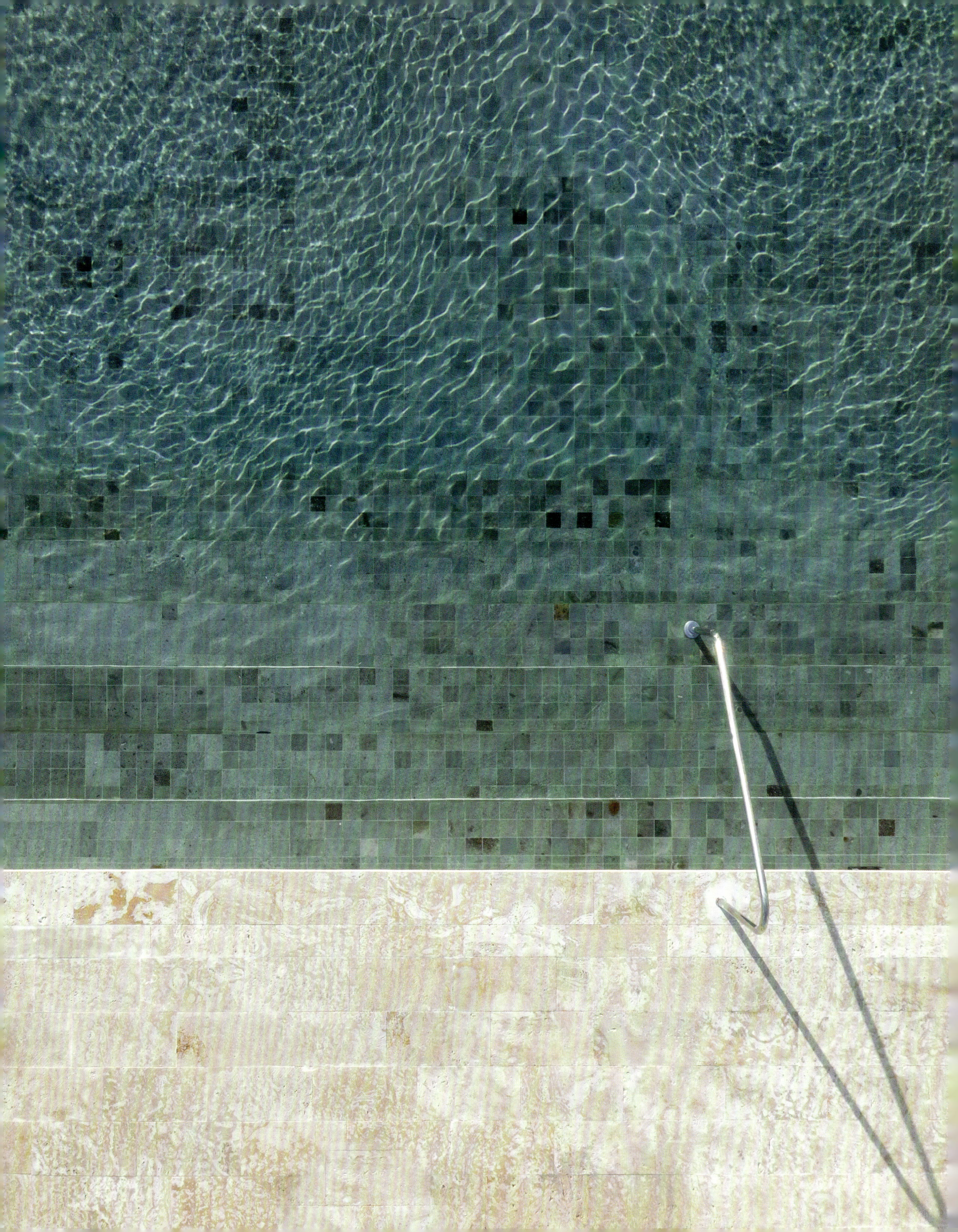

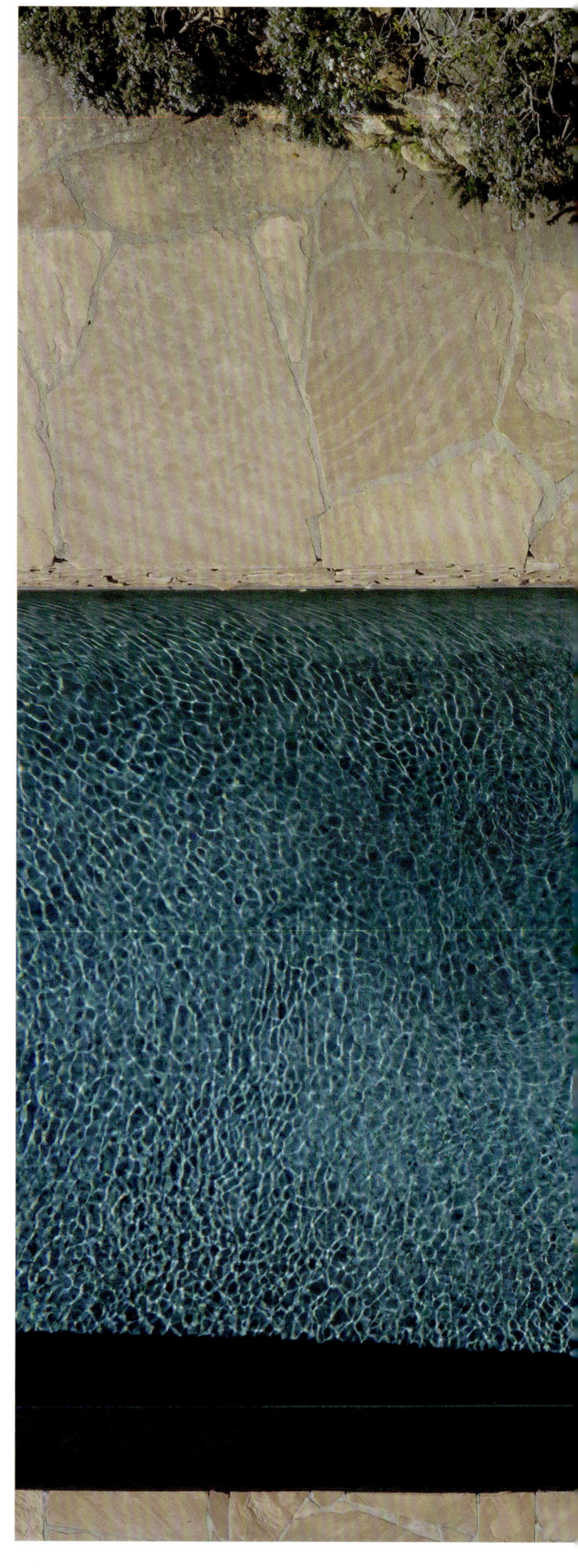

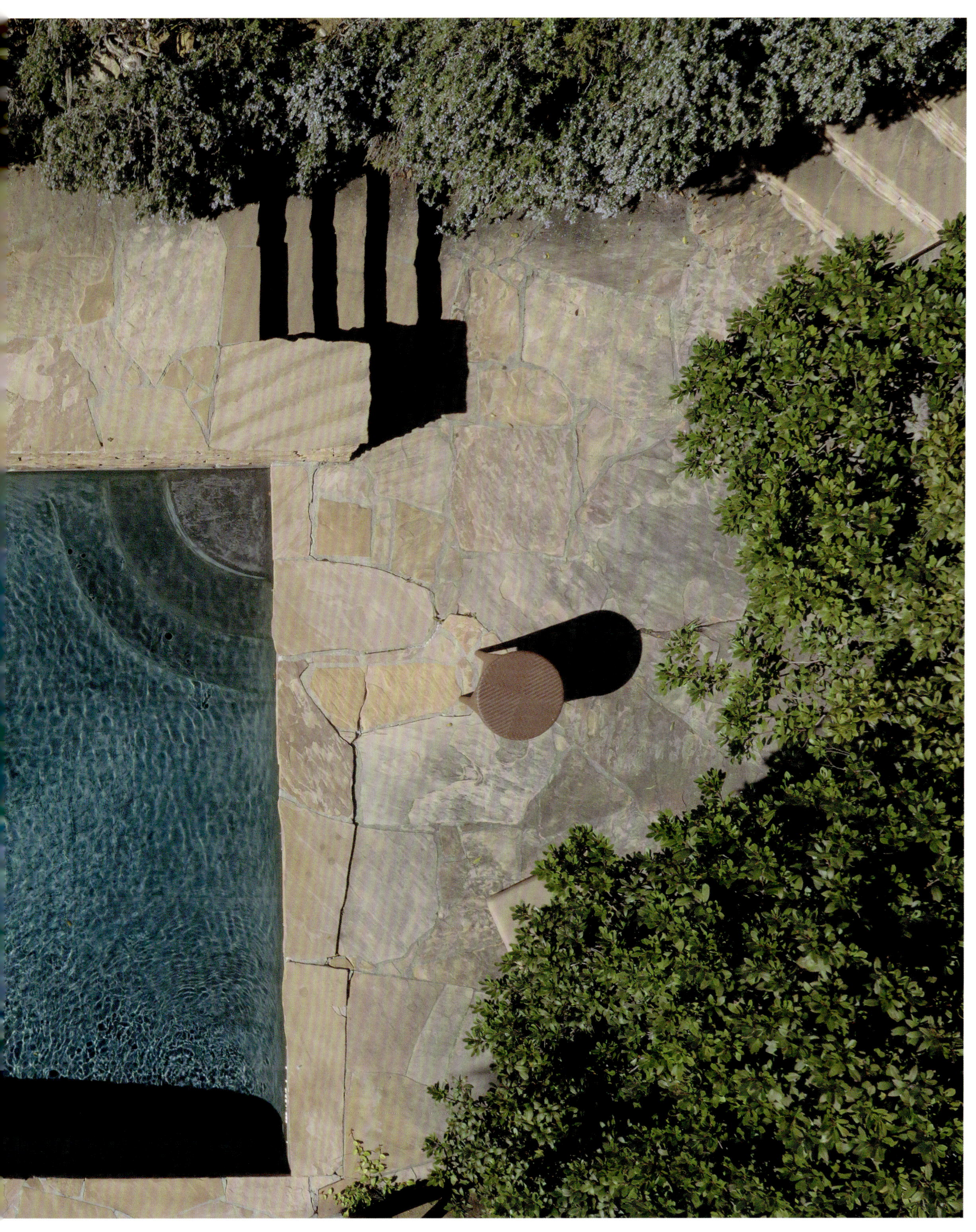

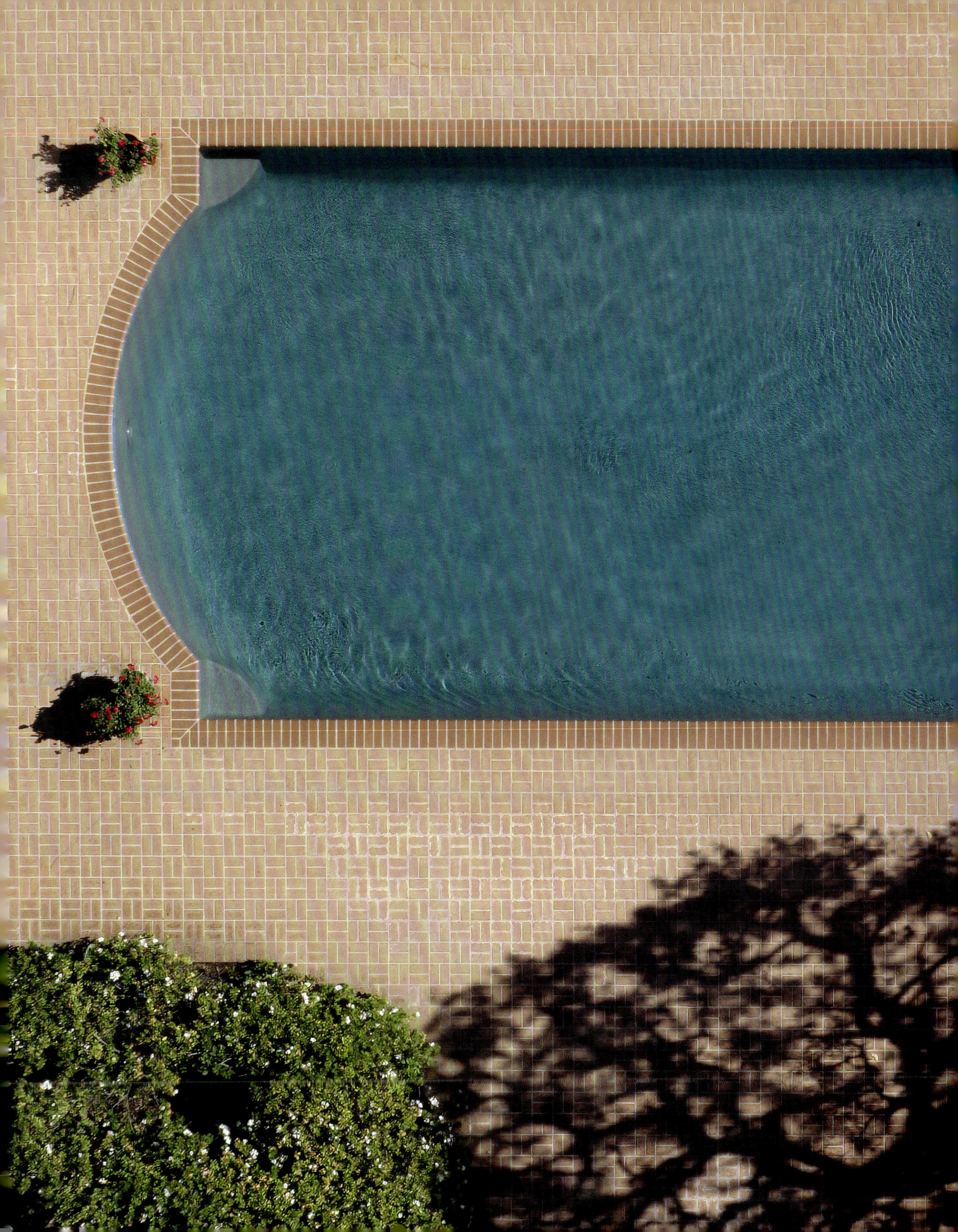

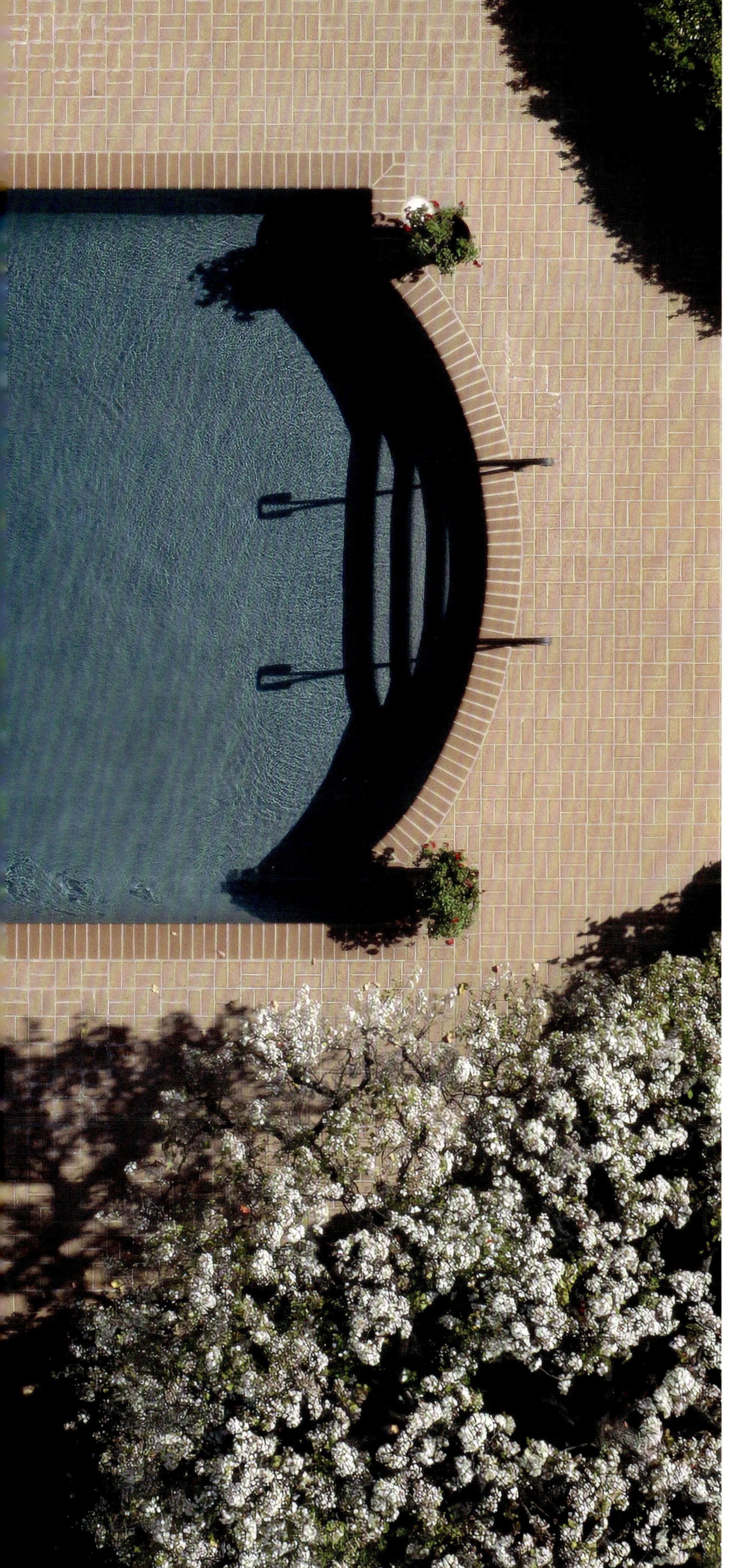

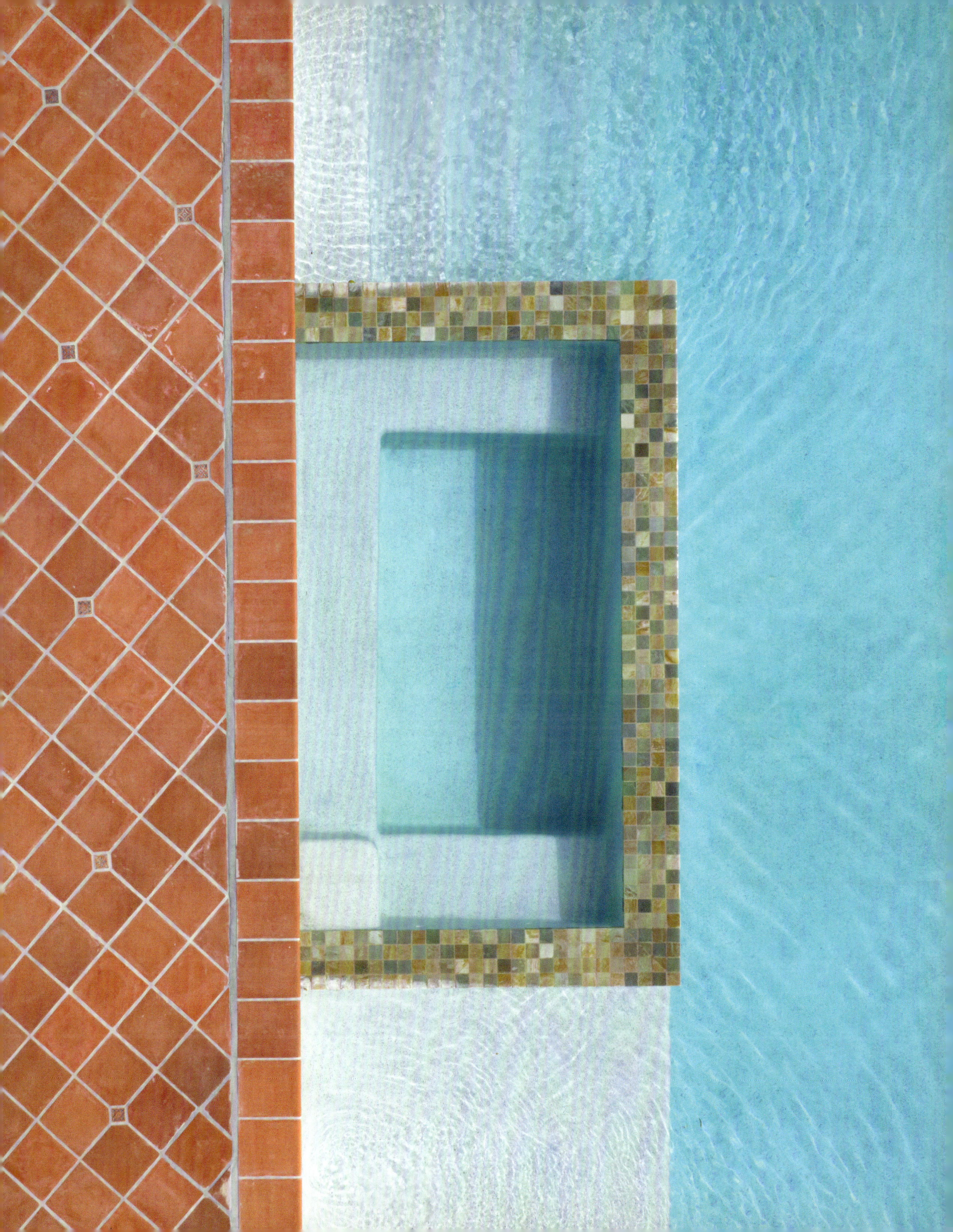

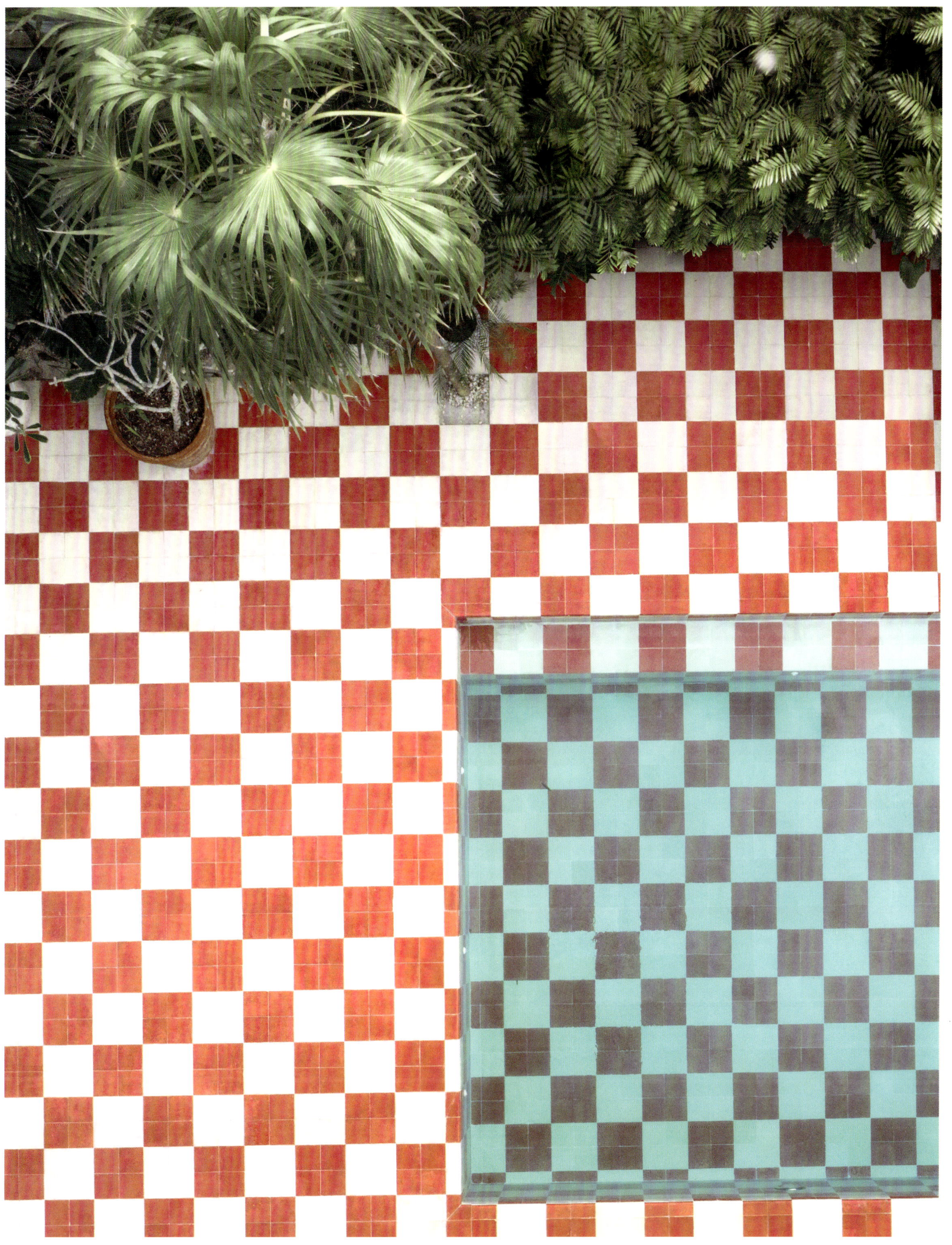

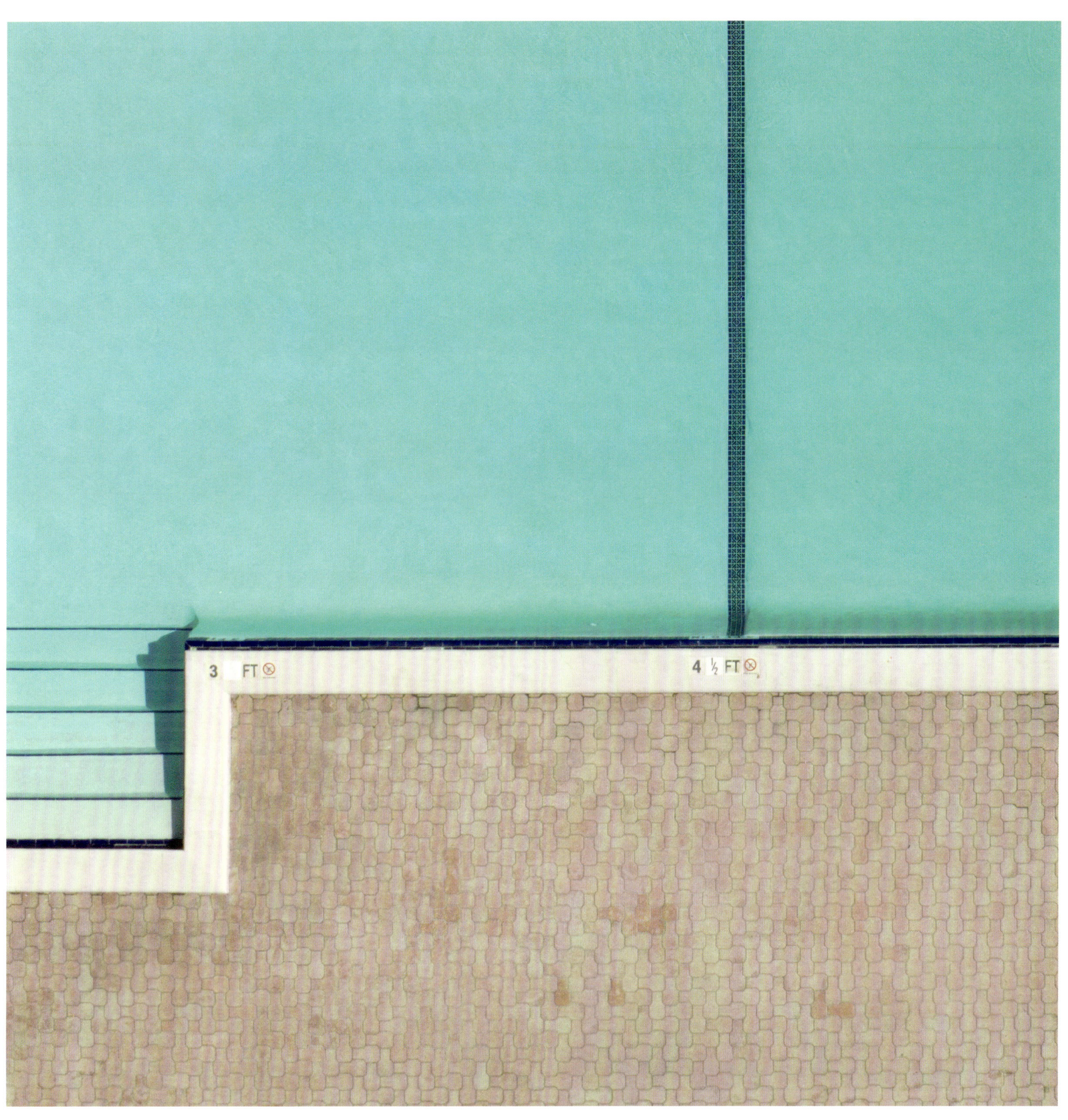

MIAMI BEACH, FLORIDA — USA THE L

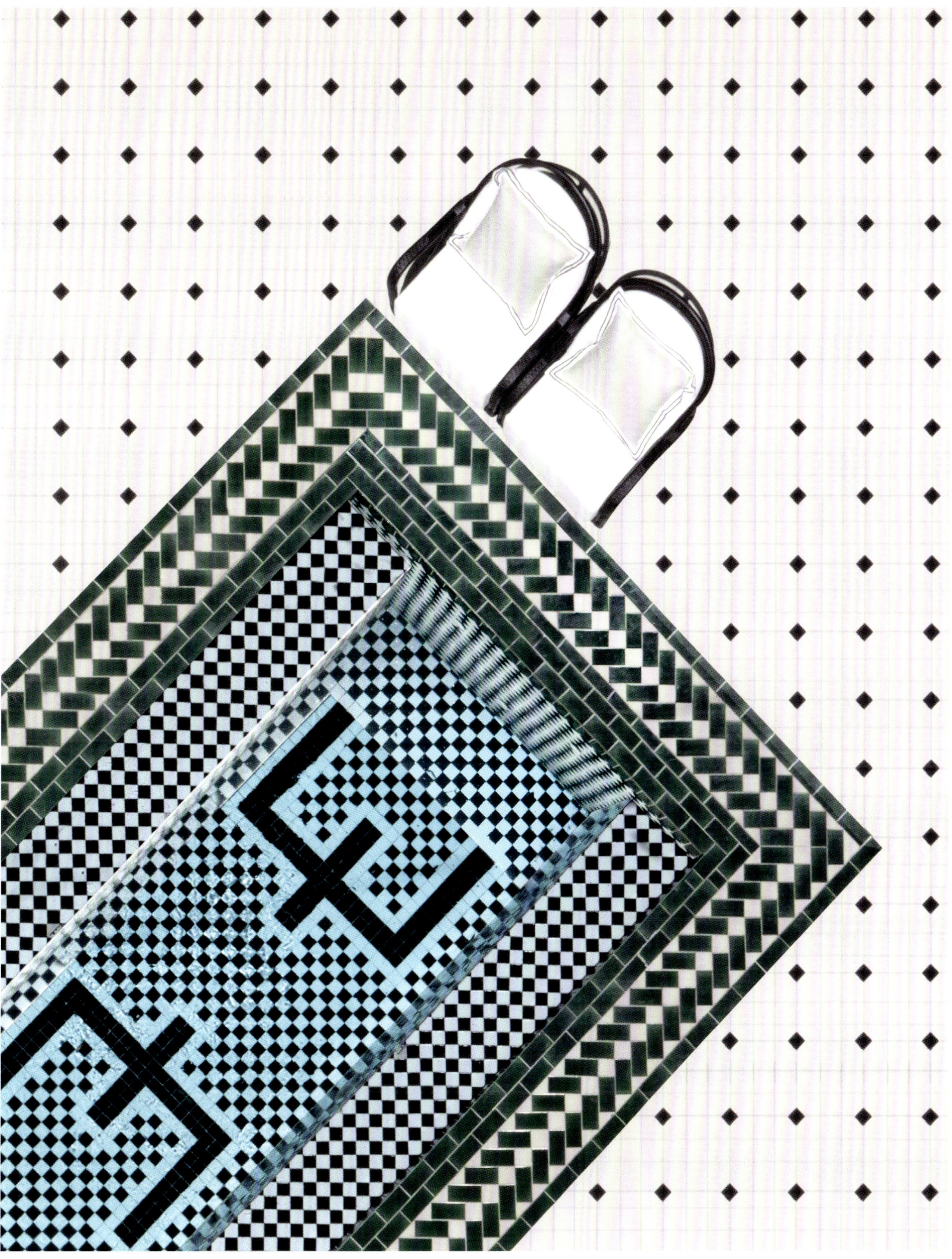

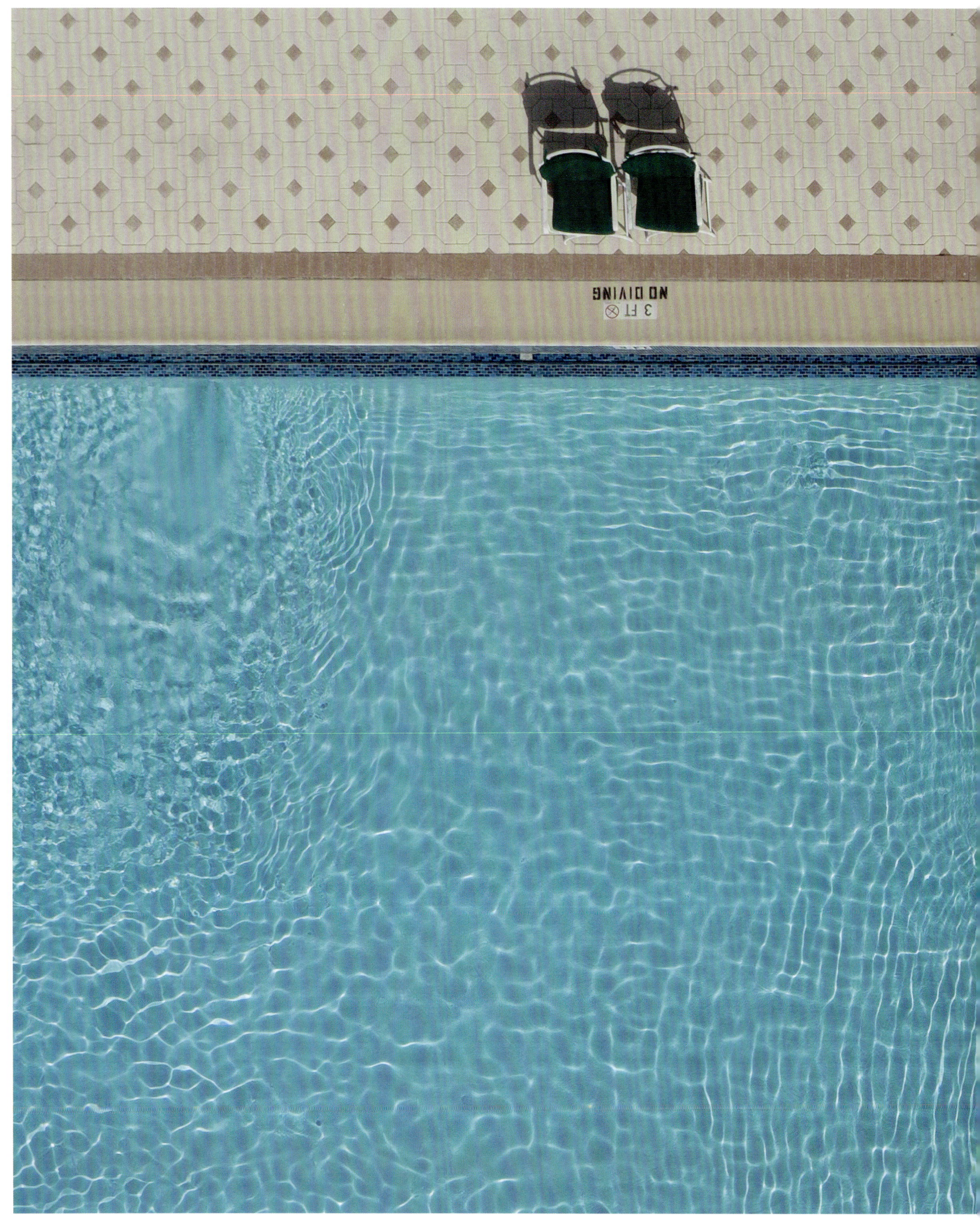
3 FT
NO DIVING

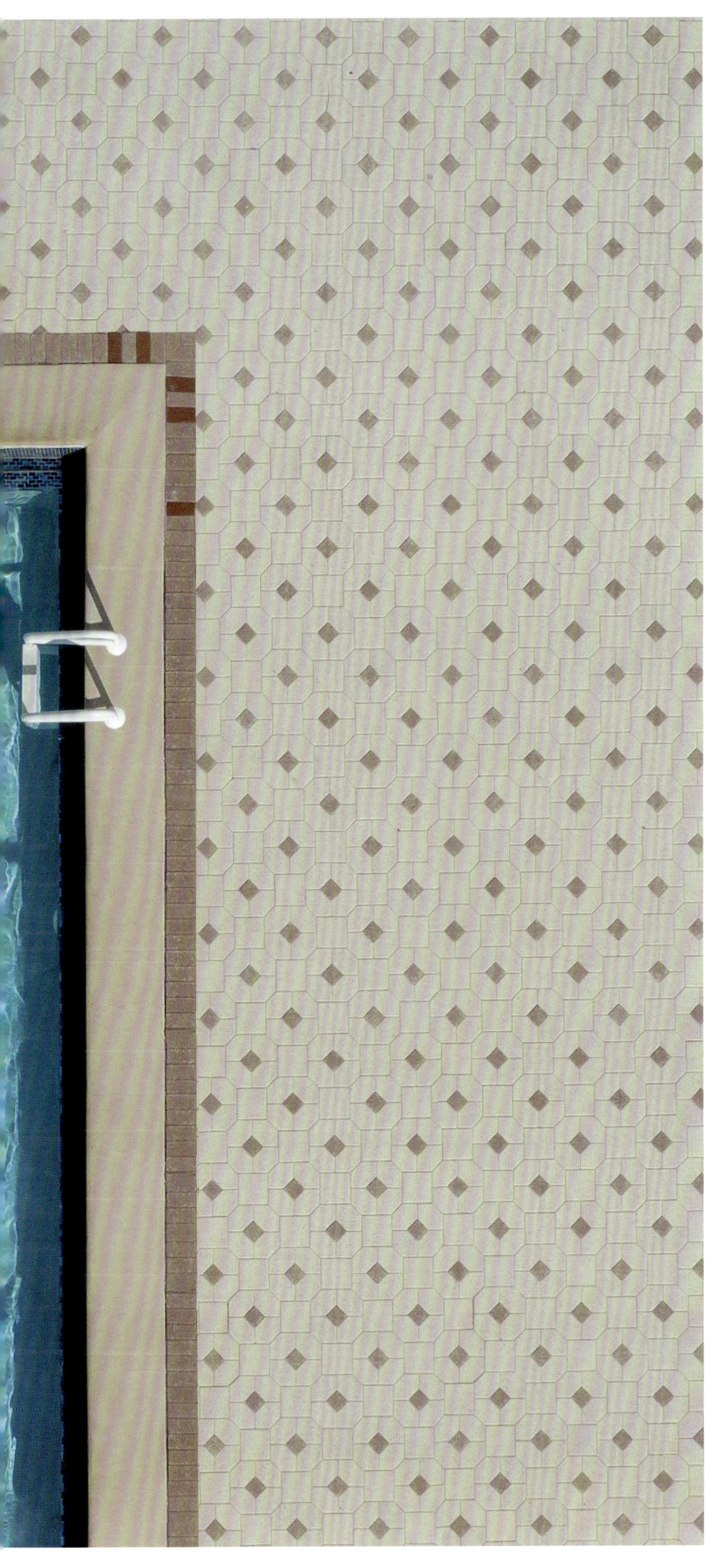

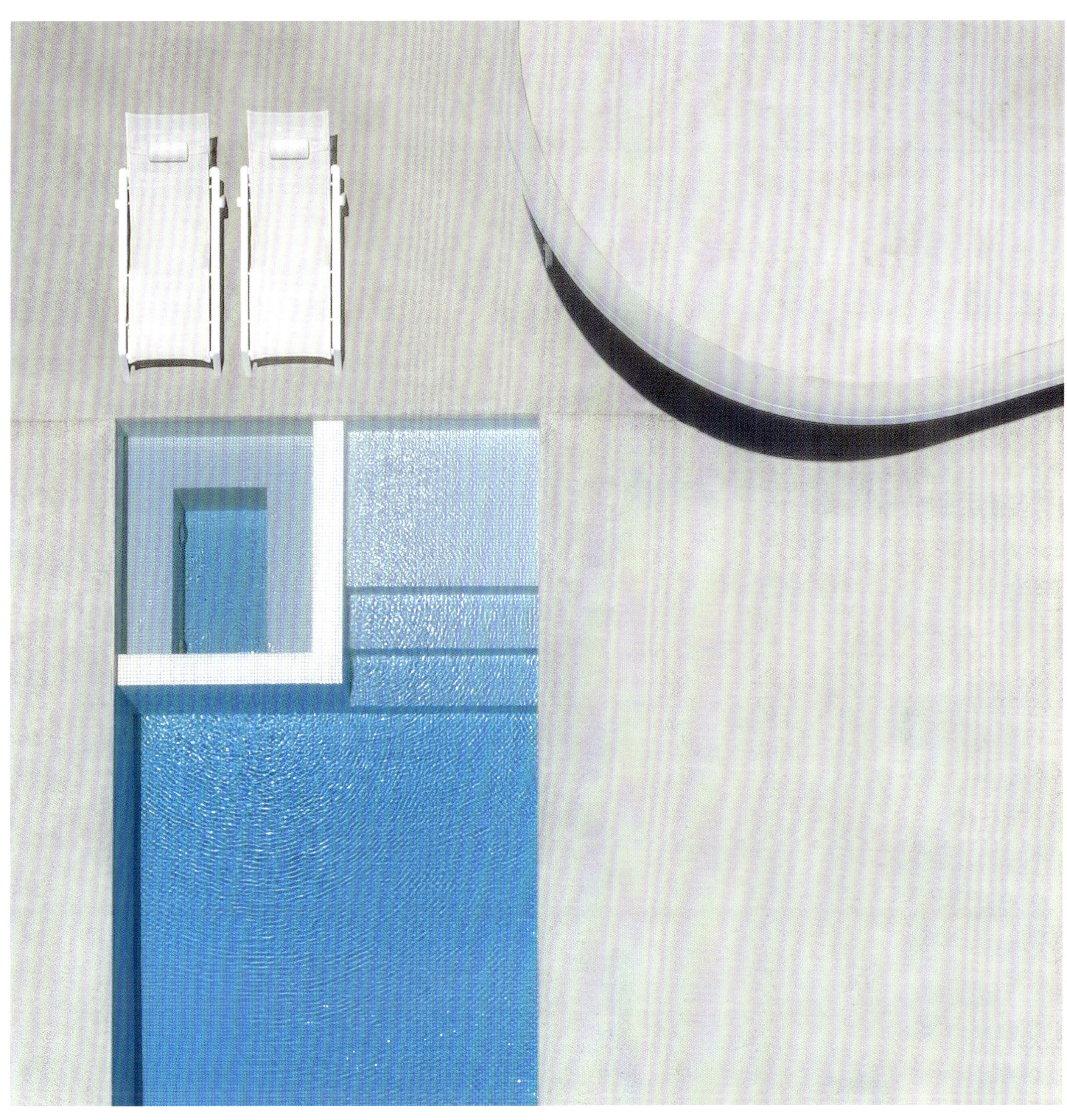

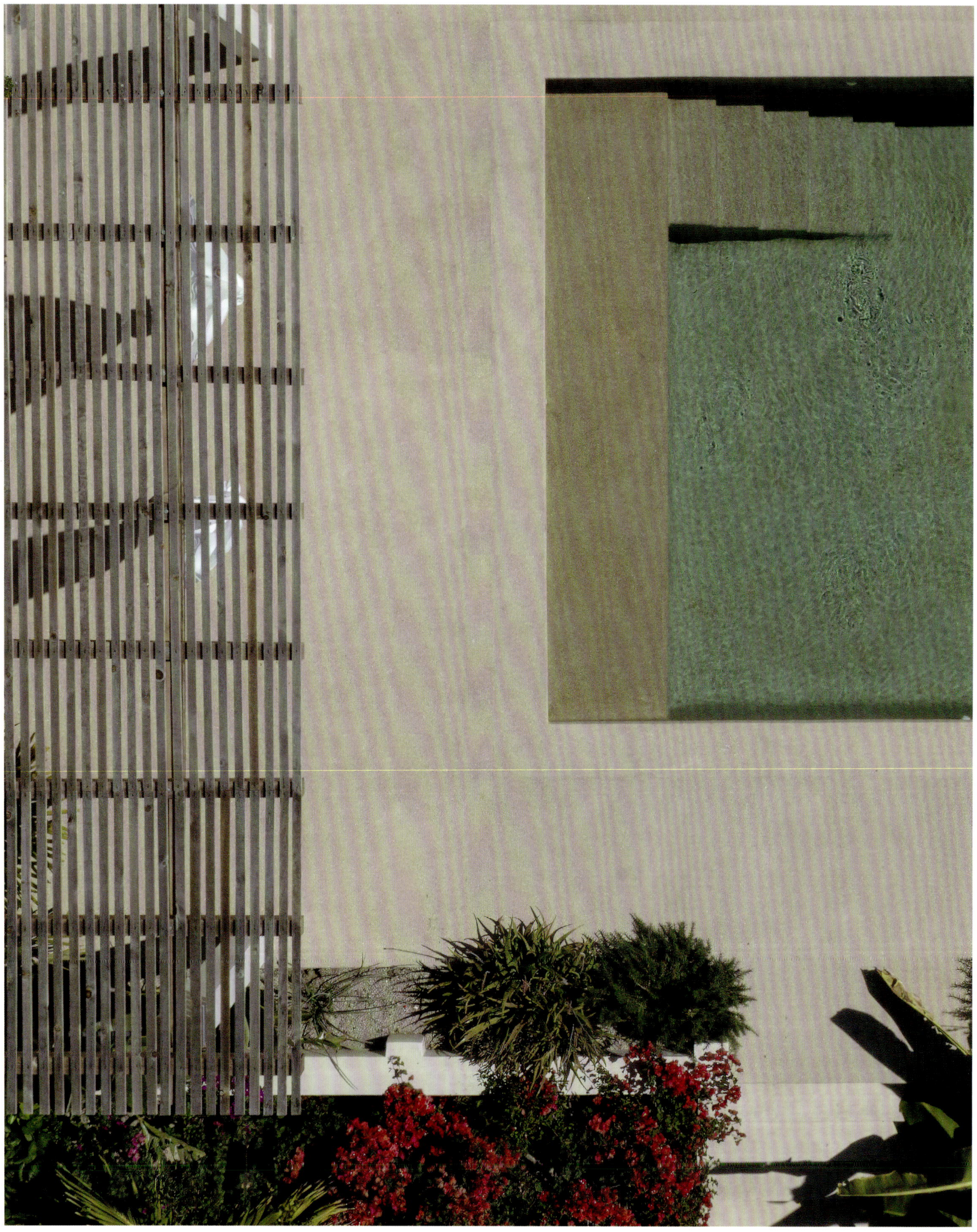

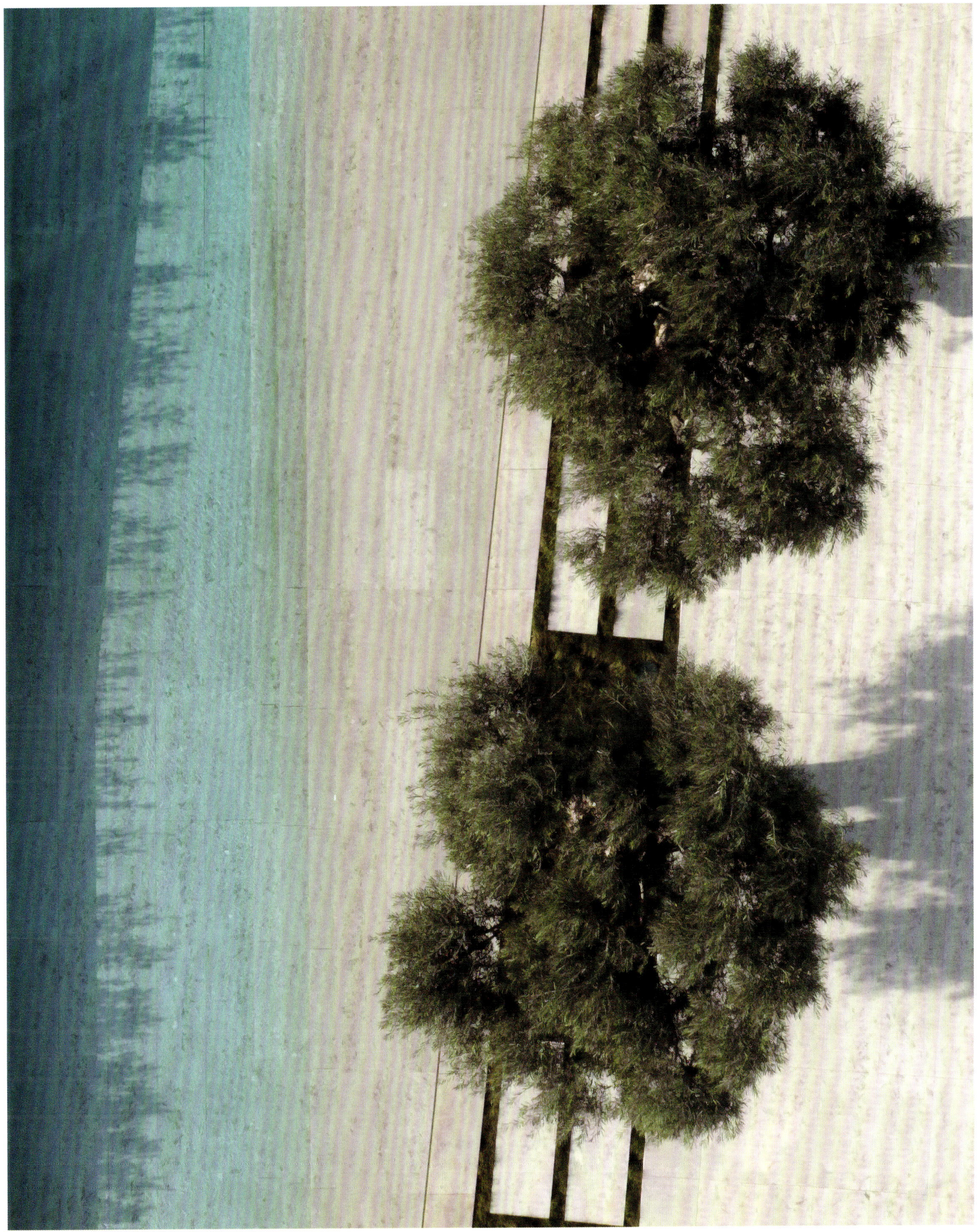

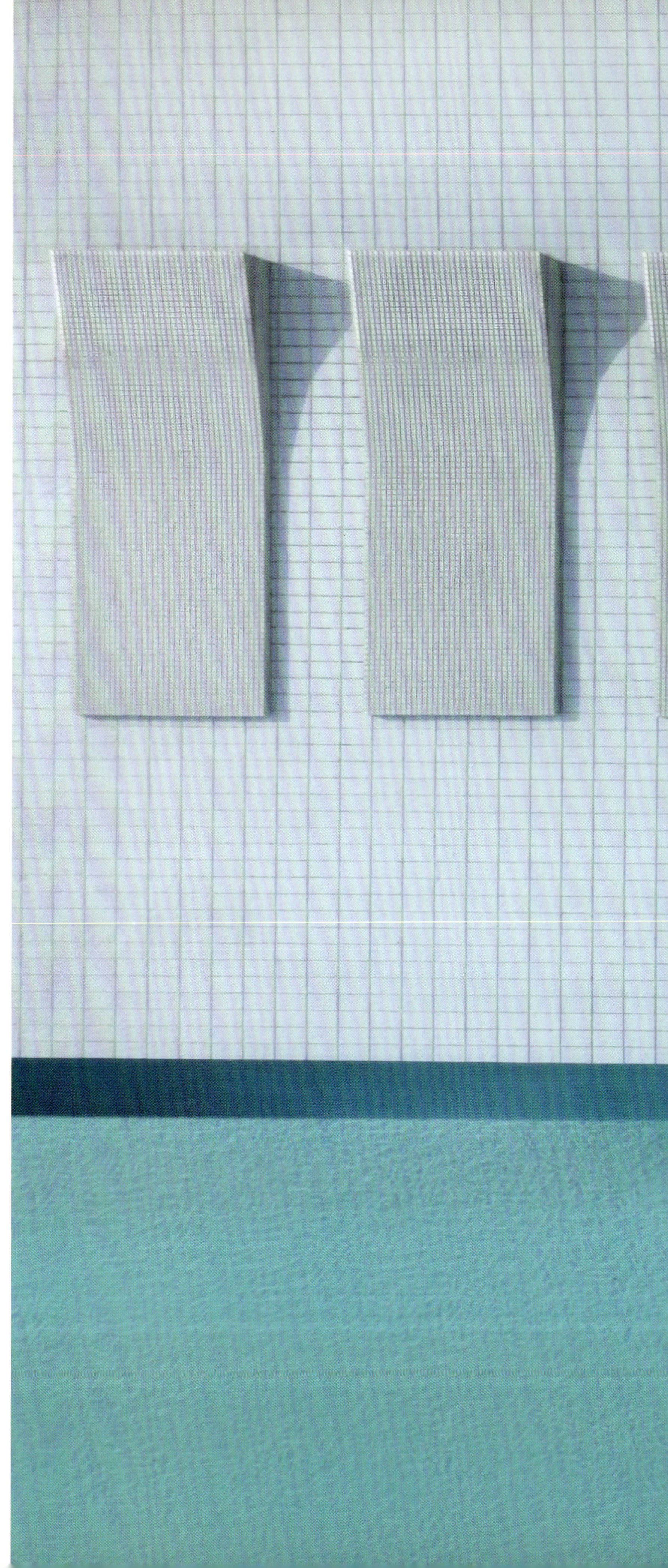

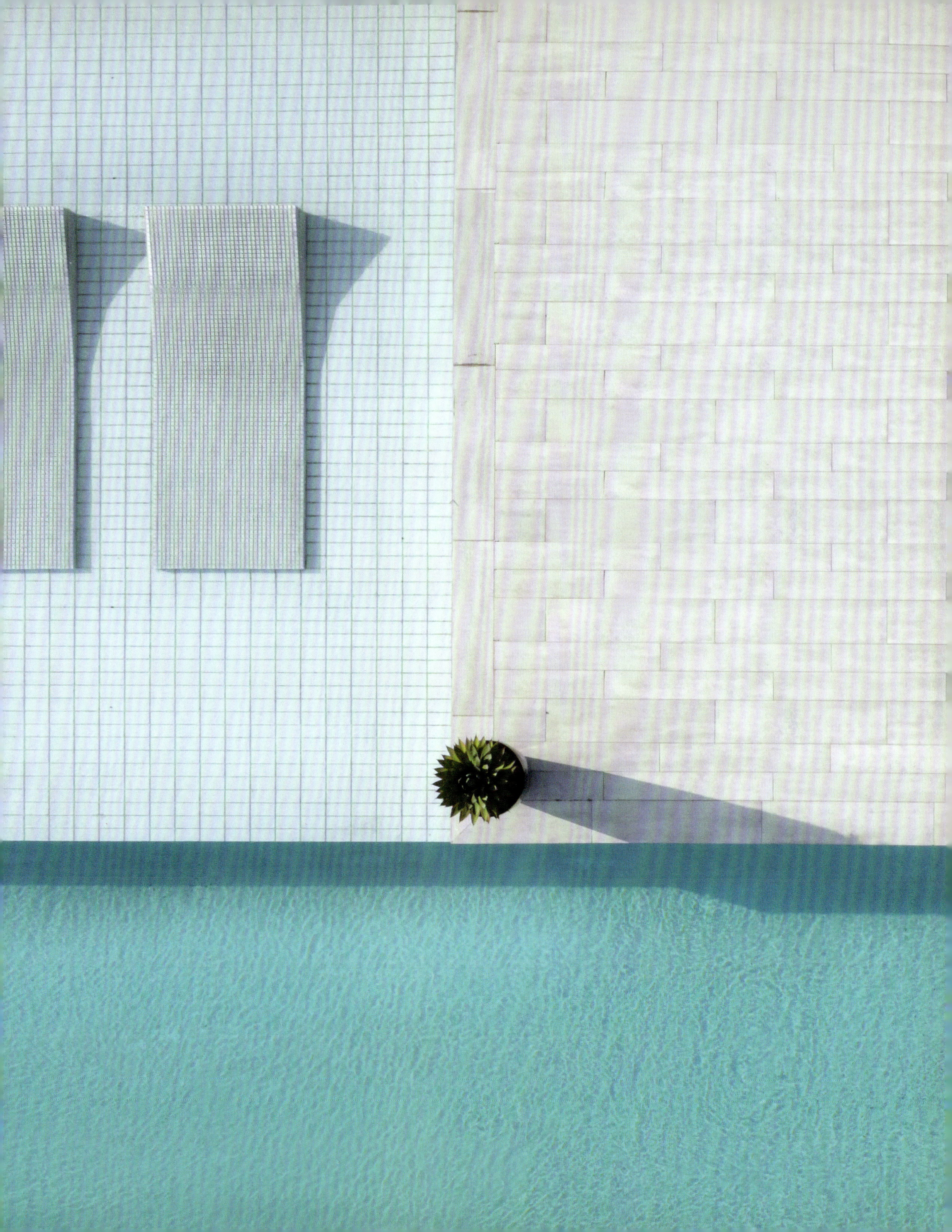

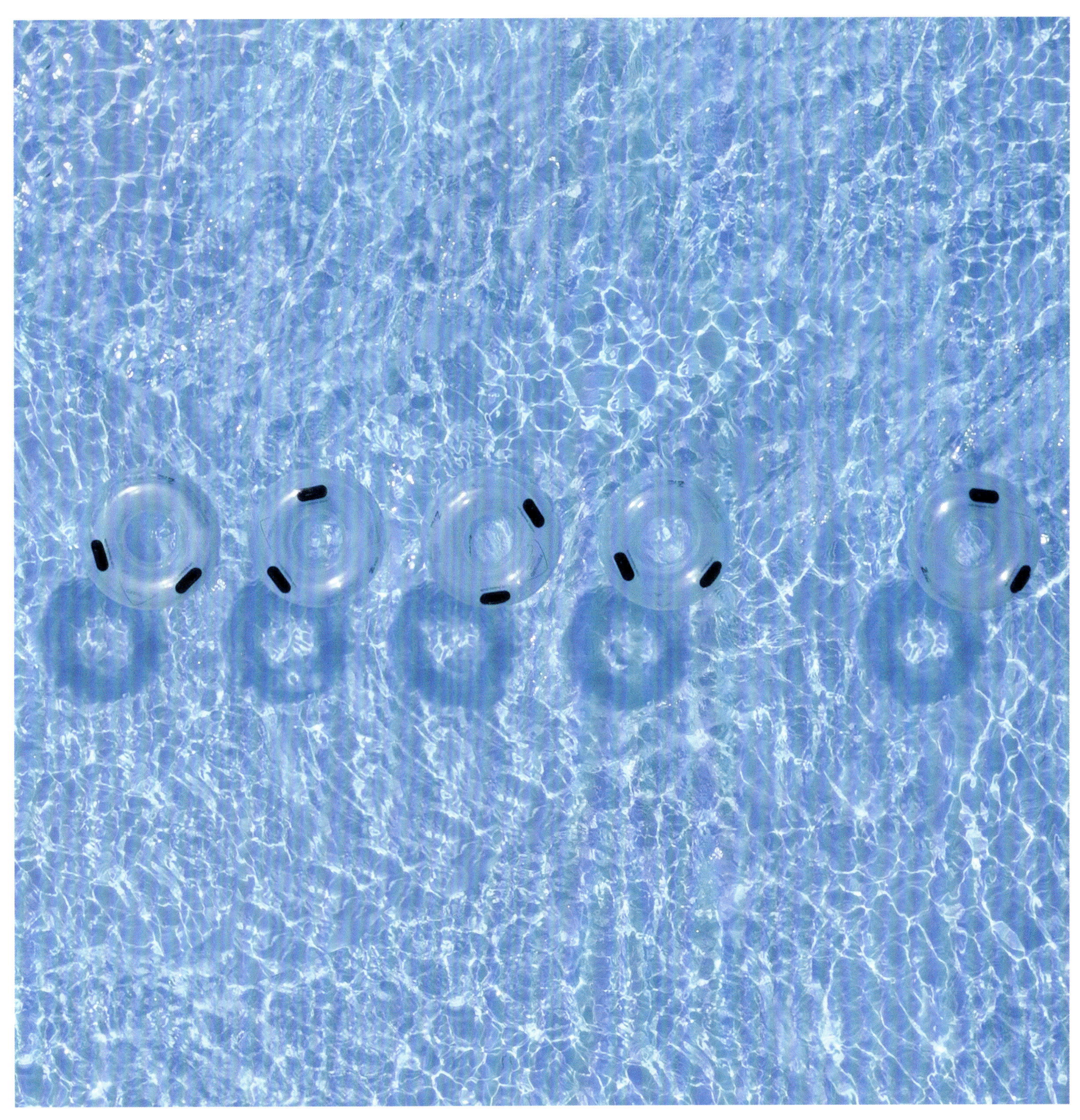

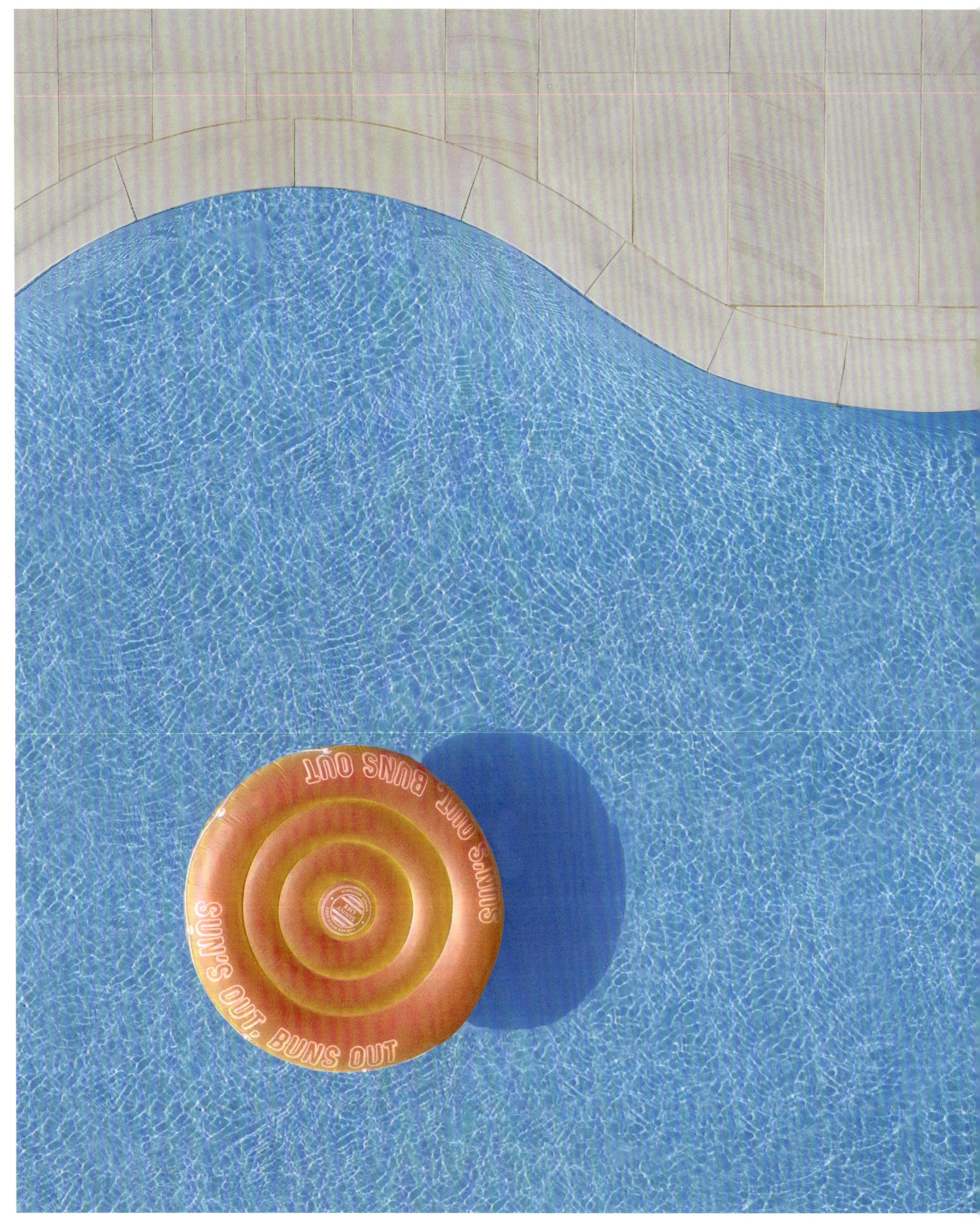
SUN'S OUT, BUNS OUT
SUN'S OUT, BUNS OUT

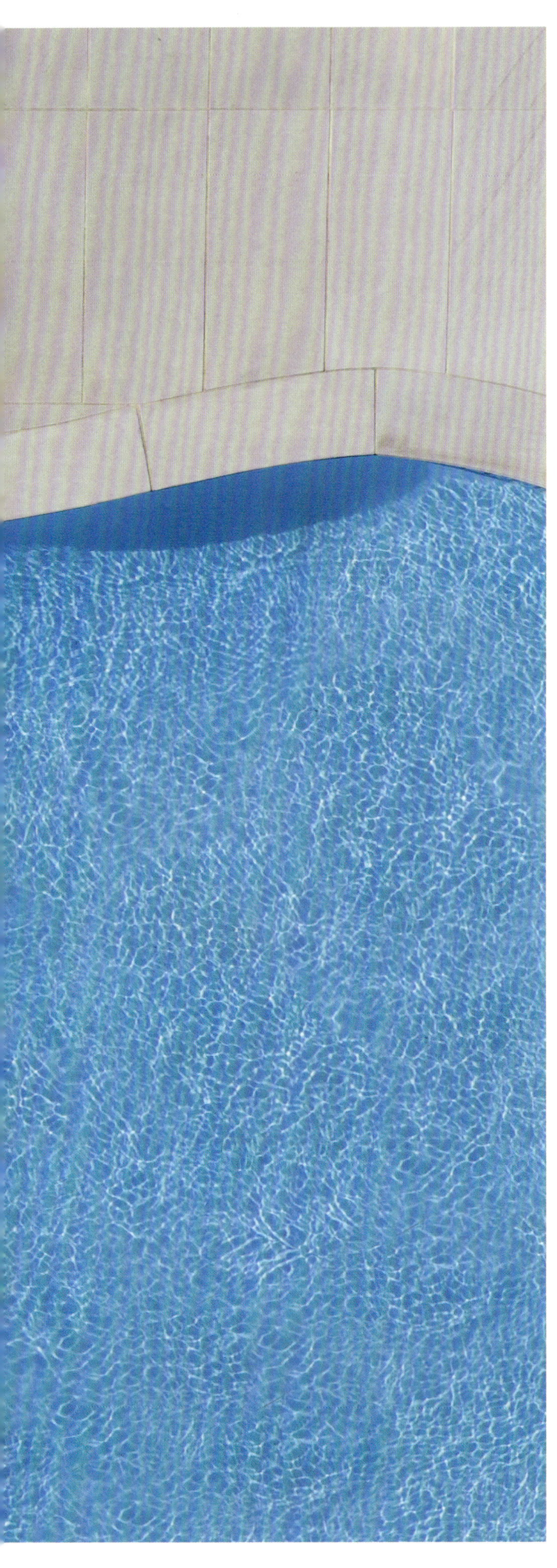

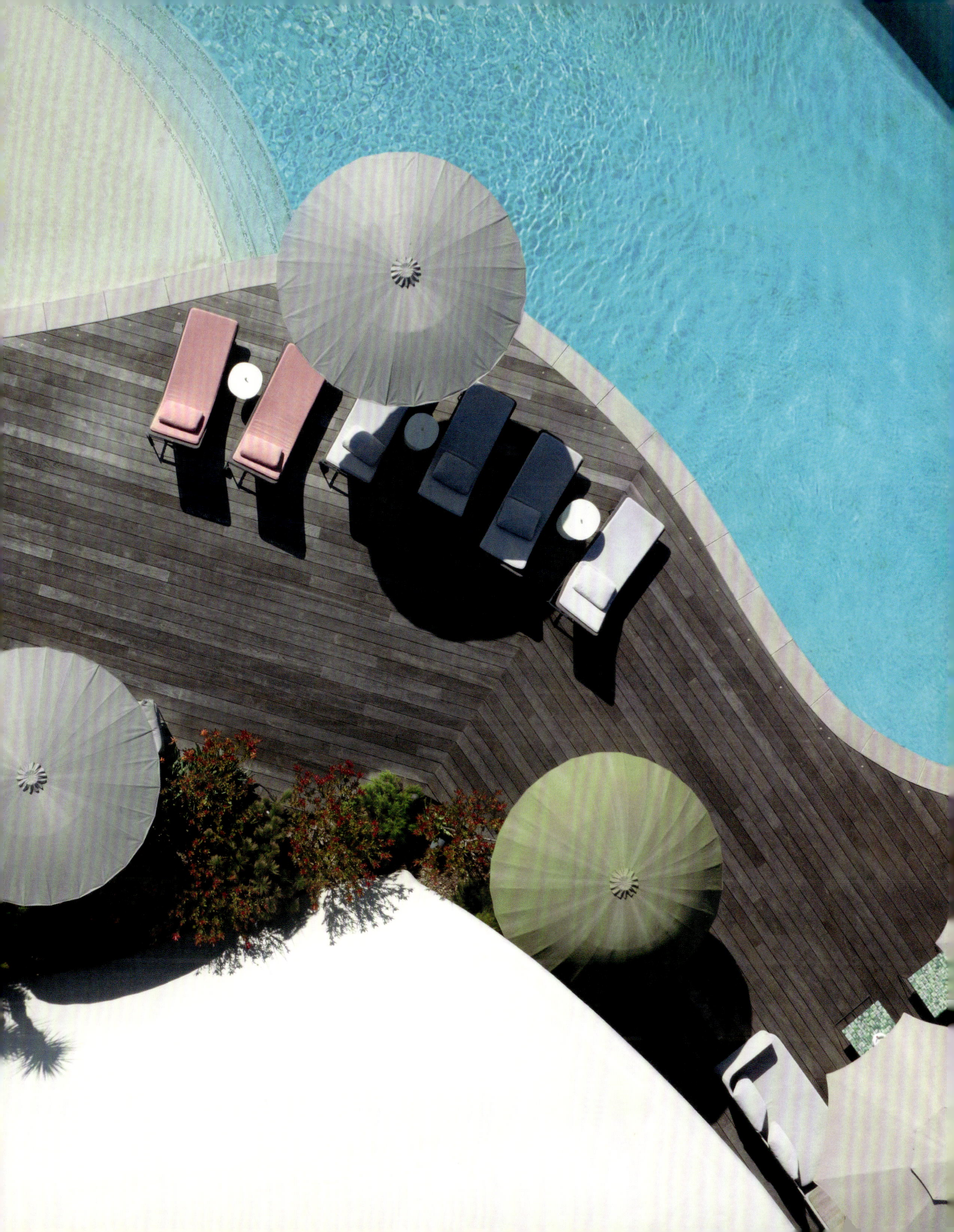

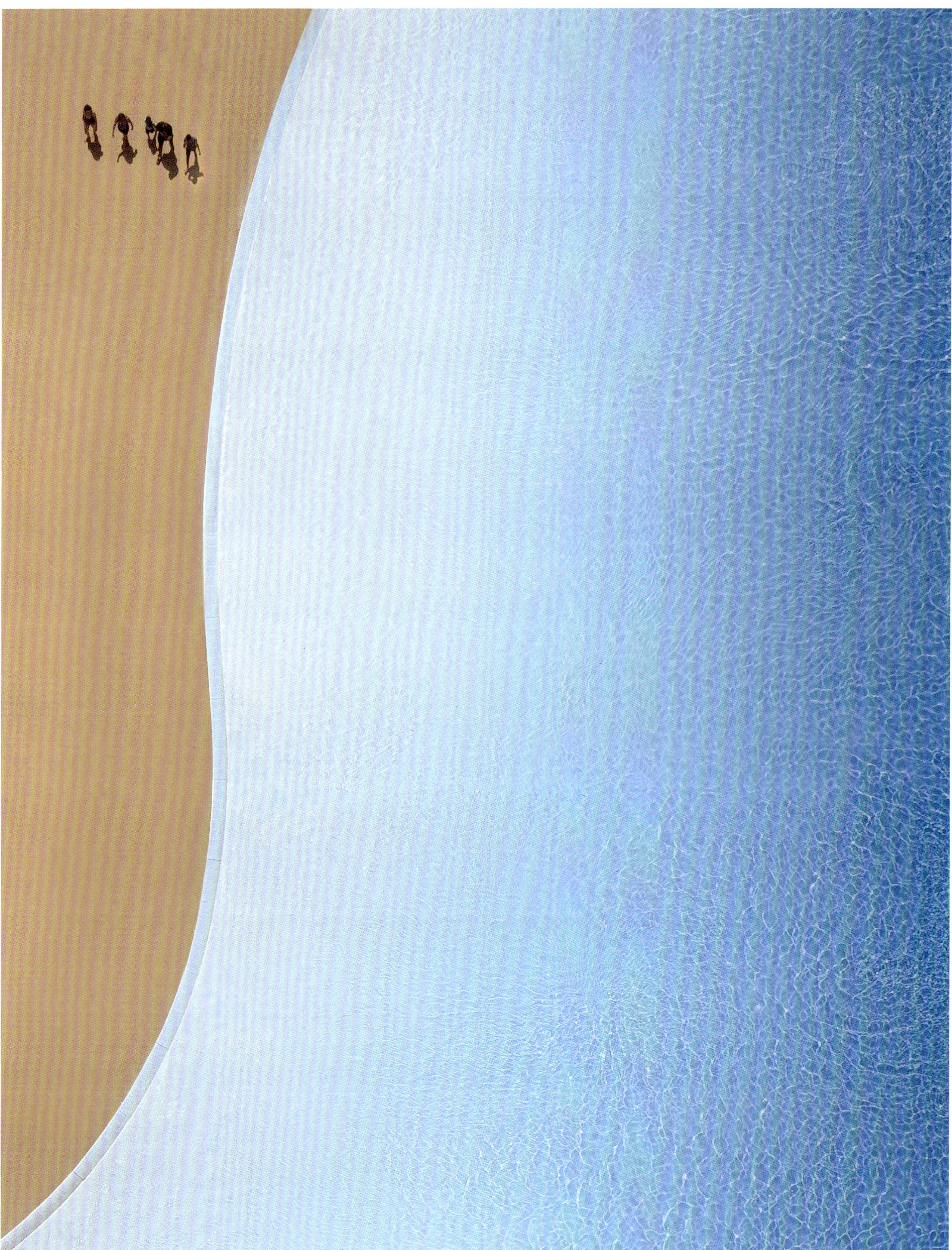

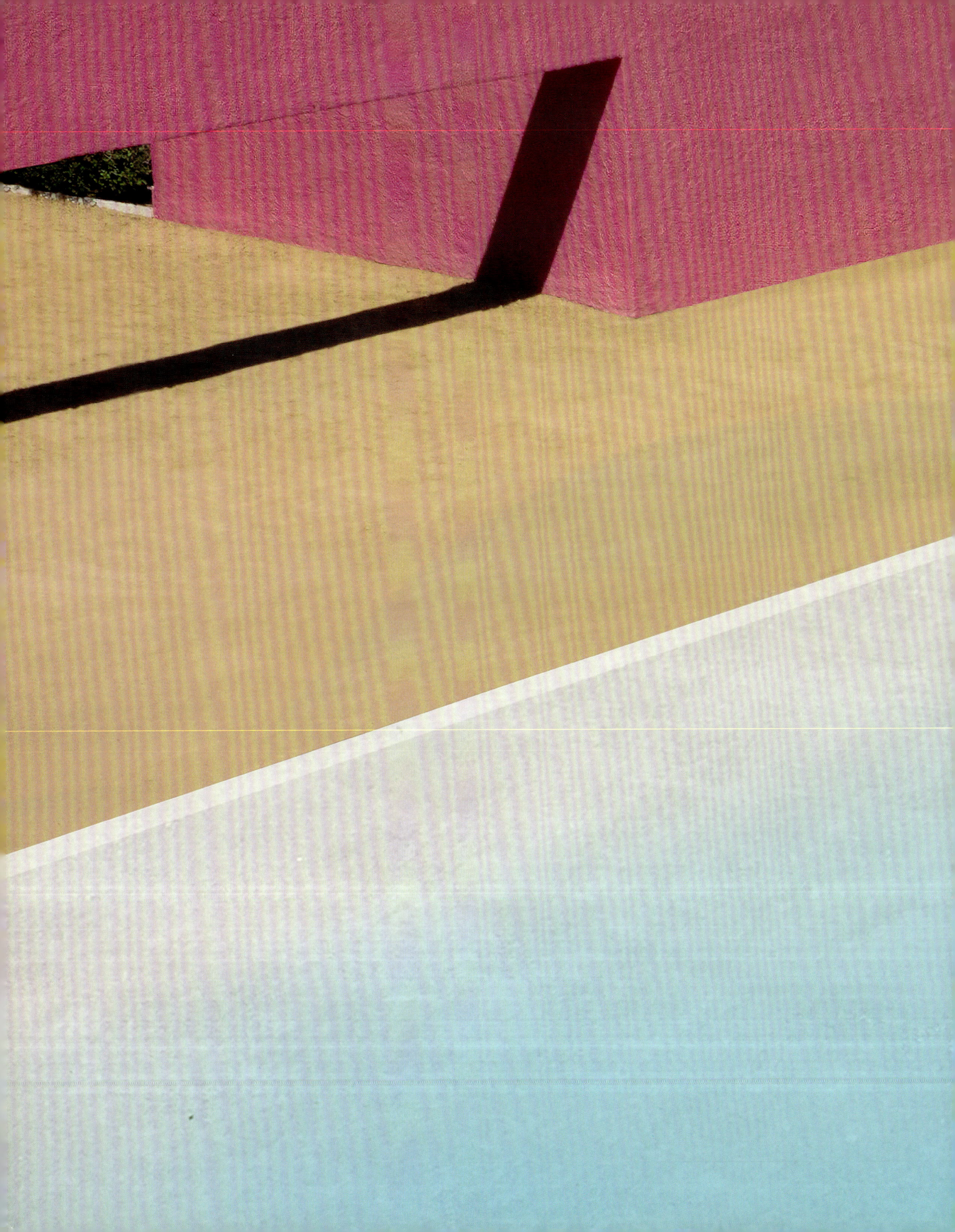

←

CIUDAD LÓPEZ MATEOS, STATE OF MEXICO — MEXICO CITY

CUADRA SAN CRISTÓBAL

BYRON BAY, NSW — AUSTRALIA

PARASOL

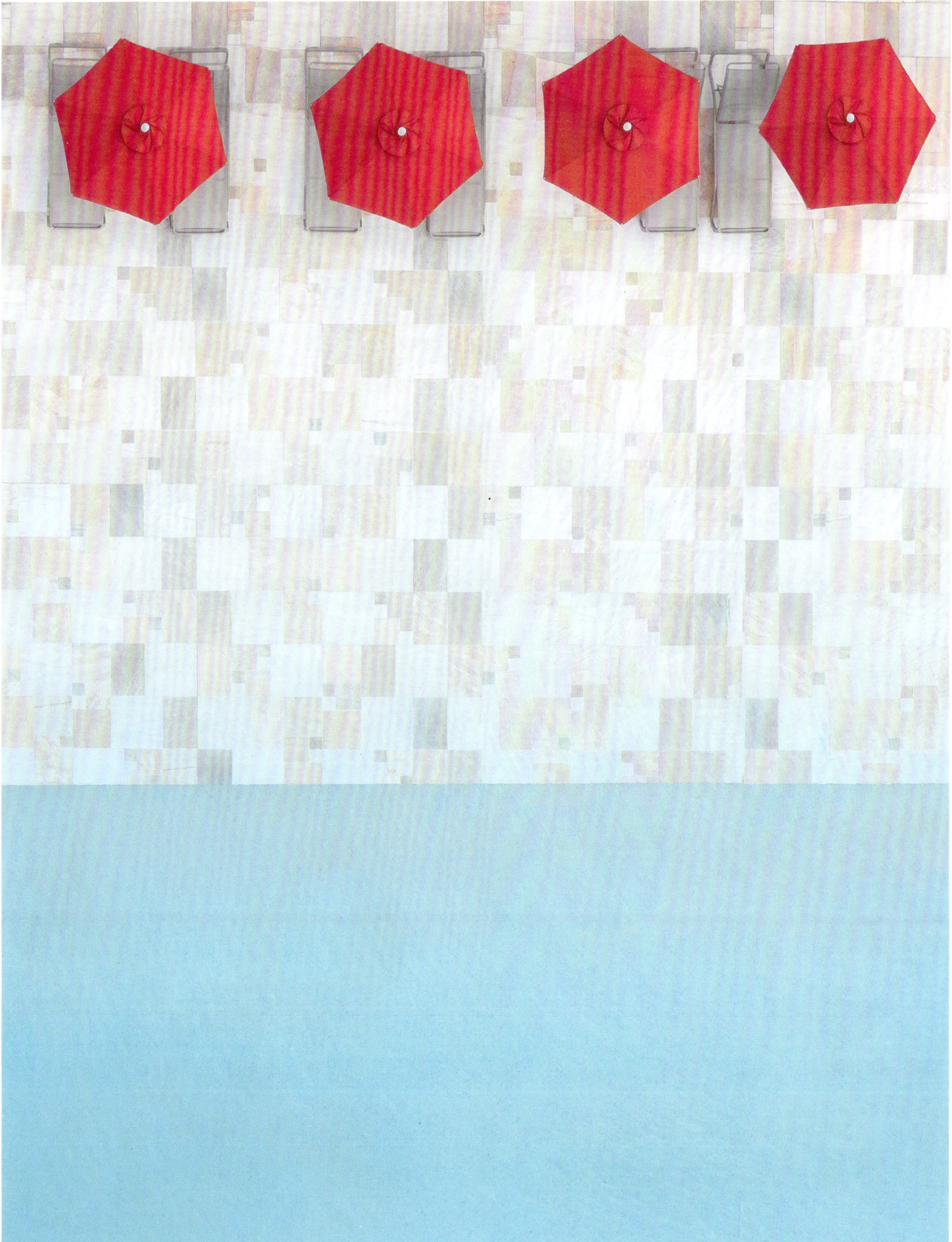

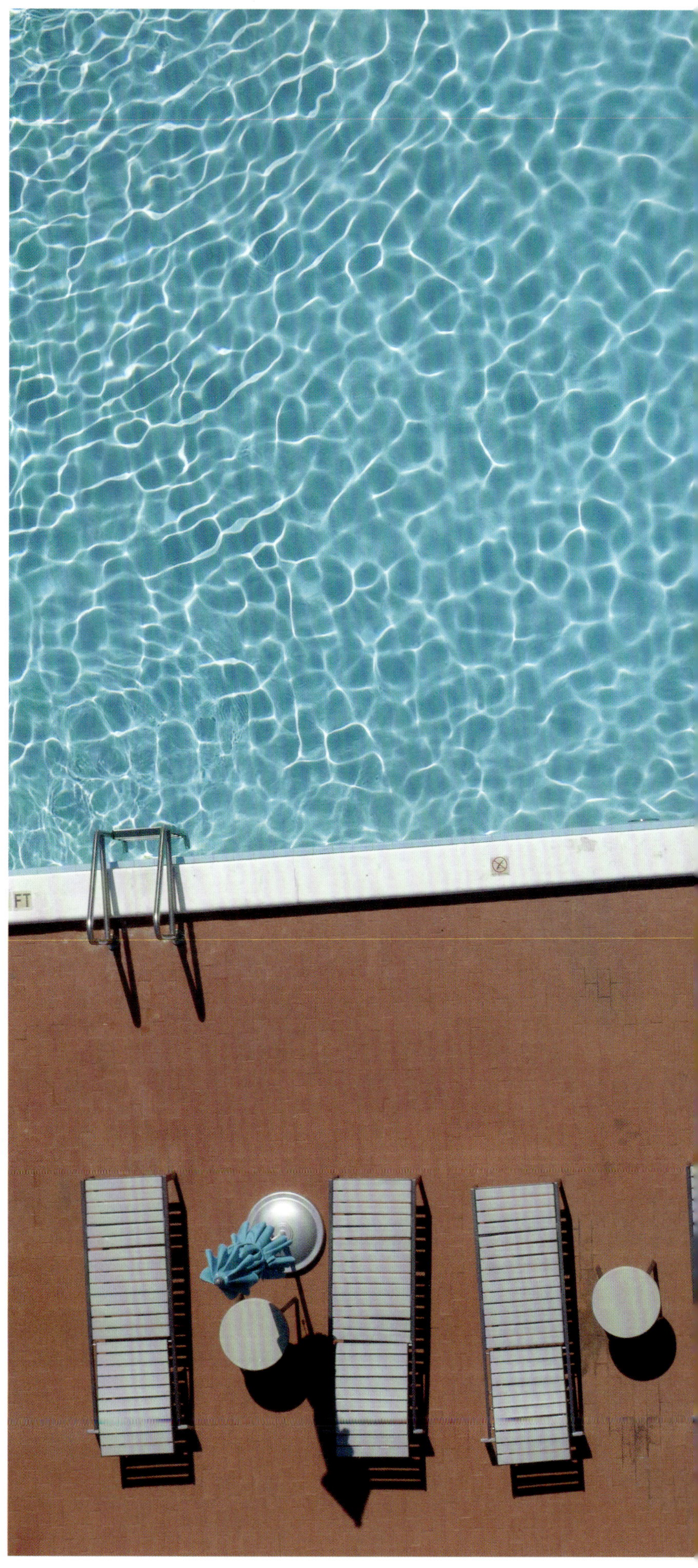
FT

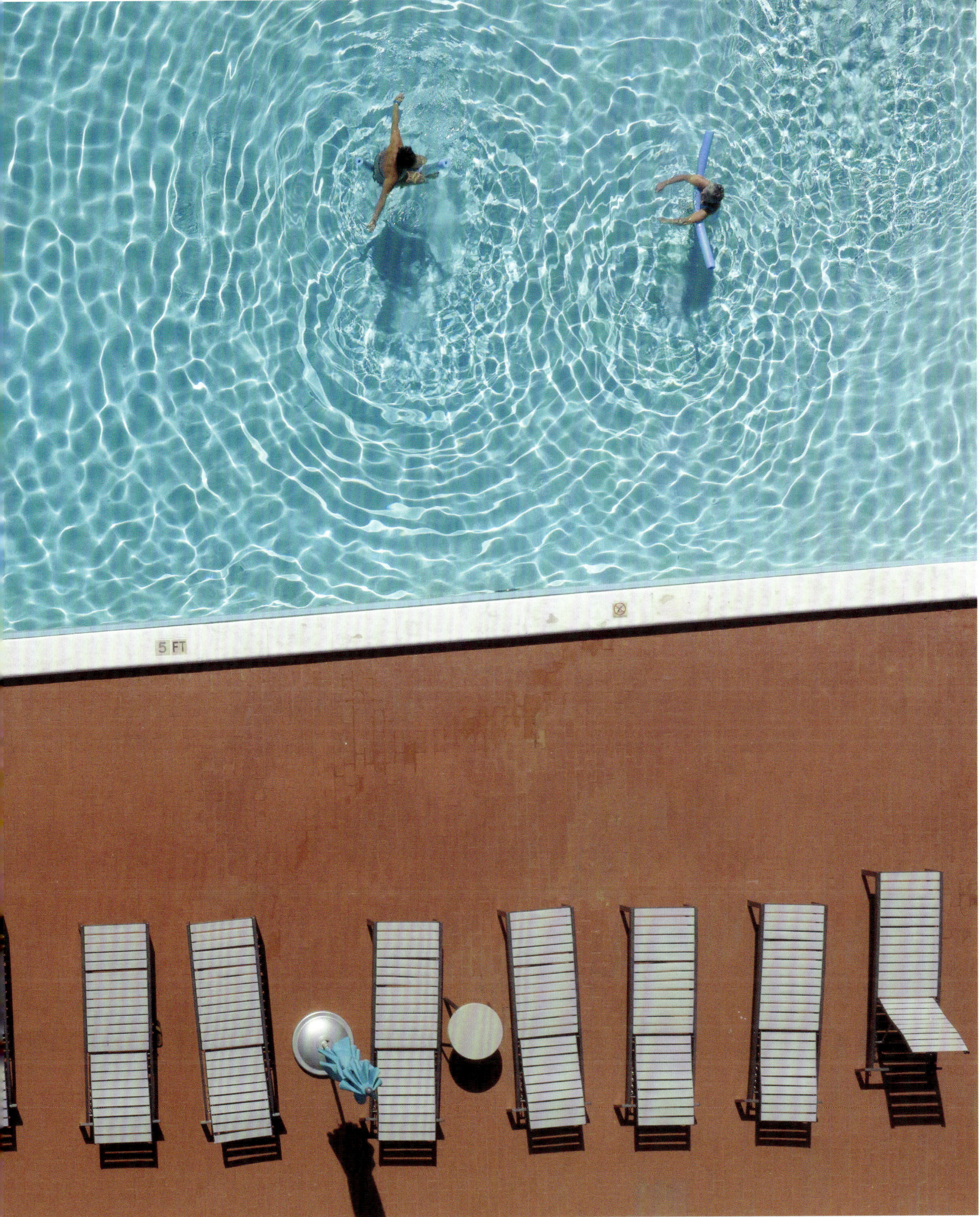
5 FT

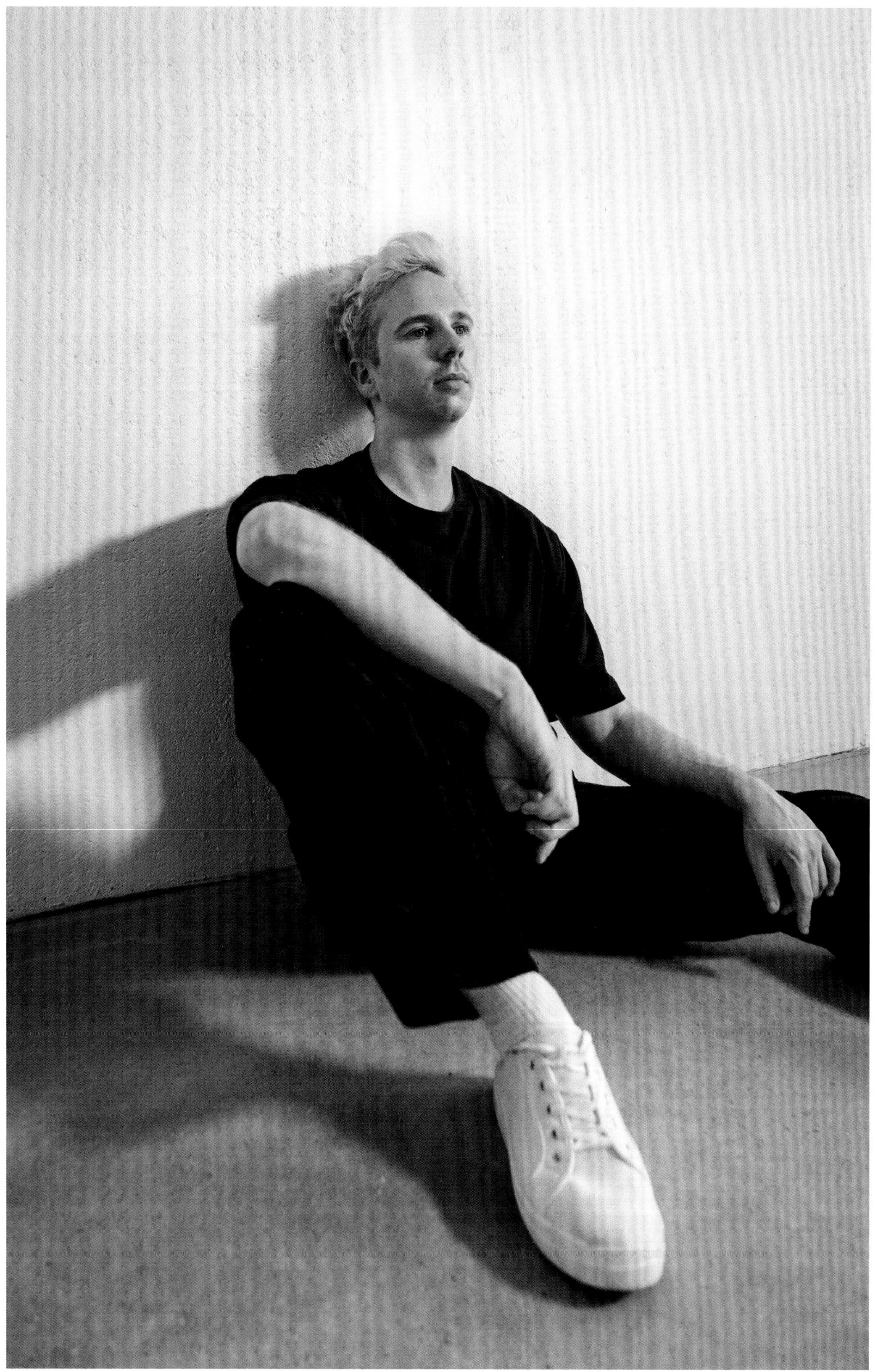

ABOUT THE AUTHOR

Brad Walls is a fine art aerial photographer hailing from Sydney, Australia. In helping to define a new genre of photography, he has been the recipient of several prestigious photography prizes, including the Pollux and Communication Arts awards, and his work has been published by *The Washington Post*, *The Guardian*, *CNN* and *The New York Times*.

Brad's style removes itself from traditional aerial photography, opting instead to focus on experimentation through the use of negative space, symmetry, geometry and leading lines. It's an intersection of his passion for design and love of the world around him.

Brad hopes that one day, we can all look back and chuckle at the idea that drones were once disliked – much like how hopping into strangers' cars was also once considered dangerous, but now we simply call that 'ridesharing'. After all, Brad's shtick is about altering our perspective.

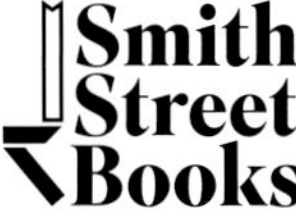

Published in 2022 by Smith Street Books
Naarm | Melbourne | Australia
smithstreetbooks.com

ISBN: 978-1-9258-1197-1

Publisher: Paul McNally
Designer: Evi-O Studio | Evi O
Design assistant: Evi-O Studio | Katherine Zhang

Printed & bound in China by C&C Offset Printing Co., Ltd.

Book 227
10 9 8 7 6 5 4 3 2 1

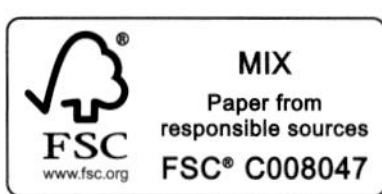